Critical Acclaim for
The True Story of the Colorad

*****

Patrick Brower didn't just report this illuminating national story of misguided hero worship; he lived it. And in KILLDOZER, he scrapes away layer after layer of accumulated paint to reveal the man at the bulldozer's controls for exactly who he was – a martyr without a cause.

Martin J. Smith, author of the nonfiction books *Poplorica*, *Ooops*, and *The Wild Duck Chase*, as well as the *Memory Series* crime novels, including *The Disappeared Girl* (Diversion Books, March 2014)

*****

Patrick Brower was there. He is the perfect writer to tell this gritty story about our society's misplaced veneration of literal and figurative bomb-throwers and oddball loners. Top-notch reporting and evocative storytelling.

Ron Franscell, bestselling author of *The Darkest Night*

*****

Snow shimmering on the Continental Divide in the background, the baby waters of the Colorado River at its feet, Granby also had a dark side exposed one June afternoon in 2004 when Marvin Heemeyer set out in his concrete-fortified, rifle-equipped Komatsu bulldozer to settle grudges. Patrick Brower has the unique position for telling this story, but this story is not that of just one mountain town, but of many towns and neighborhoods in all the barrooms and kitchens across the land where insults are imagined, conspiracies constructed, retaliations calculated. His story is about the dark-hearted side of every paradise.

Allen Best is editor and publisher of *Mountain Town News* and a contributing essayist to *The Denver Post.* He has written for *High Country News,* the *New York Times, The New Republic* and many other regional and national publications

*****

In KILLDOZER, Brower, an award-winning journalist with more than two decades of experience, recounts the traumatic day when his hometown was nearly annihilated by a madman. But Brower does not limit himself to one dark day in on otherwise quiet rural town. He puts Marvin Heemeyer and people like him — people hell-bent upon the mass destruction of innocents — in a larger context that includes the tragedies at Columbine, Aurora, Newtown and the Boston Marathon. Brower's insightful observations and commentary view these events and miscreants behind them through a prism of what he calls "a clutter of antihero veneration" that examines not only the perpetrators, but also the segments of society that have too often come to revere such blatant sociopaths as Heemeyer. KILLDOZER is a sobering and perceptive examination of a cultural dark side few of us like to admit exists.

M. John Fayhee, author of *Smoke Signals* and *Bottoms Up* and former editor and publisher of *The Mountain Gazette*

*****

KILLDOZER

The True Story of the Colorado Bulldozer Rampage

Patrick Brower

Deer Track Publishing
Centennial, CO

First Edition

Library of Congress
Control Number: 2017953304

ISBN: 978-0-9823520-1-4

Published by: Deer Track Publishing
Centennial, CO
Email: deertrackpublishers@comcast.net

Killdozer Website: killdozerbook.com

Cover: Andrew Duffy Design, Aurora, CO
Map - U.S. Geological Survey
Cracked wall texture - Lachetas

Dedication

To the people of Granby, who suffered through the Killdozer rampage with grace and restraint and who continue to endure the long-lasting impacts of that momentous day in June of 2004.

Contents

Prologue

Marv Heemeyer demolished my business, razed my town and nearly killed me as he rampaged through Granby, Colorado, on June 4, 2004. He was unstoppable in his menacing homemade tank, an 85-ton armored bulldozer that was armed with three weapons — one of them a .50-caliber sniper rifle — mounted in the impregnable steel-enshrouded cab. Gun-toting sheriff's deputies and state troopers futilely followed and fired repeatedly at the tank, their bullets ricocheting off the earth-shaking behemoth that looked like a robot rover from some dark planet sent to wreak havoc on mankind. He destroyed 13 buildings, squashed cars and fired his weapons at police and his perceived enemies. He even tried to blow up the town.

That was bad enough.

Even worse after that tumultuous day was seeing Heemeyer praised and defended for his actions based on false narratives explaining his motivation. To this day, people who should know better tell me that Heemeyer was a hero, that he didn't want to hurt anyone, that the town deserved to be punished because corrupt government and small-town cliques were out to get him.

The dust had barely settled in town when I read bloggers who falsely claimed major aspects of the event never happened at all or were staged by police and that "government" colluded with the local mainstream media. Social media pages and other web pages have cropped up over the years praising Heemeyer and boasting of his heroic status, all adopting without question the false narrative that Heemeyer was victimized by a corrupt and vindictive government. These false narratives elevated Heemeyer as a new American antihero.

While conducting my research on the elevation of Heemeyer to heroic status I discovered that many other violent rampagers and questionable characters were also elevated in the eyes of the public.

Sadly, Marv Heemeyer isn't the only violent rampager whose acts have been justified or softened by fake explanatory narratives.

For these rampaging antiheroes the consistent trait of their rhetoric, both on-line and in print, was the truth-challenged narratives that explained their actions. The narratives almost always reinforced the grudges and biases of fans of these antiheroes.

It's clear to me now, 13 years after the rampage, that we live in a "post-truth" era; a time when claims of "fake news" and a complete disregard for the facts are commonplace. The trend is so strong that the *Oxford University Press* designated "post-truth" as the international word of the year for 2016. The *Press* defines "post-truth" as "relating to or denoting circumstances in which objective facts are less influential in shaping public opinion than appeals to emotion and personal belief." Relating to the ascent of this post-truth era is the role played by social media and the Internet, mediums which make it easier for people to uncritically succumb to their emotions and personal beliefs, regardless of the facts.

I now see that the origins of our current post-truth era could be seen in the public reaction to the Killdozer rampage that took place in little Granby, Colorado, so long ago. What I initially saw as a local phenomenon suddenly was mirrored on the national stage in many ways; not only an increase in false narratives but also an increase in rampages themselves.

Two recent reports show that violent rampages in which multiple people are killed or harmed are increasing in the United States. An F.B.I. study released in September of 2014 reveals that mass shootings rose drastically in the previous half-dozen years. There were, on average, 16.4 such shootings a year from 2007 to 2013, compared with an average of 6.4 shootings annually from 2000 to 2006. In another report released in October of 2014, Harvard University researchers say U.S. mass shootings surged in the prior three years. The study states that the rate of mass shootings increased threefold since 2011, occurring on average every 64 days, compared with an average of every 200 days in the years from 1982 to 2011.

The violent rampages and mass killings have continued at a torrid pace since this study was released.

They all remind me of the Killdozer rampage.

As a longtime Granby resident and as the editor of the local newspaper, I was able to observe first-hand the events that make up this story, which is not only a story about a man who wanted to destroy a town in a homemade tank, but also about America's changing attitude about its increasingly peculiar heroes — heroes like Marv Heemeyer.

In researching this book, what I didn't see and hear first-hand, I gleaned from the personal interactions I had with Heemeyer and interviews with his friends and enemies. I also relied heavily on Heemeyer's own words about his life that he left behind in two-and-a-half hours of tapes. In addition, I had access to police files and other public records.

And so it is that I examine the story of the Killdozer, a menacing machine that destroyed my town and which set the tone for the post-truth America in which we live today.

Prologue

I. Origins

1. Attacked

I ran out into the controlled mayhem in front of the *Sky-Hi News*, a digital camera strapped around my neck and a reporter's notebook in hand. Rushing out to cover the biggest story in the history of my small town, I felt like Peter Parker or Clark Kent, a naïve and eager journalistic superhero chasing down important facts for the good of mankind. The cops in my building had told me in a grim and anxious manner that they had to evacuate our building. They said some crazed dozer driver had already smashed up the town hall, the electric co-op and the concrete batch plant. They said the dozer-tank had weapons too. They looked worried. It didn't occur to me that I was soon to be the target of a mad man.

In front of my office, cops were shouting and waving their arms, directing cars out of town. Pedestrians were walking fast to the east along the sidewalk and cars packed with people and belongings were streaming slowly in the same direction on U.S. Highway 40 in jerky, stop-and-go motions, like stunt cars on parade. I snapped a photo of an old Datsun four-door, packed with laughing and smiling children.

I jogged west a few blocks and was suddenly confronted by a strange and alarming procession that was slowly heading my way on the otherwise deserted U.S. Highway 40. A massive bulldozer crawled down the middle of the road, flanked by Colorado State Patrol vehicles on each side. The thing looked like a homemade tank. It was about 18 feet tall and wider than two cars abreast. The front blade was taller than a man and the treads alone came up to chest-height. This machine dwarfed the police cruisers at its sides, as if the cars were midget-mobiles. Sheriff's deputies jogged alongside, rifles and shotguns in-hand, their weapons carried at port arms across their chests. The cab of the bulldozer was shrouded with an odd, grey-black steel enclosure that had the look of a '30s era conception of an ominous spaceship — like Darth Vader's helmet on treads.

On the other side of the street a young man with a skateboard in one hand and a bandana-wrapped head was pumping his fist in the air, looking back at the approaching machine and shouting 'Yeah!,' as if cheering on a sports hero. In front of him I saw a couple — the woman with a swaddled infant in her arms and its head crooked on her shoulder — look back and upward as if they were escaping Godzilla, fleeing Gomorrah. A uniformed forest service employee stood at an intersection to the west, shouting orders and gesticulating frantically to cars easing out on the highway. He carried an M-16 rifle over his shoulder, the first time I had ever seen a forest service employee armed in such a manner. The once-clear sky of that Colorado bluebird day had faded in a haze of dust, leaving the sun a dull orange disc above the town. I was witnessing an exodus.

It all had an anxious and oddly festive air to it. And yet, the fear was palpable. It had a taste — the alkaline tartness of masonry dust, like quinine, wafting through the air.

I went back to our newspaper offices and decided to stay despite a reverse 911 phone call telling us to get out of the building and flee to the east of Granby. My staff, except for *Winter Park Manifest* Editor Harry Williamson, had fled. I wasn't going to miss this story, which was developing right in the small town where I had lived and worked for 24 years. As a small-town journalist slaving away in the hinterlands of the Colorado Rockies, I was excited to have a major, national news story breaking right in my backyard.

There were cops in our building using the phone and looking around nervously.

"You can't stay. Get out. You're on the list," said Sgt. Jim Campbell. He pointed at me.

"List? Whose list?" I said.

"Leave. And we've already called your house. Don't go there."

"What do you mean, 'my house'?" I said, thinking of my pregnant wife and 2-year-old son who should have been napping at that very moment.

"We're warning people out of their houses," his voice was unsteady, but loud. He seemed incredulous that I was standing in front of him. "Especially your house. Now get the Hell out," he said, even louder.

He turned and jogged in a crouch out of the front door, his hand on his holstered handgun, his eyes cast to the left, down the main thoroughfare through town, toward the approaching machine.

I frantically called my house and got no answer. Were my wife and son okay? In a quick thought that encompassed all the years I had covered the news in that small mountain community, I remembered the trepidation I felt each time I realized that the heroes and villains of our news coverage were also our neighbors and acquaintances. Many times, these people blamed the newspaper if coverage wasn't exactly to their liking. They'd say we got the facts wrong or we weren't telling the truth, or we had no right to tell the world any unflattering facts. Wife-beaters, drunk drivers, ski champions, failed politicians and thwarted activists were the first to accuse the paper if they looked bad in stories we published.

I felt the ground vibrate, like an itch on the bottom of my feet. A pen left on the clean surface of a desk jiggled and rolled with the rumbling of the dozer. The leaves on the decorative plastic plants in the front of our office, eternally green and firm, quivered. An odd rattle became more intense in the entire office as coffee mugs, computers and phones shook with increasing intensity; the entire world, it seemed, trembling underneath. It was like the tremor from an earthquake. Then I heard the loud drone of the bulldozer's engine and the clanking and creaking of the steel treads. The dozer came into my view, moving at probably five miles per hour.

The massive machine took a sharp turn to its right, toward our building, without any noticeable change in speed. I watched, mesmerized.

The blade lifted a foot or so, and then the right tread slammed over the curb. An instant later the huge blade hit the large aspen tree in front of our office. That tree was one of the largest on Agate Avenue, planted with pride by the town fathers 15 years prior as part of a beautification project I had enthusiastically endorsed in our editorial pages. That boosterish campaign and the tree seemed insignificant and foolish to me at that moment. I remember clearly how the tree collapsed with a genuflection as the shimmering aspen leaves shook and thrashed under the force of the impact. I was reminded of why they call aspen trees quakies. I felt like giggling, an odd reaction to the shock of incredulous fear flooding through me. What was this thing? It was both absurd and frightening at the same time.

The blade slammed into the building along with the tree. The 20-foot-high front wall of our newsroom and reception area crumpled like a shattered sheet of glass. The bricks, cinder blocks, drywall and windows tumbled and crashed. The bulldozer didn't slow down a bit.

The sound was overwhelming, from both the screaming engine of the bulldozer and the roar of ruin. And there was the creak and whine of the treads as metal against metal squealed under the push and pull of tons of pressure and cascades of dust, as if some giant was slamming its fingernails onto some massive chalkboard and scraping them back and forth, time and time again. Harry and I turned and ran toward the back of the building. I ran stooped over, as if I was dodging bullets. My mouth felt dry and my knees quivered as I moved instinctively through the pressroom toward the exit.

"Why?" I asked Harry as we scrambled toward the back door, looking over our shoulders toward the falling walls and ceilings. "My God," I thought, "what had I written, what had I said, what had I done?"

After we made it out the back door in a cloud of dust, I couldn't resist my urge to document the destruction. I turned to take a photo along the east side of our building, which used to be the town movie theatre before we remodeled it into our newspaper offices and pressroom. It was a long, rectangular shaped structure with walls of cinder blocks upon which rested a bowed-truss roof. Dust filled the air as the front corner of the building crumpled in a pile of cinder blocks and pink insulation, piling on the ground and on the bulldozer-tank. Deputy Roy Ybarra, who stood only about 10 feet away from the massive machine in the parking area next to our building, gestured at us with his arm, waving us away to the railroad tracks, 100 feet away down a sagebrush and weed-covered embankment.

Ybarra fired his shotgun at the machine as it methodically slammed into the side of the building where my office had been. The reports of his weapon sounded flat and inconsequential under the roar of the bulldozer and the crash of the tumbling masonry. The machine moved in jerky, mechanical motions and it never seemed to slow down or hesitate. Rubble, pink ribbons of insulation and cinder blocks cluttered the top of the armor encasing the dozer's cabin. It stopped and started with robot-like motions as it pushed into the building about six feet, and then backed out, repeating the motion. It looked absurd to me, and if I hadn't been watching it tear up our business I would have been tempted to laugh at this clunky, mechanized menace. At the same time there was something wrathful about the machine in its dauntless progress, in its howling roar and scraping treads.

I heard more loud pops, which I assumed were gun shots. I saw more sheriff's deputies standing on a balcony next door and crouching behind a corner. They held rifles. Some were aimed at the machine. I heard a snap-like whizzing sound above my head and then a sharp pop. I turned away from my office and ran toward the train tracks.

I scrambled down the steep hillside through clumps of sagebrush and tufts of meadow grass. At the bottom, only 150 feet away from my office, I saw a small throng of people standing by the train station where boxcars and coal cars were parked. I ran to the crowd. There were women, children, men and some teenagers. People looked scared and some were trying to get on the other side of the train cars where they'd be protected from the bulldozer and the firing up on the bluff. I worked my way to the other side, crawling underneath a coal car. That's when I heard it.

"It's Marv Heemeyer in that thing! Lady on the radio station said so. He's getting back at the town!" This announced by a woman leaning against the closed door of a grey Jeep Cherokee, its window open and the mumbling drone of talk radio blaring inside the car.

My anxiety sharpened into fear. Heemeyer, a muffler shop owner, snowmobiling hero and occasional political agitator from the nearby town of Grand Lake, could have any number of reasons to hate me, the newspaper and the town. Over the last 12 years I had covered and editorialized upon three sets of stories that involved Heemeyer's political activism and his business dilemmas. Heemeyer and the newspaper usually disagreed on these issues. But what truly scared me was that Marv knew where I lived, and I figured if he was after the newspaper then he was probably after me and my family.

I turned and ran as fast as I could along the railroad tracks toward my house, awkwardly stepping on the rocks along the bed of the rails and then dodging sagebrush and thistle. I ran under the U.S. Highway 40 viaduct, cut back under the train and ran through a business and warehouse area next to the tracks on the way to my neighborhood road. I caught a ride. The driver too, was listening to the local radio station's blow-by-blow account of the destruction.

By then, I was frightened and gasping for air. The driver, a distant acquaintance, was friendly enough although he grinned with a smirk, as if he knew something. This woman, Bonnie Brown, was being interviewed about the rampage on the local radio station. She was extolling the virtues of Marv Heemeyer, calling him a gentle Teddy bear of a man who would do this sort of thing only if he was wronged — grievously wronged. It was as if she were praising him; putting him on a pedestal. I could hardly believe my ears. I looked over at the driver, hoping he'd just turn the radio off.

"You've got to admit, you asked for it," he said before I quickly scrambled out of his truck at the police barricades blocking access to my road. I started to run to my house, ignoring the one sheriff's deputy shouting "Hey you! You!" from a distance.

I didn't know it then, but I was part of a story that was already getting attention on the airwaves, on television and particularly on blogs and online news services. At that moment people were already gloating about Heemeyer's rampage, cheering to themselves in front of their flickering computer screens.

I was beginning to feel like I was on the wrong side of this story, the biggest news story of my life.

2. The Landscape of Heroic Imagination

How did I end up in Granby, Colorado, the target of a mad man, running a group of small newspapers where this bizarre yet historical event took place?

Once known as the Dude Ranch Capital of America, Granby epitomizes the terrain of the wild American West, evoking the feeling of a virginal, pre-civilized landscape with spacious skies and room to roam. The town sits at an elevation of 7,892 feet 85 miles northwest of Denver. The town straddles the Fraser River along a series of undulating stair-stepped mesas that rise from the meandering, cottonwood- and willow-lined river. Just two miles downstream the Fraser merges with the Colorado River, the waters passing through massive canyons, deserts and reservoirs all the way to California.

With 2,000 permanent inhabitants, Granby is the most populous town in Grand County. The deckle-edged Continental Divide, with its 12,000- and 13,000-foot peaks, lances skyward of the town to the east. Below the peaks stretch olive green expanses of tundra, with massive lodgepole pine and aspen forests cascading below, spreading to valleys traced by streams and willows with meadows of grass and sagebrush. Here and there, lakes and reservoirs reflect the blue sky like splashes of earth-bound turquoise. It is like something out of the movies.

After my first visit to Granby in 1979, I fell in love with the place. Originally a military brat who had lived on bland naval bases, I was immediately captivated by Colorado and the mountains. But it was the people of Granby who sustained my attention. The small-town heroes, cowards and muddlers-in-between enlivened the pages of our newspapers. I became one of them.

Grand County is a cold and wild place. It's wild enough that a beloved, 91-year-old former mayor of Grand Lake was attacked and killed by a moose in 2003 while walking to church in that town's business sector. A seven-year-old boy was attacked and killed by a mountain lion in Rocky Mountain National Park only one mile from the town boundary. White water river drownings and avalanche deaths are common news stories. The county's natural beauty has a treacherous side to it.

The people of Grand County make their living from tourism, real estate, construction of second homes, some ranching, a little bit of mining, logging and working for the government. Two-thirds of the county is owned by public entities such as the U.S. Forest Service, the Bureau of Land Management, the National Park Service, the Denver Water Department and the state of Colorado. The southeastern part of the county thrives off Winter Park, the fourth-busiest ski area in Colorado, and tourism in general. The center of the county, including Granby, is dependent on summer and winter tourism. Grand Lake, a town 16 miles north of Granby on the shores of Colorado's largest natural lake, sits at the western portal to Rocky Mountain National Park. Kremmling, to the west, is a traditional ranching community.

Grand County is a tough place to make a living. It's also the sort of place that some people might pigeonhole as a semi-rural backwater where the character of the local population has been hardened and refined by hard living in a tough but beautiful environment. Yet it still has a level of sophistication created by a tourist industry that brings in extensive outside influence, including successful retirees from other parts of the country. It's not all forest rangers, ski bums, cowboys and miners.

I arrived in Granby as a reporter who needed a job, inspired in part by the golden age of journalism in America. Carl Bernstein and Bob Woodward of Watergate fame and Walter Cronkite on television epitomized the newsmen who had given journalism its glow during those times. Their newspaper and television reporting had helped bring about the United States' withdrawal from the Vietnam War and had helped topple a president. They ferreted out the facts and proclaimed the truth to a nation that needed to know the reality of its imperfect experiment in Democracy.

American journalism was at its peak of influence and sway throughout the '70s and '80s, long before the rise of the Internet. The more I worked at the newspaper in Granby, the more I wanted to be a part of that journalistic tradition while living in a place that was the epitome of the American West. I took my job at the *Sky-Hi News* hoping to stay for one or two years so I could get some real experience at a small paper in a beautiful place where skiing, fishing and hiking would be added benefits of the job. I had imagined I'd get a call from the *New York Times* or the *Washington Post* and I'd work my way up the journalism career ladder. That phone call never came. I never left.

I couldn't have known then that my decision would make me a leading character in a story just as dramatic as anything I'd ever seen in the movies or on television.

Buried as an afterthought behind my ambition was the idea that small and isolated communities in the hinterlands could harbor an assortment of odd and violent characters, including the stereotypical disgruntled loner who was good with guns and his hands while hiding away in seething anger and nursing grudges. The countrified locals from the film *Deliverance* came to mind. It never occurred to me that perhaps I should take that stereotype seriously. I wasn't in Appalachia, after all. I was in the exotic and romantic Colorado Rockies, the land of Champagne powder, ritzy ski resorts and endless recreation. Yet, when I started writing about my new community, I saw that even the Rocky Mountains harbored their share of petty, sordid and violent crimes mingled with an assortment of odd characters. And yet, murder is rare in this small county. In 28 years we'd cover a murder only about once every four years.

I liked the semi-state of isolation and natural beauty I enjoyed way up in the Rocky Mountains. I skied, hiked, fished and lived outdoors as much as possible while working hard at the same time. By the turn of the century I was running a thriving community group of newspapers. In the course of this work, Marv Heemeyer started to become more prominent. When he wasn't out exploring the backcountry on his snowmobile or ATV, he was agitating for his local political causes and business interests. Increasingly, he was becoming a big part of the local news.

"Hey you! You can't go over there!" the cop shouted after I had stepped out of the pickup truck. The look on my face must have been one of fear and confusion.

The cop recognized me and he waved me on. I looked back toward town and saw the distant image of the bulldozer tank, surrounded by gun-toting deputies, rumbling toward me and my house. I had to get home, fast.

I couldn't have known in that panicked moment of the attack, as sirens blared and cops shouted, that Heemeyer and his defenders would conflate the facts of his predicament and challenge my writing, my life and my town in a spectacular and ominous way. Was this another Columbine High School shooting situation, right here in Granby? Was this another case of outlaws gone berserk, like the two cop killers in Cortez who went on a spree and prompted the largest manhunt in U.S. history? Was Heemeyer another crazed American patriot, like Timothy McVeigh of the Oklahoma City federal building bombing that left 168 people dead? The idea of the rampage and the bulldozer, despite the danger, was intoxicating somehow to me and, as I would discover, increasingly to the outside world. This was something bigger than Granby.

I had a hard time imagining Heemeyer as some crazed, rampaging fiend. He had a large group of loyal friends in Grand Lake and Granby. They had gotten to know him through his snowmobiling excursions and his near-daily morning visits to the Corner Cupboard Café in Grand Lake. He wasn't shy about being seen in public with his girlfriends and he had even managed a sustained relationship with a prominent Grand Lake woman for several years. He attended church somewhat regularly for his preferred denomination, which had locations in Denver. He participated in the bowling leagues and had earnest if not stern opinions about local issues, which he expressed well in public hearings and in letters to the editor. He could seem brooding and a little menacing at times when he didn't get his way, but in general he got along well in the community.

All these thoughts raced through my mind. I ran, confused and scared.

At that moment I decided I was going to find out what it was that prompted Marv Heemeyer to embark on this grandiose scheme to destroy our business and the town of Granby. This was going to be a journey down a long road that would require a close examination of the day-to-day news coverage at the newspapers — much of it my own — that took place in the lead up to this startling event.

I was going to remember and re-remember and comb through public records, police files and town minutes. I was going to re-read my own news stories and editorials and ponder and listen to the writings and recordings that Marv had left behind. I wanted to know.

What had I done — what had we done — to become such vulnerable targets of his mechanized and indifferent fury?

3. A Winning Bid

In a bland hotel in Denver on west Colfax Avenue, at an innocuous real estate auction of distressed properties, the seeds of a dispute that would change Granby forever were planted.

"On the docket now is property number 67. Asset of Middle Park Bank in Granby, Colorado. Two acres with concrete-form garage and shop on site. Zoning is commercial and industrial. Minimum bid of $20,000."

The auctioneer uttered this introduction to the property in a monotone, as if he were reading it from an audit, which, in fact, he was. He seemed to anticipate a lack of interest in the property, but he would soon be surprised.

The auctioneer was clad in a dark brown suit that was too large for his frame, a simple Navy blue tie and a white, buttoned-down shirt that had the smooth-but-rumpled look of a permanent-press shirt washed too many times. I was familiar with this near caricature of a federal employee, having covered the spectacular failure of Middle Park Bank — the very bank that had owned this property — five years earlier, winning a National Newspaper Association award with reporter Martha Williams. It was the arrival of such earnest and suit-clad FDIC examiners in Granby, marching almost in step around the town and carrying large, box-like briefcases, that set off the panic that prompted people to dash to the bank to withdraw all their money. Since then, to see such formally dressed strangers in town — people seldom wore suits and ties to work in Granby — has generally been agreed upon as cause for alarm.

Marvin Heemeyer, one of the attendees who had come to the auction to buy this very property, sat in a back row of the audience on one of the folding metal chairs that had been neatly aligned in the sterile, neon-lit room. He doubted that anyone else would show up to bid on this property. It had been on the market for three years.

"Granby is located here." The lackadaisical auctioneer pointed to a map of Colorado with a telescoping pen, which stretched out like the antenna to a portable radio. "This is the first of seven Granby parcels up for auction today."

"The starting price on this property is $20,000." He was almost apologetic. He flipped a sheet of paper over on the podium, looking at the reverse side. It rattled into his lapel-pinned microphone and through the public address system. "Do I hear a number? Do I hear a price?"

This agent of the FDIC was reflecting, perhaps, the mood in general of a federal lending insurance agency that had ended up with too many distressed properties in the last four years as banks and savings and loans failed all across America. For him, this drab parcel was probably just one of many similar parcels, all representing to some extent a trail of woe and loss. He was auctioning the detritus of failed dreams and squandered fortunes.

Heemeyer, then a new resident of Grand Lake, saw nothing but opportunity in this offering. He wanted to buy the parcel for a snowmobiling friend, John Kleiner, who needed a location for an auto repair shop as he wanted to move his business from Boulder to the mountains. Heemeyer had worked with Kleiner in Boulder, repairing mufflers, and they had become snowmobiling buddies while riding on the trails in and around Grand Lake. This parcel was perfect. There was a large, two-bay garage, office area and plenty of room on site for storage and parking. And it was zoned just right, near the intersection of U.S. Highways 34 and 40. Heemeyer hoped he could buy it for a song, lease it or sell it back to Kleiner on favorable terms and add to his already fairly comfortable income stream. The auction was the way to go. Two Granby realtors had shown the property to him before, asking prices well over $100,000. He knew those prices were way too high for such a parcel in depressed times.

Heemeyer raised his hand and waved the white card with his bidding number, 57, on it.

"Twenty thousand," he said. He might get it for less than a song.

"Mark," the auctioneer said, acknowledging the bid. "I hear twenty thousand."

Accordion-like walls descended from the dropped-panel ceiling, creating a large rectangular space inside an even larger convention space. Windows behind the auctioneer presented a broad view of west Denver. The smell of burnt coffee filled the room. There was muffled conversation from the front of the room and then a literal throat-clearing.

"We'll go to twenty-five thousand."

"OK. Any more interest here?" the auctioneer said, seemingly resigned that there might actually be some real bidding on one of the parcels he had to dispose of. He looked at Heemeyer.

"Well alright then. Thirty thousand."

"Thirty-five," came the bid in the front of the room.

"Yeah, thirty-five," another voice echoed. This wasn't a sole bidder, apparently. It was a bidding duo.

Heemeyer stood up this time and looked at these mysterious bidders. He loomed large in the group of seated men, his six-foot-four frame garbed in pressed denim bib overalls with a striped-pattern shirt underneath. He was trim and robust with broad shoulders and no sign of any sort of a pot belly. He glared at the other bidders and looked at the auctioneer.

"Thirty-seven," Heemeyer said.

"Thirty-eight," came the response from up front. The man doing the bidding, Gus Harris, was a former mayor of Granby who had run a paving business on land near the parcel up for auction. He now stood up, revealing a man of a tall but slight build, wearing khaki pants and a grey cotton work shirt with a calculator and two pens in his right breast pocket. Another man stood up next to him. Shorter and wearing a pearl-buttoned western-style shirt and Levi jeans, this man rocked from foot to-foot and cajoled Harris forward, tapping his elbow.

This man was Metro Cody Docheff, the one-time owner and operator of a concrete plant in Granby. His hair was combed back in a wavy cascade, evoking the image of a bantam rooster. Docheff, of average build, is a high-energy sparkplug of a man. With the leathery skin on his face and neck, he had the look of a salt-of-the-earth businessman. You would never confuse Cody Docheff with an office worker. He's prone to speak his mind forcefully and honestly, at times inspiring fear or anger in those who might differ with him. At one time Docheff had owned the property now up for auction, but he had sold the land with his concrete business. The new owner had failed three years ago as business dried up in the county. The bank had taken the land back and now the FDIC was getting rid of it. This land was, indeed, the dregs of the dregs.

Heemeyer now turned back toward the lackluster auctioneer, shaking his head in an obvious way, as if to let the room know he thought there was something odd about such people who would dare to bid against him. He had a budget of $66,000, but there was no sense in leaving any money on the table.

"Forty-two thousand." He could see Docheff and Harris talking in urgent whispers. Heemeyer started to grin.

"Well?" said the auctioneer.

Harris and Docheff sat down, mute. There was only a brief pause. Harris had set aside $40,000 for the property. That was his limit.

"OK, I have $42,000 from here for the property." He pointed to Heemeyer and nodded toward an associate in the room, as if to say "don't let him get away. He's committed now." "It's going once. It's going twice." He paused, for effect. "Sold to this gentleman, card number 57, for $42,000."

Heemeyer walked to the assistant and stood almost too close, and they walked off to a corner, both with papers in hand.

"Now for the next parcel from Middle Park Bank, in that same neighborhood . . ."

Steve Borda, another Granby business man in the concrete and foundation business, had shown up to bid on that parcel. Borda and Heemeyer were soon to be neighbors.

Harris and Docheff ambled over to Heemeyer during a pause in the bidding a few minutes later.

Heemeyer must have already been forming in his mind all the negative thoughts he could muster about Docheff. In his tapes, Heemeyer claims they spoke for a few minutes, after introductions, and he thought Docheff was "the rudest, most arrogant person . . . a fucking asshole." Heemeyer remembered in his tapes that Docheff had "come back and just introduced himself kind of by just giving me a tongue lashing for about 10 minutes about who I thought I was and what I was going to do with the property. And I explained to him I was buying it for John Kleiner."

Heemeyer says he then offered to sell it to Docheff right there for $66,000.

"Well, I'm sorry," Heemeyer recollects on his tapes, "but I can't just not come down here and spend my money and waste my time and not get . . . make some money on it."

Harris and Docheff were disappointed about not getting the property.

As related in his tapes, Heemeyer watched and thought to himself: "I mean 160 people, for 160 properties that are being sold and this is the only fool that didn't come down there with enough money to buy his property. I mean he's – this shows you how day-late-and-a-dollar short this fool is. This guy's pretty dramatic."

No deal was reached.

Docheff doesn't remember talking to Heemeyer at the auction. Harris remembers saying only, "Well, it looks like you got yourself a piece of property." Steve Borda, another Granby businessman at the auction that day, doesn't remember any verbal confrontations during or after the auction.

Heemeyer thought Docheff was the one who wanted the property and that he had brought along Harris to pony up the money. But in reality, Harris wanted the property for himself, for equipment storage, and he had thought if he could get it for a song, he'd buy it. He already owned two acres adjoining the parcel to the south. Harris remembers that he had $40,000 and that was where the bidding ended for him, not the $42,000 remembered by Heemeyer.

Heemeyer, though, was sure that Docheff was behind it all.

Heemeyer signed the documents for the quit claim deed being processed by the FDIC on May 16, 1992. He left the room knowing he had bought the property at a good price. That Granby Realtor had wanted $110,000 for the very same parcel! Heemeyer was already nearly $70,000 ahead on his investment. He would make money and a steady stream of income in leasing it back to Kleiner; he had done his snowmobiling friend a favor and he had shown those other two yokels a bit about how to do business. He had won.

He couldn't have known on that triumphant spring day that he had just purchased the very ground on which he would last walk alive.

Although Heemeyer had rural roots, he grew to become accustomed to getting his way in land and business dealings. He had grown up as a farm boy on land between Clear Lake and Castlewood, South Dakota. His brother said Marv was like any other farm boy: good at repairing machinery and shooting the gophers that plagued farms in that region. He wasn't an exceptional student in school although he did hold the record in the half-mile at his high school for a year. He worked on the yearbook and the school paper.

Marv would say he wasn't really "book smart." But others would say he was handy, a fast learner and very practical-minded when it came to machinery. After leaving the farm in South Dakota he attended trade school and then went on to serve in the U.S. Air Force. During his military service he spent time stationed in Germany. He was honorably discharged at the rank of sergeant. And even though he mostly worked as an inventory and processing clerk, he enjoyed the military. In the Air Force he got his first taste of Colorado and he liked it. He had excellent mechanical skills and the ability to learn most any trade quickly. He had always been good at welding from his farm days and he decided to get into the muffler repair business in Colorado.

It didn't take him long, working at shops in North Denver and Boulder, to see that he was better than his bosses at the mechanics and the business-side of muffler repair. He opened his own shop with help from a partner and before long he had two more shops in Boulder and Denver. Through the ups and downs of the economy he had managed to buy land for the shops at low prices and sell them high. He made money on real estate and he still owned a shop that was making good money. He'd keep it, hire a manager, and move to the mountains to enjoy the good life.

And the land was perfect. Granby is the ideal location for a business that hopes to serve Grand County. It's centrally located in east Grand County at the intersection of U.S. Highways 40 and 34 near the confluence of the Colorado and Fraser Rivers. Granby offers expansive views of the national forest and valleys all around, and it has its own ski resort, Ski Granby Ranch, then called Silver Creek. Yet the town is more of a service town than a resort, unlike the nearby villages of Winter Park and Grand Lake, where tourists flock in winter and summer.

For Marv Heemeyer, it was beginning to look like Granby was a great place to be doing business.

4. Turd Polishing

It didn't take long for Heemeyer to realize that his good life in the mountains was going to be disturbed by what he saw as needless and escalating hassles over owning a small piece of land in a puny town high in the Colorado Rockies.

"Stinks in here," Heemeyer said to Bud Wilson, the manager of the Granby Sanitation District.

"What do you expect," Wilson said. "This is a sewer plant."

They both smiled. Wilson liked Heemeyer because this new owner of two acres in western Granby seemed all common sense and no-nonsense. Wilson had learned that Heemeyer was a one-time farm boy who was just a straight shooter who knew his way around a piece of equipment.

"So this is where you work?" Heemeyer said.

"Only if I have to. Yes, we run this plant. The work I prefer is out in the field. But you know what they say about the smell here. That's the smell of sanitized shit."

They laughed. Heemeyer shook his head appreciatively, expressing the mutual sort of admiration these two men had for each other. Wilson was an atypical bureaucrat who was more concerned about getting things done than paperwork, forms and legal precedent. It was that attitude, in fact, that had prompted Heemeyer to show up at the Sanitation district board of directors meeting that night. Wilson had told him he could annex into the district and hook on to the sewer lines down by his new property, but he'd have to go through the board first.

"Just a formality," he had said. "Don't bring a lawyer." Heemeyer believed him and got on the agenda.

They were early for the meeting, sitting in the simple and plain boardroom where fluorescent lights cast a flat-white glow on the laminated board table and the row of hard, wooden chairs for the audience. The hum of the sewer plant in operation filled the silent moments, like the engines of a ship at sea. Occasional splashes could be heard as the massive white plastic tumblers that served as aerators and purifiers rolled and sloshed through the murky water of the town's sewage.

At 7 p.m. sharp the board members all filed into the room from the outside, as if they had been together as a group before the meeting. Heemeyer might have wondered if they had already met beforehand, discussing the issues out of the public eye. But the easy cordiality of the greetings exchanged between Wilson and the board members put Heemeyer at ease. They looked like an OK bunch, if not a little countrified. There was even a woman on the board.

Routine matters such as meeting minutes and the payment of bills were taken care of quickly before the first item on the agenda came up. It read: "Annexation of Heemeyer Parcel to district and provision of services thereof."

"You must be Heemeyer, the one who got that parcel at auction."

That was from the one who had the name "Ron Thompson, Vice President" on a plastic nameplate in front of him. He wore a red, shiny jacket that had Thompson and Sons Excavation emblazoned across the front in cursive black letters. He wore a John Deere baseball-style cap.

"Got the quit claim deed here to prove it," Heemeyer said. He held up the document from the FDIC.

"Well, what's this about, Bud?"

That was from Randy Schmuck, the board president. He owned the auto body shop in town. He also served as a trustee on the town board. He took a quiet pride in assuming the less-savory roles of local governance.

"Like it says here. He wants to annex into the district first, so he can get sewer for that place he bought. It's not got a proper system down there now. Just an old mixer truck barrel buried underneath, holding it all. Not exactly legal. He's on well water. It'd be nice to get him in the district, filling a gap in service and all down there."

Board member Pete Robinson, the longtime owner of Pete's Service, a gas station on Granby's main street, summed up the real problem that was screaming to be related, despite the quiet nature of it all.

"But there ain't no service down there."

"Well, what do we have down there, Bud," Schmuck asked.

Wilson said Heemeyer's two-acre parcel was about 100 feet from a non-pressurized sewer line that ran from an active sewer main farther east. To use it, Heemeyer would have to put in a lift station. And he'd have to run at least 100 feet of service line to the main.

Heemeyer looked at Wilson as he spoke. He had a sinking feeling, knowing this news was not good, but that Wilson had said something could be worked out.

"You do know what this means, don't you, Mr. Heemeyer?" Ron Thompson leaned forward in his chair. He wiggled a toothpick around under his mustache with an unseen tongue behind those closed, pursed lips.

"I just want to get sewer, that's all. Shouldn't be complicated."

"Nothing money can't uncomplicate," Thompson said. "That'll cost you a pretty penny to put in that lift station and run that service line from your property. And a lift station has year-round costs. Electricity for the grinder pump and lifter."

It was quiet again for a moment.

"You sure you want to do this?" Thompson said. "I mean, leach field'd be cheaper and all. And legal."

The board members stared at Heemeyer without any strong facial expression one way or another.

"Now look. I just want to do the right thing and get on the public sewer. You should want that. It's the best thing. I'll pay to get my property annexed then have to pay those property taxes from then on. But you've got to hook me up," Heemeyer said defensively.

"Well, we just can't willy-nilly hook you up," Schmuck said. "This little district isn't made of money. We can't let the other people, people here before you, pay for you. Why, we just took on a pile of debt just for this plant here. We'll pay to annex. You have to pay to hook on.

Those are the rules. Development has to pay its own way, otherwise we'd go broke."

"Well, that's just not . . . not worth it. That's seventy, eighty thousand dollars, just all that." Heemeyer looked over at Bud Wilson, who now was rubbing his forehead, looking down at a ledger book on the desk in front of him.

"We just did a job like that for an ol' boy up there at Three Lakes, near Grand Lake," Ron Thompson said. "Lift station. Service line. Me and my brothers. Why, the lift station alone was forty thousand dollars. You add in that service line, you've got a chunk of change in this."

"I can operate equipment. Do it myself. That'd save a lot."

"It might," Thompson said. "But it's got to be inspected. Material costs are big here. Our engineers, they'd come in and look over your shoulder. Big job."

At this point Heemeyer believed that Thompson was trying to set up his family's excavation company for a bunch of work to be paid by him. But the cost would be more than seventy thousand dollars — more than he'd paid for the land itself. This was getting to be highway robbery.

"You should want to hook me on. I'll bring business and fees to you. I'd become part of the community with a nice little business down there. Even more. I could expand. I mean, what do you do then?"

"We polish turds and purify pee," Pete Robinson said with not a smile or a chuckle. He just looked straight at Heemeyer. Nancy Anderson, the board member who was also the board secretary, was writing in a legal pad in front of her. Randy Schmuck was looking over at Robinson, not really smiling but subtly nodding his head in approval. Ron Thompson fiddled with a pencil on the table in front of him, spinning it like a dial on a compass. The toothpick moved vigorously in his mouth.

Now Heemeyer stood up. He had a rolled-up piece of paper in his hand, a photo copy of his quit-claim deed.

"Well now I've heard just about all I need to hear." He spoke evenly, but with the appearance of clenched teeth in his facial muscles. "You can't expect to grow if this is your policy. It's extortion by government fiat. I don't need you. You need me. Can't you see that? And I want to be part of your district. But I will leave now."

"And this isn't any clean shit," Heemeyer said, talking back to Wilson over his shoulder, as he exited, the door slightly open. "It's bullshit."

Heemeyer was beginning to realize that he owned land that had no legal water or sewer service.

The door slammed and the board sat quietly, the only sound being the soft whoosh of thousands of gallons of sewage water washing in the massive aeration tumblers.

"He didn't withdraw his annexation request, as far as I could tell," Wilson said, looking sheepish. "We can do that for him. Things could change down there. Wouldn't cost him as much. Doing him a favor."

And so the board unanimously agreed to annex the Heemeyer parcel, which was duly advertised in the local newspaper and then made a matter of the public record. Heemeyer didn't notice these actions. He was done with the sewer district.

Heemeyer and the board members couldn't have known it at the time, but that effort to placate Heemeyer would greatly complicate everybody's life in the not-too-distant future.

5. Betting on Gambling

Marv Heemeyer was still a relative newcomer to the community when he started making himself known in the summer of 1991. It wasn't long before members of my newspaper staff had their own run-ins with him, partly because Heemeyer published two editions of his own newspaper — a newspaper he wrote and produced — called *The Grand Lake Gazette*. He published it as a foil to our newspapers, which he considered to be biased against what he saw as an opportunity to bring legalized gambling to the tourist town of Grand Lake. Our Grand Lake reporter and columnist Cece Krewson had the first contentious contact with Heemeyer.

Cece Krewson was a sophisticated sort of rural wag. In an earlier life he had owned and operated newspapers in Tunkhannock, Pennsylvania, winning many prestigious journalism awards and herding the family newspapers to a dependable sort of prosperity. When his first wife died he descended into a nearly suicidal funk, only to snap out of it to marry a young woman on his staff, sell the newspapers and buy a dude ranch in the Rocky Mountains of Colorado, near Kremmling, 40 miles west of Granby. He relished his move to the Rocky Mountain West. He frequently dressed the part of his new persona.

During the summer months he set aside his well-worn brown felt cowboy hat and wore one made of breathable woven straw mesh with a turned-down front brim. The summer hat featured a resplendent ostrich feather tucked in the front of the hat band that cast a swath of colors like fresh oil on water.

He was wearing that hat when he unexpectedly encountered Marv Heemeyer on the boardwalk of Grand Lake just as the high season for summer tourists was starting. Heemeyer stood with his newspapers in his hand between the Grand Lake Pharmacy and the Lariat Saloon, then the most popular watering hole in Grand Lake, celebrated in the *Denver Post* as a place that harbored "denizens of Grand Lake in a dark, dusky and smoke-filled backroom." Heemeyer stood so still and proud a person might have thought he was a classic drug store Indian peddling nickel cigars and posing nobly for all to see in the early evening light. But Marv Heemeyer was no Indian that night and he wasn't selling cigars. He was a man with a mission. He was spreading the right word about the gambling debate in Grand Lake, handing out *The Grand Lake Gazette.*

Cece, on his way to the pharmacy to buy a pack of cigarettes before meeting me for our weekly editorial meeting over beers at the Grand Lake Lodge, stopped short upon seeing Heemeyer hulking on the sidewalk. Cece took one of the newspapers.

"I know who you are," Marv said after Cece snapped the four-page tabloid paper open. He looked askance at the front page. The tone of Heemeyer's words did not have the sound of a greeting.

The paper's slogan read: "Promoting a Better Economy for All in Grand Lake." In a matter of seconds Cece's seasoned eyes took in all that he needed to know about this publication. Clunky typography, butting headlines in all caps with awkward line breaks, spelling errors and unrestrained boosterism about the benefits of gambling screaming from each story prompted him to chuckle. This was an ugly newspaper that was nothing more than crude propaganda.

"So it's come to this," Cece said, wagging the paper at Heemeyer with both hands.

He read the lead story, a short piece that was crafted as this newspaper's mission statement.

"Now Read This! The Fair Truth Revealed!"

The story stated there was a need for "other points of view" in the important debate over gambling since the local newspaper, in his reference to the paper Cece and I produced, was "telling lies and slandering the reputations of upstanding local businessmen who favored legal gambling in our town. So Now Read This and learn the fair and balanced truth!"

"Well I don't know you. I'm Cece Krewson," Cece said.

"I'm Marvin Heemeyer. The publisher. You don't have a monopoly on the news anymore, Cece (which he pronounced see-see)."

"It's 'Cece,' as in Cease and Desist," Cece said.

There was a pause. Heemeyer didn't seem to acknowledge Krewson's comment one way or another.

"Oh, so you're the one," Cece said. "You're the new leader of their crusade. You're their hero, leading the way to bring casinos and high rises to the shores of Grand Lake."

"Why yes, Cece (see-see again) I'm the one they came to in an effort to get the right word out that your paper won't publish. So I'm leading the way. They asked and I know what to do."

"It's Cece," Krewson said, giving the proper pronunciation again.

"It looks like see-see to me," Heemeyer said. "Rhymes with pee-pee."

At this Cece tilted his head back and looked up into Heemeyer's face. It was broad and round with a smirk on the lips.

"Well then please let me know the specific lie we've published. Just one. Just tell me. Give me an example. We would correct it, you know."

This statement, uttered in the tone of a question but perhaps too solicitous, too earnest-sounding, like the baiting comment of a cross-examining attorney, got Heemeyer's attention. Heemeyer seemed to stand taller in front of the faux log siding of the building behind him. Now Heemeyer's large and erect frame stood in stark contrast to Cece's tall (six one) yet slight physique. A few disinterested tourists passed by on the boardwalk, their footfalls clunking on the wooden planks, their heels scraping the lumber occasionally.

The boardwalk had become an object of great pride for the town fathers. It reflected, they thought, the quaint western heritage of their small town, a town that was the most scenic in the county. The boardwalk lined both sides of the main street, setting off the fake hitching posts scattered here and there and giving definition to the rickety overhangs that protected the wooden walkway in places.

The street's business establishments consisted of a few art galleries selling brightly glazed pottery and paintings portraying idealized and fuzzy portrayals of the scenic Rocky Mountain beauty in the area, bars and restaurants that had western-themed names (The Lariat, The Little Bear, Grumpy's, The Stagecoach, Pancho and Lefty's), ice-cream and candy shops, real estate offices trying to sell high-end homes that sat on the shores of Grand Lake and run down "rustic" cabins hidden on windy back roads for the economically minded.

There was even the mandatory putt-putt golf course, full of gewgaws and rube Goldberg-type wonders, earning it at one time the distinction of being a *Mechanix Illustrated* award-winning establishment. And then there were the touristy boutiques selling rubber tomahawks, true gold nuggets, leather moccasins, tom-tom drums and pop-guns alongside racks of postcards, some of which portray jack-a-lopes and donkeys carrying 10-foot-long rainbow trout. This town was the epitome of a small summer tourist haven high in the Rockies.

But Grand Lake also has a wild and isolated side to it. During the winter months and most of the year, Trail Ridge Road, the highway through Rocky Mountain National Park that links the town to Estes Park, is closed due to heavy snows. For many months, Grand Lake is literally the town at the end of the road with only one way in and out. This heavy snow is why Grand Lake labels itself as the Snowmobiling Capital of Colorado. It's a cold and wild place, but beautiful.

Cece couldn't help but notice that there wasn't any sort of real news in Marv Heemeyer's *Grand Lake Gazette.* Cece stood there on the boardwalk, reading and scanning the publication when a couple sauntered by and the man paused long enough near Heemeyer to stick his hand out and ask for a copy.

"Here you go sir," Heemeyer said. "Here's all you need to know about important issues facing our town."

"We're just passing through," the man said, reaching up to tip the brim of his International Harvester cap, as if in a polite salute upon leaving.

"You'll want to come back once we get our way with these important economic issues. We want prosperity in our town," Heemeyer said.

"Well that's fine and dandy," the man said. His wife, with a grey and white bonnet in the style of a Mennonite, had walked along. Now she looked back.

"Don't believe everything you read," Cece said to the man as he walked toward his wife. They held hands and looked back at Cece and Marv.

"Well you should know that, you hypocrite," Heemeyer hissed under his breath, so the couple couldn't hear.

"But of course I was referring to this great little publication here," Cece said, holding it up higher, as if the couple was still looking back, which they weren't.

The cloudless sky glowed in an azure blue that darkened subtly with every passing second as the sun dropped in the western sky toward the still snow-covered ridges and peaks on the western horizon, marking Bowen Peak, Baker Mountain, Blue Ridge and Rocky Mountain National Park.

"Oh no you don't," Heemeyer said, stepping a little bit closer to Krewson. "It's your bias, your slant. You've said it. You don't want the gambling that will save this struggling town that doesn't have any business to start with. The people here need the business. They're starving here! Starving! And you people here, you don't even know it. You can't see it."

When the idea of bringing legalized gambling to the small town of Grand Lake cropped up a year and a half earlier, in the wake of the statewide voter approval of low-stakes legalized gambling in Central City, Blackhawk and Cripple Creek, Colorado, our newspaper came out strongly opposed to the idea. We felt it would ruin the spirit and feel of the picturesque and quaint Grand Lake and we thought it wasn't right for a town at the western entrance to a natural wonder of the nation, Rocky Mountain National Park.

We felt it would crassly commercialize Grand Lake, named for the state's largest natural lake, which sat right next to the town. In tandem with our newspaper's stance, a loud and persistent contingent of citizens had stepped forward to fight the pro-gambling effort. Most of those pushing for legalized gambling were Grand Lake businessmen who hoped to cash in on gambling fever in Colorado.

Land values soared in Central City and Blackhawk on a wave of gambling speculation, and since gambling was legal there, those once-sleepy mountain towns, which before could boast of nothing more than a glorious mining past, now saw huge increases in business. The pro-gambling crowd wanted that in Grand Lake. But many other citizens didn't want it at all. They wanted to protect the picturesque village-like qualities of Grand Lake from the depredations of legalized gambling. They wanted to protect the pristine and wilderness-like qualities of Rocky Mountain National Park.

The fight had been intense during the last year, with shoving matches in town meetings, vandalism, battles on the letters-to-the-editor page and many ruined friendships. Priests and ministers even got into the act, decrying the negative impacts of gambling from their pulpits. Some had stood up and ostentatiously walked out of church during those sermons. The gambling debate was splitting the town.

"We've been presenting both sides of the story," Cece said, "going out of our way. Many of your supporters advertise with us."

"Not for long," Heemeyer retorted, his voice rising. "You and Brower, you write with a poisoned pen that writes only in yellow ink. You spin a web of lies and deceit, you do. I know. You're just making a well-meaning group of businessmen look like fools and idiots."

"And how is it you're qualified to write all this crap?" Krewson said, shaking the paper at Heemeyer now.

Heemeyer stood and glowered, not saying a word. He must not have wanted to say he had worked on his high school newspaper and yearbook.

"I speak for those who agree with me and my newspaper. Who embrace this new publication. They scorn your rag and you. They would smite you for your falsehoods."

Cece was beginning to see that he was not getting anywhere having this conversation and he was believing that Heemeyer was one of those people who couldn't differentiate opinion from fact and who couldn't agree to disagree.

"You can write us a letter to the editor. In fact, we ran a letter from you. We've run many, many pro-gambling letters and pro-gambling columns, balancing it all out."

"I don't need your letter to the editor," Heemeyer said, now stepping even closer to Krewson, forcing Cece to step back. "I've got this." He held up in the shape of a tube a bunch of hand-rolled copies of his *Grand Lake Gazette.*

He held it up toward that beautiful sky in such a way that Cece felt he might be preparing to hit him with this roll of papers as a man would beat a dog with a rolled newspaper.

He stepped back again, turning his left side away from Marv, raising his right elbow and shoulder as if to shield himself from a blow. He ducked his head and his hat fell to the boardwalk, rolling awkwardly to Heemeyer's feet.

And Heemeyer merely stood there, his arm raised, the cowboy hat spinning to a stop at his feet. Cece's thinning and grey hair was matted on his scalp and strung in moist whisps down his forehead. He looked back up at Heemeyer from this near-cowering position and he felt ashamed and afraid, all at once.

"My hat," he said, after a long pause.

"Get it yourself." Heemeyer walked away heavily, his steel-toed work boots stomping loudly and triumphantly down the boardwalk in a militaristic and march-like cadence, sure and relentless. Never once did his heels scrape the surface mid-stride.

Cece's hand shook as he reached for his bottle of Coors.

"I was to have been smitten," Cece said to me, a sardonic smile on his face. "It was all very Biblical, him lecturing me and raising the word in his hands above his head, like Moses decrying false prophets. God. Smite. One of my favorite puzzle words."

Every week Cece composed a crossword puzzle for our newspapers, using clever local clues and place names. It was a popular feature.

We sat on what boosters called "Colorado's favorite front porch" at the Grand Lake Lodge, a classic old-style resort that sat on a ridge overlooking the town and its eponymous lake. In the distance shimmered Shadow Mountain Reservoir and Lake Granby, all set off by mountain peaks and ridges. The puny white triangles of sailboats on Grand Lake, like over-large specks of stray confetti, dappled the dark rippled surface of the water. It was a stunning view.

Cece's hand shook even more as he lit his Marlboro with a well-worn Zippo.

"He scared me and now we've got more of a fight on our hands," he said, putting the *Grand Lake Gazette* on the table in front of me. It was the first I had seen of it.

We had already lost advertisers and been threatened with lawsuits over our stance in the fight over bringing gambling to Grand Lake. And now there was this. I thought with a tinge of worry about the threat of competition to our already struggling little newspaper. Cece, I could tell, worried about physical violence.

"This big brute is their leader, their hero. No wonder it's gotten out of hand."

His rimless bifocals reflected the dark-green mountainside of Shadow Mountain, obscuring his eyes.

After two years of hate and discontent, a vote on gambling in Grand Lake took place three months later in November of 1992. The people of Grand Lake overwhelmingly voted down the question that would have allowed gambling in the town. Cece and I both looked at the result of that vote as a victory for the newspaper and the right cause. After that vote the question of legalized gambling in Grand Lake was seldom brought up, as if people were more afraid of the feelings such a topic might recall.

Marvin Heemeyer would never forget that fight, which he saw as a crusade in which he had tried to help save the hapless inhabitants of Grand Lake from their own economic misfortune. He had hoped to help save the town. He would never forget how he had lost that fight and the role our newspaper and I had played.

While Marv wouldn't forget the gambling fight, we moved forward at the newspaper, covering the weekly news in Granby and Grand Lake that revealed a modest turn-around in the local economy. By 1993, new businesses were opening, families were moving to the area and the tourist trade was picking up. Marv's muffler shop was one of those new businesses.

Heemeyer had opened the muffler shop on that property in western Granby he had purchased from the FDIC. He wanted to buy some ads for his business. His doors had been open for about six months and now he wanted people to know he was an expert at repairing and replacing mufflers. He had painted the concrete, two-bay garage building yellow and in red ink he had written Mountain View Muffler. The building was now obvious from both U.S. Highway 40 in western Granby and U.S Highway 34.

"Who are you?" he said to me when I showed up at his shop. He stood tall and looked fit and seemed proud and suspicious all at the same time. He didn't smile, at least not at first. He wore neatly pressed bib overalls over a plaid button-down shirt. His face was broad and his eyes were wide. It was a warm day in early June. He had a cramped reception area and office by the front door. Inside, a selection of brightly gleaming muffler pipes was spread out on the high counter.

"The newspaper. I'm Patrick. You called," I said.

"Oh. You," he said. "It's not that Cece?" (He pronounced it see-see).

"He's in Grand Lake. I've got Granby."

Marv stared down at me with his broad eyes and flat gaze. The car he had been working on when I showed up was elevated seven feet in the air. A welding torch sat underneath.

"Well, what's the best deal on some advertising? And I want a story too. You do those new business stories."

I went into an explanation of ad rates and possibilities with him, to which he didn't seem to be listening. I said we'd have to set up an appointment for the interview for the story. He said he wanted the cheapest ad deal I could give him. He said he could meet me for the story interview on a Monday.

"Okay," I said.

"You know I didn't really want to do this here. But it's turned out OK," he said.

I nodded.

"The first guy I was going to lease to, Dr. J, he backed out on me. It was going to be a garage," he jerked his head toward the east, toward Dr. J's garage in Granby, located at the other side of town. "So I'm doing this now on my own. For me. I know how to make this work. I've owned and run shops like this in Boulder, Denver, Wheat Ridge, Aurora. Sure, I won't be as busy here, but heck, this is OK."

The hydraulic lift looked brand new. Large red steel toolboxes on wheels sat in a corner. An older Chevrolet pick-up truck sat in the other garage bay, the paint chipping away and the hood wide-open. An engine hoist sat poised over the engine compartment, cables stretched taut into the place where the engine sat.

I took down some basic information and said I'd be back Monday for his interview. We shook hands. I welcomed him to Granby. He followed me out of his garage and he gestured toward a barren lot, littered with three car chassis, two engines, wooden crates and empty pallets. Weeds grew up through the slats in the pallets. A tall pile of rusted and stained catalytic converters, like over-sized ancient tin cans, cascaded off the side of his garage in a conical pile.

"I've got plans here," he said. "There's possibility here. I can make it work. Could mean more for you."

My first impression of Heemeyer after that meeting is that he wasn't exactly friendly, but he wasn't hostile either. He seemed to be appraising me in a skeptical sort of way. I remembered that he had a connection to the gambling fight in Grand Lake and that we had been on opposite sides of the fight. By then, most people were anxious to move forward and forget about that episode, which seemed like ancient history.

I showed up at his shop the following Monday, with my camera in hand so I could do a new business story, and the shop was closed up. I tried again the next Friday, and it was closed again. I called Marv up and tried to set a date and he said show up Tuesday this week and I did, and he wasn't there. Two weeks later the shop was closed every day of the week. His ad was still running in the paper but I gave up. A month later, in July, I showed up and he told me to pull his ads since I hadn't done the story. I said I had tried but I never found him and yet he insisted. I offered to do the story right then and get a photo later. He sternly insisted that it was too late. I began to feel uncomfortable.

So I offered a solution.

"Look, since we missed that I'll give you a quarter page ad free in our Meet Your Merchants section. That includes a photo, description. It's popular. Free. Normally costs $250."

He said nothing. A customer dropped off a car and he parked it. He came back in the shop and looked down at me from behind the counter. The same brightly shined tail pipes gleamed on the counter top.

"I'll do it. Come back tomorrow for the photo."

I left him some paper work. He kept his little ad in the paper and I took a photo of him the next day, with those brightly gleaming tail pipes as props in the foreground. In his free ad he described his business as a muffler repair shop, nineteen years of experience, satisfaction guaranteed. He was smiling broadly in the photo.

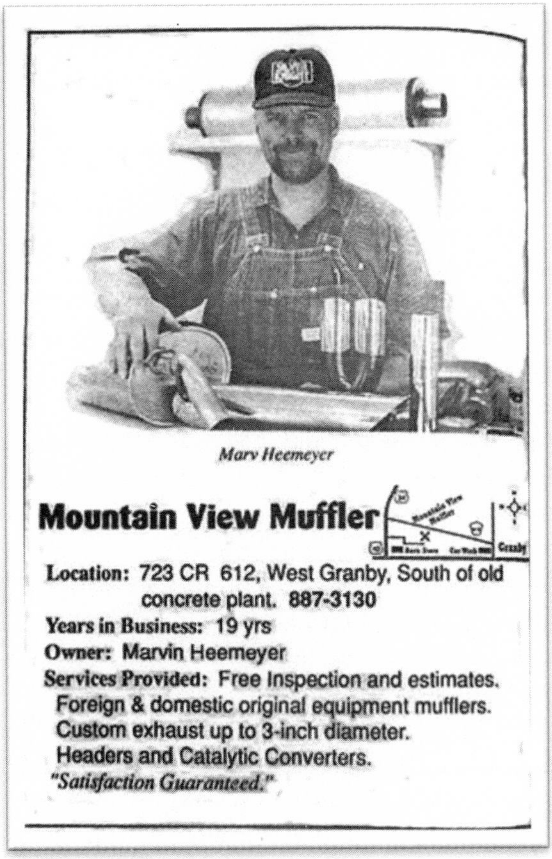
Marv Heemeyer
Mountain View Muffler
Location: 723 CR 612, West Granby, South of old concrete plant. 887-3130
Years in Business: 19 yrs
Owner: Marvin Heemeyer
Services Provided: Free Inspection and estimates.
Foreign & domestic original equipment mufflers.
Custom exhaust up to 3-inch diameter.
Headers and Catalytic Converters.
"Satisfaction Guaranteed."

Sky-Hi News

His smile, however, belied an anger that he felt toward me. He was angry that I hadn't done the story on his shop and he wasn't satisfied with my make-up offer of the free ad in our business profile special section. He was convinced that I was a liar, spinning webs of lies, and that I was a part of a local conspiracy of Granby good ol' boys who were doing all we could to keep the newcomer down.

But this wasn't at all clear to me that July day as I walked away past the pile of rusting mufflers. He had seemed happy and content with our arrangement. It wasn't until later — two years later — that I sensed Heemeyer's anger.

My friend Ted Kellner had transplanted a barn from Kansas to property he owned in Granby and I was enchanted with the idea. He told me how to do it because I had the idea that I would do the same thing and turn my transplanted barn into my home. Ted cautioned me, however, that I'd need to have at least two bigger pickups to haul tools and machines out there and to haul the disassembled barn back. He knew a friend of his who'd probably let me borrow a pick-up. His name was Marv Heemeyer.

Marv happily agreed to rent me his truck. It was going to cost me $400 for four days. I'd be responsible for gas and oil. But he warned me.

"It's losing transmission fluid," he said. "You've got to check it out every 300 miles or so. You've got to lift the hood here and fill 'er up. Be careful of this hood."

It took some manipulating and jimmying to get the hood to open smoothly, but we figured it out. A week later, after two trips to Kansas, I returned the truck. But when he came out to take the keys and my check, he was no longer the smiling Marv I had seen a week before.

"What did you do to that hood?"

He looked at me sternly as he walked around to open it. He had to pound on the hood to get it to pop away from the latch and it awkwardly yawned open, just as it had before the trip.

"You've ruined this hood. I told you to be careful."

He was clearly angry. He pointed at me as if to scold me.

I protested, but meekly, because I felt intimidated by it all. His mood had changed so quickly from seeming accommodating to angry that I felt a wave of fear pass through me. I felt small in front of him. We had done exactly as he had said and the hood seemed the same as it was before the trip: damaged but operable.

"I can't even close it," he shouted, slamming it down in a deliberately hard manner, as if to force it shut, which is just what he had told us not to do.

"Now look, Marv, we didn't do that. It was working OK."

"You've damaged this and you must pay. You will pay or I'll take you to court."

"What?"

"You heard me. I'm taking you to court. You ruined this. You won't take advantage of me!"

There we stood next to his Dodge dually pickup under a massive cottonwood tree in a yard littered with the carcasses of other cars and piles of mufflers and catalytic converters.

"Well what can we do short of court, Marv?"

Too quickly he said it.

"Eight hundred dollars. Right now and I'll feel settled."

He stared down at me while he leaned against the right front fender of the truck. It wasn't a casual sort of lean. It was more like the position a man would take if he were preparing to climb up on top of the hood and leap at me. I felt intimidated.

So I paid him right there. I wrote out the check, he took it, folded it in half and stuffed it neatly into the breast pocket of his coveralls. He smiled happily and smugly and turned to walk back to his shop.

I felt then as if I had been had. He had set me up but I felt there wasn't much else I could do, other than dare him to sue me. And as I was to learn later, that's probably exactly what he would have done.

6. Leader of the Pack

During this time in the mid-90s it might have been easy to dismiss Marv as a disgruntled schemer prone to angry outbursts. For instance, it was well known that Marv had let his sensitivity about money and being "taken" intrude into his passion for snowmobiling. He had purchased a snowmobile from a Grand Lake dealer based on ads that claimed the sled would ride the powder well. But it didn't ride the powder well for Heemeyer, which he claimed was because of a change in manufacturing specs. He demanded a refund because it wasn't as advertised and when that didn't happen he sued, going all the way to court. Representing himself, Heemeyer wanted his money back, plus damages. But the case was dismissed and Heemeyer ended up throwing cash into the face of the snowmobile dealer after it was all said and done. He had played the victim and lost.

So he switched snowmobile brands, bad-mouthed his former favorite brand to his wide group of friends and revealed a deep distrust of people when it came to money and commerce, even his friends and fellow snowmobilers. And yet, his business thrived as he smartly captured the muffler repair market in the county. He remained the friendly town character in Grand Lake over coffee at the Corner Cupboard most every morning. He socialized evenings at Pancho and Lefty's. He continued to enjoy snowmobiling.

Troy Hilton learned that the ultimate goal of this Thursday's ride was the tuning fork tree at the apex of the North Supply Trail, on the way to Bowen Mountain. He had never heard of such a thing. All they said was if you didn't turn at the tuning fork tree, you'd get mired in the downed trees and deep snow, all in the steeps. Heemeyer knew exactly how to find the tuning fork tree.

The planning started, as it usually did for the renowned Thursday rides, at the Chuck Hole Café in Grand Lake, where plowed and drifted snow sat in banks six feet high along the boardwalk. Dan Schneller, even though he wasn't going on that day's ride, joined Heemeyer at their usual table. Schneller, who built and remodeled homes in Grand Lake, had grown up in the town and he had come to like the affable Heemeyer. They exchanged pleasantries and small talk on those early mornings before Schneller headed off to his most recent job. John Linton, the owner of a small grocery store in town, the Mountain Food Market, would likely have been a part of the Thursday group that day. A few others showed up in their bulky snowmobile outfits, helmets under their arms. They were all locals. All ready to ride.

Most of them knew that Marv was the undisputed leader for the Thursday rides, although he himself wasn't one to insist on any such label. He was the fastest, loudest and most audacious of any of the riders assembled that day. He had rebored his sled so he had 1300 ccs and the pipes were modified to allow the most efficient system he could assemble, which also meant it was very loud. Not only that, he had equipped his sled with a modified bumper system that allowed him to pass through forests of small trees and quagmires of willow bushes and small cottonwoods, knocking them over or pushing them out of the way.

The Marv bumper was a popular thing with the more extreme snowmobilers in town. Most everyone's sled that day came with Marv bumpers. If you didn't, you stood a good chance of getting stuck way out there in the wilderness, miles away from the town and an easy rescue. The important thing, they all agreed, was to stay with the group so if any one rider got into trouble, the others could help. But it wasn't always an easy task to stay with the group when Marv was in the lead.

Over coffee, eggs, pancakes and massive smothered cinnamon rolls it was agreed that they'd take the trails to the tuning fork tree and from there it was cross country powder and tree bashing.

The crew left the Chuck Hole in different cars, most with snowmobile-laden trailers in tow. They went to John's Mountain Food Market. There, sandwiches, bags of chips and candy bars were grabbed and slammed into packs for that day's lunch. John, a soft-spoken store keeper known for his skillful persistence on a sled, was known to make great deals for the Thursday riders: Three dollars for a sandwich, chips, a drink and a candy bar. They all left the market stocked, stoked and ready to ride.

It was a four-mile drive to the trailhead where groomed trails on what were dirt roads in summer led the way up toward Blue Ridge, the Gilsonite Trail, Lost Lake, North and South Supply Creek, Cascade Mountain and the Bowen Mountain area. Some of the terrain was certified federal wilderness, where snowmobiles weren't allowed, some was private land, yet most of it was wide open public land where snow machines were free to roam. The Thursday group loved to cruise on all that land with what some would call reckless abandon.

One newcomer with the group that day was Gary Hilton, a Granby resident who was the son of the owner of Middle Park Glass. He was an avid snowmobiler who shared Marv Heemeyer's love of old Chevrolets and Oldsmobiles especially the Toronado, a unique car with a dubious reputation that was nonetheless loved by stock car enthusiasts. Heemeyer and Hilton had traded many a story about old Chevys and Toronados, mostly while Hilton was waiting for Heemeyer to repair a muffler. Hilton thought Heemeyer's muffler work was expensive, but it was almost always expertly done. Eventually, Hilton was invited to go on one of the Thursday rides.

It was snowing off and on that winter day, as Hilton remembered it, with snow flurries coming and going in the mild-to-gusty wind that blew out of the west. At 20 degrees it was considered to be relatively warm, but to the group of eight riders heading up the county road to North Supply, the weather made no difference at all. The thick and bulky snowmobile suits, the well-insulated helmets, down gloves and snowmobile riding boots rendered the riders immune to the weather. They were in their own, insulated worlds, as if wrapped in wintry cocoons. This left them free to sense acceleration, speed and pure mechanical power without worrying about freezing or overheating. Hilton loved that pure feeling of speed and power that only a snowmobile can give, especially when it does so in a pristine environment like the mountains around Grand Lake.

As they climbed up the forest service road, Hilton looked back as Lake Granby and Shadow Mountain Reservoir, flat pans of white, opened up below them. The lakes were rimmed by Shadow Mountain and the ridges and peaks of Twin Peaks. To the north, Mt. Baldy nudged toward the sky at the east end of Grand Lake. The mountainous terrain of Rocky Mountain National Park, off limits to snowmobiles, loomed to the northwest. The parade of snowmobiles whined along the well-groomed trails, the train of sleds seeming to go faster and faster the higher it got. Marv Heemeyer on his souped-up Polaris was at the lead, his sled emanating a slightly deeper growl than the higher-pitched whine of the other sleds. Some of the riders sat on their sleds while others stood on the runners, their rear ends awkwardly jutting backwards to give weight and traction to the snowmobile tracks.

It was at a spot on the county road about a mile before the junction with the North Supply Creek that Gary Hilton decided to show his stuff. The line of sleds, even though it was moving fast, bored him a little. He quickly turned his snowmobile out from last place in the line and jerked the throttle full back and wide open. The sled screamed and Gary lowered his ass over the seat while pushing down on the handles as hard as he could to keep the bucking machine from flipping backward. That's how hard he pushed it. Once the runners were on snow at a speed approaching fifty miles per hour his tracks were sending up a rooster tail of snow that flew higher than the lodgepole pines surrounding the road in the national forest. He jetted to the lead of the group.

Hilton learned only moments later that Heemeyer wouldn't have that sort of behavior.

From his position in the lead Heemeyer didn't bother with a drastic twist of his wrist to bring his modified Polaris to full speed. He just gradually rolled his throttle back until it stopped, wide open. Now Heemeyer was gaining on Hilton. His sled out-raced Hilton's easily, emitting such a loud, authoritative and deeply guttural growl from the modified engine that Hilton felt scared.

As Heemeyer roared past, he deliberately jerked to the right, turning the back of the sled toward Hilton like a dog turning its rear end to a passing foe and sending a heavy spray of cold snow over

Hilton. Hilton immediately down-throttled, leaning forward again but this time because of the braking power of his engine. He knew he had pissed off Heemeyer. If you wanted to take the lead, you asked his permission and that was all there was to it.

Up North Supply, Heemeyer had slowed enough to allow the entourage of snowmobiles to catch up and he turned into a meadow where he raced through deep powder to the far edge, where a copse of aspen trees was edged by willows with a looming forest of spruce trees all around. Here there were oddly out-of-place steel poles with mesh wire stands, a massive fire pit buried in the snow with an ingenious angling lever on a steel pole for cooking over the fire pit and a cleverly concealed covered area behind the willows. All the riders dismounted their sleds here, sinking deeply into the snow, but laughing and lunging about all the same. A fire burst into the gray day in the fire pit and thermoses were opened, candy bars unwrapped. Wet gloves and two sodden jackets were placed on the crane-operated grate to warm over the blazing fire and steam rose from the garments.

This whole meadow was a renowned and almost sacred spot for the Thursday riders. Here, Doug Ohde had gunned his sled years ago in some off-trail stunt but had fallen off with the throttle wide open. The unmanned sled, with its malfunctioning kill switch that didn't properly shut down, careened wildly through the snow into the aspen trees where it crashed, sending a plume of snow to the ground. Those who witnessed that odd event said it was surreal how the riderless snowmobile sped wildly and with leaps and bounds across the snow-covered meadow right into a tree. From then on the meadow was known as the ODE.

Over the last two summers Heemeyer had sped up to the ODE with a specially tricked-out ATV that could tow a trailer. In the trailer Heemeyer had packed pre-measured and hammered and cut steel for making his glove-drying racks, fire pit crane and shelter. All hand made. All made by a master welder with an eye toward practicality.

For Heemeyer it must have been something like bliss to see his snowmobiling crew carousing around and laughing in this high cold place, their snowmobiles nearby and on the verge of a higher trip into the high country. To see his friends all so happy while using the tools of his trade probably made the day for Heemeyer. They trudged back to their sleds and powered out of the meadow onto the narrow and twisting Gilsonite Trail, bobbing and sliding as they went until Cascade Mountain came into view. They were just at timberline heading toward an expanse of wilderness on a wild ridge where the wind blew and the snow flurried about.

The other riders followed Heemeyer closely, knowing he knew the way. It was a team of fun-loving riders on a powder day high in the Rockies.

Through it all Gary Hilton wondered about Heemeyer, the guy who had happily urged him to come along on a Thursday ride and who had so often shared stories about renovating old cars. And yet Heemeyer had rudely asserted his place over Hilton with a show of speed and power that was unexpected and intimidating. He had heard about Marv and his lawsuits and he had witnessed his sternly pronounced opinions. Heemeyer ignored Hilton during the rest of the ride.

7. Offer, Counteroffer, Escalating Prices

Joe Docheff, the son of Cody and Suzy Docheff of Mountain Parks Concrete, had a proposal for Marv. Joe was the voice of reason and friendly banter for the management team of Mountain Parks Concrete. Slight and wiry with an engaging glance and open demeanor, he was the opposite of his opinionated and outspoken father. He was the negotiator of the family, usually dressed in toned-down western apparel that spoke of his moderate western way.

Joe, Cody and Suzy had gone to the Granby town board saying they wanted to put in an indoor concrete batch plant, like they had proposed in 1992. But now, in 1997, the town said it would be amenable if they could merge their land with Marv Heemeyer's two acres, the same parcel they used to own. That way the plant could be placed farther away from neighboring hotels and the highway.

Joe drove down the hill from their concrete plant operation up on the mesa west of Granby. He had rehearsed what he would say to Marv. He thought it might go well since Marv had worked on Cody's truck and some other company vehicles. Marv had even bought their concrete for the slab of the new steel building he had built on his property.

Marv was waiting for him in his office at the muffler shop.

"Good Morning Marv," Joe said.

"Right on time," Marv said.

"No sense in being late."

"So you want my property, huh? I already tried to sell it to your dad once."

"I know that Marv, but now we want to talk again."

"Talk away."

Joe had hoped there would be a place to sit down and chat, but Marv stood behind his high counter. He towered over Joe, who was a relatively short man, like his father. Joe projected his smooth demeanor and a conciliatory personality.

"Well, Marv, we'd like to buy our old property back."

"Well, it's $250,000," Marv said.

"Seems high, Marv. But I'll talk to Mom and Dad and I'll be back."

Marv was smiling when Joe walked out of the office. He went back to work on the muffler pack he was installing in a Ford 250.

Two days later Joe returned.

"OK, we've got a deal."

Marv, standing behind the counter as before, looked down at Joe with a smirk on his face. Joe didn't like the feeling he got. A customer came in, paid Marv for a job and left. While Joe waited he saw the clipping of the newspaper's Meet Your Merchants ad, with Marv's smiling face in it, posted on the wall in a cheap black frame.

Marv said, "I'm sorry Joe, but we don't have a deal." Marv was now leaning forward on the counter, where three sheets of paper were laid out in front of him.

"I just had this appraised. It's worth more than your offer. I want $375,000. That's what it's worth."

"Oh, come on Marv, now we can't come up with that. It won't pay."

Heemeyer slid the appraisal out to Joe. Joe stepped forward and quickly glanced at it, leaving it on the counter.

"Well I'm not so optimistic now Marv. I've got to go back to Mom and Dad. Is there any wiggle room in that?"

Marv responded positively, but there was a smile on his face that Joe thought was more of a smirk.

Joe was back two months later. Summer was winding down. Marv was working on a snowmobile in his garage.

Marv stepped out and stood behind the same tall counter and looked down on Joe.

"You're finally back," Marv said, this time with an easy grin.

"Sorry it took so long Marv, but we had to see if we could find the money. You said $375,000. Well, that's a hard pill to swallow. But we found an investor and I think we can swing $350,000. What do you say?"

Now Marv started to laugh softly, shaking his head left and right. He hitched up his bib overalls and took a pencil out of the front pocket. A pad of paper on the counter inscribed with the logo of Ferris and Cohn Muffler Patches sat open to a blank page. He had had another appraisal done.

Joe felt a sinking feeling in his stomach, as Marv quickly wrote out a new number on the pad.

Though Heemeyer offered to partially finance the deal if he got a good down payment, when Joe looked down and saw $450,000 staring him back in the face, it was like a slap.

"I don't think I can even take that back to Cody and Mom."

Marv pulled the pad back to his side of the counter and in a neat, small signature, he made his offer official. "It's in writing now — my writing."

"Oh come on Marv . . . Really?"

Marv didn't say a word. He turned to go back out into his work area.

And Yet Another Failed Offer

Joe, Suzy and Cody Docheff were ready to present their plans for their concrete plant to the Granby Planning Commission. There were a few dissenters at the meeting, including Heemeyer. Joe was hoping that Heemeyer had his appraisal done, so he could finalize the latest deal to buy Heemeyer's two acres.

Heemeyer had proposed a land swap where the Docheffs would give him a prime lot in their new subdivision they had purchased to allow more land for their plant. They couldn't buy Marv's land so they bought the defunct commercial subdivision on the other side of their parcel. When Heemeyer learned of that purchase he countered to buy the same subdivision out from under the Docheffs, but it was too late. Now they could swap land in that subdivision in exchange for the two-acre muffler shop parcel. The Docheffs liked that idea.

But Marv had come back with a counteroffer just a week prior to the planning commission meeting, which involved a 4,000 square foot structure in addition to the land.

Joe thought that was too much, but they had agreed to bring individual appraisals to the meeting.

Joe had his doubts since the building Heemeyer had proposed would cost the Docheffs at least $150,000 and the land was worth a lot. It was a prime lot.

And now, at their negotiation meeting before the first hearing, Heemeyer was looking down at the Docheffs. Heemeyer pointed as if to lecture them and said they had no appraisals he'd accept and therefore there would be no contract. He said he would oppose them all the way. Cody turned red and just walked away with Suzy. Joe told Marv that he thought they had it all worked out.

"You heard me," Heemeyer said. He walked back into the town meeting room where a small throng of people stood. He had rounded them up to speak out against the concrete plant proposal.

Marv Heemeyer had enjoyed his new efforts to create community interest in opposition to the concrete plant. He had set himself up as the person who would help save an entire neighborhood from the environmental impacts of the proposed concrete plant. He had gone door-to-door, petition in hand. Most had signed on and agreed to be at the meeting. People who had not agreed to sign were greeted by a cold stare and a simple admonition delivered with a firm phrase: "You'll be sorry about your foolish decision."

Marv sat across from me, in front of my desk, holding a sheet of paper in his hand. Our office was officially closed but I was working late, as I usually did on Wednesday nights, and he agreed to come by after he had finished working at his shop. He had called about a letter to the editor he wanted to run in connection with his fight against a proposed concrete batch plant on the Docheff property next to his muffler shop. We agreed I would go over his letter with him, allowing him to clarify and understand any changes or deletions I might want to make. He wore bib overalls with steel-toed boots. There was an acrid smell about him that I recognized as the smell of welding.

"Well, here it is."

He handed me the letter.

"Thanks Marv," I said. "I think your letter will be better if we go over it together and so you see what might need to be edited out or in, so you have that control of your message."

"OK."

He didn't smile, frown or make any facial expression at all. He looked at me with a sort of wide-eyed intensity.

The letter began:

"The proposed construction of a new concrete batch plant will negatively affect the quality of life in our town for years to come. We must rally together as a community in order for our concerns to be heard."

Good enough. I agreed we could run that.

But then he had written:

"The illegal rezoning of the Granby West Subdivision, which was pre-approved in secret meetings at the coffee shop and other undisclosed locations, clearly distorts the intent of the zoning ordinance in the following ways:"

With Marv looking on, and with his approval, I took out the unfounded and speculative. We didn't know yet if it was illegal and there was no proof or even any reason to believe there had been secret meetings at any place.

His letter then clearly spelled out his points in opposition to the plant:

1) *I read that the ordinance states that a Planned Development Overlay must constitute a unique and truly innovative project. The concrete plant does neither by being common and only that, in my opinion.*
2) *The rezoning of the Granby West subdivision will detract from existing commercial, industrial, residential and education facilities in our town.*
3) *The ordinance states that the rezoning must benefit the community as a whole. To me, it's clear that it does not.*
4) *According to the ordinance, the PDO must reduce the burden of traffic on current streets and highways. The proposed rezoning and subsequent construction of the concrete plant will increase traffic and congestion on our roads.*
5) *Rezoning is supposed to conserve the value of the land while preserving environmental qualities. I believe the proposed plant will result in a decrease in property values and an increase in pollution.*

6) *The rezoning does not encourage preservation of the natural site characteristics as required by the ordinance.*
7) *The proposal has not encouraged integrated community planning and development, going against, in my opinion, virtually all of the town's zoning guidelines.*
8) *The ordinance states that no building permits will be issued unless a final Planned Development Overlay Plan has been approved. Has this PDO been approved? A building permit was issued in March of 2000 would suggest that it has. Doesn't this in effect tend to negate any public hearings thereafter and in addition make a mockery of the entire ordinance? If this proposal can dance around these requirements today, won't we see that same type of dance in the future?*
9) *In addition to the ongoing ordinance concerns I have listed above, I also have these worries: The proposal will generate no appreciable new sales tax, it will create few if any permanent new jobs, and it is not compatible with surrounding forestry, tourist and HGB (Highway General Business) zoning, which comprise a large percentage of the surrounding properties.*

With a few minor changes, all that was OK. But his last paragraph needed more than a few changes. His sentence originally read: *"Don't let the lying good ol' boys and backstabbers, who get away with whatever they want for their profit and power, dump this on the community of Granby and Grand County."*

Marv objected, but only mildly, when we changed it to read:

"Don't let this get dumped on the community of Granby and Grand County. Please help to defeat this proposal by writing more letters to your town trustees at P.O Box 440, Granby CO 80446. Please be at the final meeting at the Granby Community Center on July 25.

Marvin Heemeyer
Granby and Grand Lake

"Well, is that OK, Marv?"

"Yes, it'll have to do."

He stood up and we shook hands. He didn't seem angry. He didn't seem happy. I tried to make small talk as he walked toward the front door. He said nothing in reply.

"Good night Marv."

"Yes," he said.

He climbed into his pick-up truck parked in front of the newspaper office and drove away. There was a rainbow arcing across the dark blue sky to the northeast. It sprang from a northern and higher aspect of the Continental Divide at Pawnee Peak and brightened the dusk. The rainbow appeared to go right into the roof of the Gambles building just across the street. I went inside, grabbed my camera and snapped a few photos of the rainbow arcing into Gambles.

A week later I gave Casey Farrell, the owner of Gambles with his wife Rhonda, an 8 by 10 print of that photo. Casey hung that print on the front wall of his store. It stayed there for more than four years.

8. Town Meeting

Snow fell heavily during Heemeyer's drive to Granby from Grand Lake. The usually unreliable local weather report on the radio had accurately predicted it would be unusually cold that January evening in 2001. Near the bottom of his long descent to Granby at Coffey Divide, elk were likely milling in the snow-obscured distance.

Heemeyer had been desperately hoping for a massive crowd of his friends and allies to turn out for this hearing, probably the final hearing in the approval process for the new concrete batch plant that the Docheffs wanted to build right next to his muffler shop in western Granby. Despite his initial willingness to sell to the Docheffs, Heemeyer had been protesting the proposed plant in hearing after hearing and just recently in a lawsuit he had filed against the town.

Heemeyer had argued that it would hurt his business, ruin the value of his property, create all kinds of environmental problems, compromise a nearby residential neighborhood and limit his hopes of expanding his new steel building into a retail and wholesale facility. That new steel building, he hoped, would be his ticket to a secure retirement. But the Docheffs and their indoor batch plant, he was convinced, were about to ruin it all.

The brightly lit room was only halfway full, and he saw not one person there who he thought would speak out in behalf of his position against the plant. No one other, that is, than his Boulder lawyer, Peter Dietze, who was being paid handsomely to be there. The other people, as far as he could tell, were lackeys and employees for the Docheffs, all there to blindly plead for the right of their employer to build a new batch plant, add jobs and expand the local economy. All in the Docheffs' pocket, Heemeyer thought to himself. All brainwashed.

The table where the town board members sat dominated the room. In front of it sat another table where a scale model of the proposed batch plant was displayed in all its childish glory. It was something like a diorama, with little models of the new batch plant building, its storage silo, streets and rolling green fields around it. A few cottonwood trees were depicted by matchsticks with balls of cotton painted green at the tops. *Papier mache* hillocks and willow bushes lined the irrigation ditch, shown as a crease in the ground with glinting plastic water depicted by plastic wrap streaming by as if on a clear summer day.

But the little Matchbook cars and Matchbook concrete trucks, and the dinky little human forms shown blissfully walking from a truck to the office, riled Heemeyer the most. It all looked so ideal and silly at the same time. The little diorama gave a pristine image of the Docheffs' proposal, and Heemeyer had to admit that in its simplicity and charm it had been a prop that helped the Docheffs sell their case to the citizens and the town board.

He hated that little scene and he wanted to walk over to it and crush it, smashing the little buildings and stick figures with his fists. The newspaper had even run a photo of the little depiction of the plant.

How his fortunes had changed in only six tumultuous months.

Before, at the first, second and third town meetings on the plant proposal, Heemeyer had been able to pack the town hall hearing room with people who were all on his side. Those were the days of summer, when the setting sun streaming into the town's meeting room created a cauldron of heat and steamy breath, making town board members irritable and defensive. The people cramming the room on his side were neighbors in the New Church Circle community, the closest neighborhood to the proposed plant and Marv's shop. They were well-intentioned mothers of children in the grade school that would be downwind of the batch plant's dust. They were the avid anti-development types who never saw a project they liked. They had been there, in force, defending Marv Heemeyer's valiant and just effort to stop by legal means this God-awful concrete plant.

At those meetings there were fifteen, twenty and even thirty people clamoring for a chance to tell the hapless town board that the concrete plant should be stopped. Heemeyer had gone door-to-door with fliers and petitions to get these people away from their TVs and in front of the town pleading for a just cause. He had been proud. He would never forget how Pam Cornett had courageously stood up and told the board the plant was a terrible idea. He would never forget how his letters to the editor of the newspaper ran side-by-side with letters from other citizens, all decrying the proposed new plant. She was one of many who had pleaded his case. But none was present that Tuesday night, the penultimate night for the batch plant proposal.

Now he was the lone citizen pleading for the town to vote against allowing the new plant that he was sure would ruin his business and devalue his property. He sat in the back row of the folding chairs that had been carefully set out. Heemeyer had made it clear that he thought these interminable public meetings were nothing more than rigged spectacles designed solely for the purpose of subjecting anyone who dared to defy the town to a simmering sort of public rebuke. But it was all part of the game, and he was willing to play along.

The meeting began with the usual formalities and Heemeyer looked even more galled than usual at the slow and tedious method of presenting all sides, of hearing all opinions. Mel and Lana, his former friends, came in and sat in front of him. They turned to say hello, but Heemeyer looked at them hard, stood up and moved to the other side of his row. Even they had betrayed him, hiring the very same fat lawyer that the Docheffs were using to ruin him and his life. They had hired the lawyer for another, unrelated dispute of their own, and yet he hated them for it. They had betrayed him and he no longer cared about their nights of bowling together, their steak dinners and the snowmobile rides. He regretted ever confiding anything to Mel and Lana; especially Lana. He had told her that he hated his mother because she was so fat. And now he had to put up with their corpulent lawyer. What a mistake.

Richard Daly, the lawyer for the Docheffs, was first to plead his case. Just the sight of him made Heemeyer seethe deep inside. Even worse, Daly was delighted to make points about the ideal nature of the batch plant by blissfully pointing out cosmetic details and highlights, using the diorama to drive his points home. Heemeyer must have known then that Daly, from the Front Range, had been the one who thought of that scale model of the entire property, setting it up in glee and playing with it like a pudgy little boy and his new HO railroad set.

Though he must have been seething inside, Heemeyer watched, expressionless, as the plant's proponents once again told the board in sworn statements that they favored the plant for the usual reasons. All of them sat right there, by that childlike diorama. Then it was time for Heemeyer's proponents. No one other than Marv spoke up. He read this handwritten letter, which he then submitted to the town and asked that it be made a part of the record: "*Based on all previously presented information, I'd like to say I am opposed to the approval of this application and would encourage the members of the board to vote against it.*" It was signed: "*Thank you, Marv Heemeyer.*"

The tone was much less aggressive than previous communications. Perhaps Heemeyer felt he had already made his point by filing a lawsuit against the town the prior November in District Court. He and his lawyer claimed that the town had not followed state law and in general abused the process, causing harm to Heemeyer. They had filed the suit after the town had been caught in a procedural error that sent the entire batch plant application back to square one.

Heemeyer even thought he had caught the Docheffs building structures for the plant before any approval was given, but was proven wrong when it turned out the work they were doing was for a storage tank, not the plant itself. And yet everyone knew the town had blundered in the process, but it was also perfectly legal, the town said, to go back and start over. And in doing so, the entire proposal had become better for the town and the neighbors.

But the most stinging aspect of the town's retort to Heemeyer's legal complaint was this: How could Heemeyer legitimately claim the town had damaged him if it hadn't even yet approved the batch plant?

Heemeyer cringed when his lawyer presented the opposing case to the board. Were his efforts fruitless and a waste of time? Was there any chance they would still prevail in the lawsuit? Had filing the lawsuit been a mistake? For now it was obvious that people on the board who might have been sympathetic to Heemeyer's cause were changing their minds. When the town board members stated their positions, Trustee Casey Farrell, owner of Gambles, a main street business, summed it up best. He, like other trustees on the board, had initially wavered on the need and value of the new batch plant. They had agreed with many of Heemeyer's points. At first, it wasn't by any means a sure thing that the Docheffs would get their batch plant. But things change. That night he said the proponents of the batch plant had now dotted all the 'I's and crossed all the 'T's.

At that January 9, 2001 meeting Heemeyer believed, but in a resigned way, his propaganda about why the plant should be stopped. He couldn't see that town board members, many of his earlier backers and the town staff were aware of what was really going on.

It was Faye Rumsey, the town clerk pro-tem, who wrote in a letter to the editor what people were beginning to understand about the entire fight. She notes that at first Heemeyer's concerns had some support, but she adds that the support waned as the Docheffs improved the project. She states: "As the process continued and people were convinced their concerns had been taken care of and were comfortable with the batch plant in their neighborhood, fewer and fewer people attended the public meetings. However, Marv Heemeyer seemed to have a personal vendetta against the Docheffs, caused by matters other than the concrete batch plant — the refusal of the Docheffs to buy Heemeyer's property at an exorbitant asking price."

It was true that Heemeyer had been badgering the Docheffs to buy his property in a series of ever-escalating debates with ever-escalating prices, all the way from 1996 to 2000, maybe even all the way back to the day Heemeyer bought the property in 1992. When the highest price Heemeyer wanted was refused by the Docheffs, he vowed to Joe Docheff that he would fight the project tooth and nail. And that's just what he was doing.

And yet when his one-time allies learned it was largely about negotiations to force a sale at a high price, they deserted Heemeyer's cause. Many had felt they had been set up just so Heemeyer could make a sweet bundle on the property. But by January of 2001, Heemeyer couldn't see this.

The preliminary plat and PDO for the batch plant were unanimously approved that night, setting the course for a smooth final approval.

Heemeyer simply stood up and walked out of the room. It was still snowing, but more lightly now. He must have driven carefully in his GMC pickup back to Grand Lake. Through the billowing explosions of the windblown snow he probably saw some of the elk that frequently gathered at the base of Coffey Divide. He would have seen that they stood among the dead bodies of other elk that had been hit and then pushed off the road into the barrow ditch. He might have thought it odd that the living elk stood so indifferently yet alert among their fallen brethren. The town meeting that night in Granby marked a turning point for Marv Heemeyer. His quiet and stoic perseverance in front of the town and the community had changed into a sort of stolid determination. The situation had changed and something inside him became clear.

9. God Wants Me to Do It

Heemeyer couldn't get that meeting out of his head. Even as he relaxed the next night in his hot tub, beer in hand, on his outdoor deck, high on a hillside overlooking Grand Lake, he remembered the drone of public commentary. The town meeting had not gone well. It's likely he hadn't slept the night after the meeting. The town would vote against him. The lawsuit didn't look good, either. He had to be thinking about how he was spending money left and right on Dietze, the Boulder lawyer, and it was still clear: He was going to lose.

Though the hot water must have felt so good in such stark contrast to the bitter cold air, he started to cry. He wouldn't have been ashamed of his tears for no one was there to see them and, besides, these were not tears of submission. He had to have known that these were tears of decision, determination and a sort of peace. He was giving up on a normal, restful life; a family life with a wife and kids, for this sort of bliss. He was alone in his righteousness. He was losing.

It must have come to him not as a flash of inspiration nor a burst of light from on high. It had to have been a conflation of memories and his love and fear of a stern and just God, a God that he knew was on his side. Perhaps he felt calm and relaxed. He could act now as he wanted.

He would smash it up and he knew how he would smash it all up, like the fists of God in bolts of retribution.

He thought it all out to himself that night.

"If I had been married . . . have a family. You know, things may have gone different. But God built me for this job. He rewarded me for 45-50 years with a lifestyle that I am so thankful for. And it's unfortunate. The poor people in Granby. So many of them were so jealous of my lifestyle — that I could come and go as I pleased. Well, God blessed me in advance for the task that I am about to undertake."

He had lived a certain way for so long and now it all began to make sense, even his childhood and his struggles in school.

"I graduated from high school the 28th of my class of 29. That's no big deal. I wasn't intelligent. I wasn't smart. I wasn't stupid. But I wasn't educated. I didn't have the knack to sit in the classroom and be a bookworm. I don't know why. I mean I may have. But God built me . . . maybe clear back in the fourth grade when I broke my arm. Because that's when my grades started falling off. I don't know. He had this plan clear back then."

He sat in the hot tub with tears streaming down his face.

The hot tub on Heemeyer's deck where he experienced his revelation from God. (Photo by the author)

"I'm trying to understand why this was happening to me. And, to do what I have to do — to make these people listen. A peace is coming over me that has only come over me a few times before in my life; where I know that what I will do is tough but it is the right thing and that it is above me. It wasn't me. I am doing this because God wanted me to do it. And I didn't understand it. I said 'Why did you ask me to do this? Is that why I've never been married? So I didn't have a family? Is that why I've always been successful? So that I would realize my reward before doing this task?' I don't know. There are other things I can ask. Why had I not carried my cross earlier, and now God has prepared me to carry this cross? I believe so."

"And I'm carrying the cross willingly now. At first I fought it. But it has to be done. And the world will write stories about how wrong I am. And everything. And without a doubt I wish it could be done a different way. But there is no way to make this right."

"I'd shoot the truth in their face (sic), and they couldn't deal with it. And I'm sorry. They're going to have to deal with it. I guarantee you, I'm going to make them deal with it. It is my duty. God has asked me to do this."

Heemeyer was feeling inspired like a holy warrior, a crusader. The steaming water of the hot tub would have bubbled and hissed around him.

Marv must have felt it was all so contradictory and that he just didn't deserve it. He's a self-made man with money in the bank and a free-wheeling life doing what he loves and yet he's taken on a just cause for himself that has failed. He is a success and he's not getting what he deserves. And despite all his friends in town, his bantering clique at the café and his long list of happy clients, he's still in this fight alone, on the outside. That meeting made it all clear, where he pleaded in a persevering way. Now he would no longer plead. He would act, alone, determined.

"You know you could call it revenge … But, hopefully, the community will learn something from this and become wiser. Instead of hating their neighbor and keeping your neighbor down, they will love their neighbor. You know, there may not be a lot of love here because you can look at it and say it's coming from me. I've developed malice towards these people. I couldn't live with myself the rest of my life if I didn't have a plan to make this right. I feel pretty worthless and I know I probably shouldn't. But to know that for 10 years the people in the town of Granby did not want me there. And the fact that I was making good money . . . I'm sure everything about me made them jealous. I'm sorry that they felt that way. That is a bad way to feel."

Heemeyer felt he was predestined for the task he was about to carry out:

"I am at peace."

It was an odd sort of peace. Heemeyer had wanted to smash up the little diorama of the batch plant. And perhaps Heemeyer knew that he wanted to show people what their envy of his great life would cost them. He had to feel that they would never deserve what he had earned. He had to feel that in the end the victory would be his because he would show them all what he was capable of, and they wouldn't even suspect it.

"People will say that 'why did he do that?' He had such a good life. He had a better life than me anyway. I can understand that to a point. It's not what I deserved. You meddled in my business and took what I deserved away. You took advantage of my good nature. Oh I think there's something you should learn here. For as good as a man can be, also can he be as bad. And another thing you should learn is that when you visit evil upon someone, be assured, it will revisit you, and that is what is happening. It is a good thing. Because I think the community of Granby will be stronger. I think that they will understand, after years."

"Only their malice, their resentment towards the outsiders, is their motive for making sure that that concrete plant gets in town. And it is just uncanny, that after it got started, how I tried to stop it. How every time I did it failed. It told me one thing. That God wants these people to learn. And he knew that I eventually would get to the point where I wouldn't put up with what they were taking away from me. With what they had denied me. God knew Marv Heemeyer very well. He put me up here."

Heemeyer's mind must have been racing there in that moment of inspiration.

"All I ever wanted was what I deserved. You denied me of that. You are there thinking you have gotten away with destroying a person

— an outsider — and you have gotten your way. And that's wrong . . You will learn this lesson. That this is not the way to do it. I'm going to sacrifice my life, my future to show you — my miserable future that you gave me — to show you, to show you that what you did was wrong."

There was a sort of morality play going on in Heemeyer's mind. He needed to convince himself that acting in such a way — to prove that people have been wrong and are wrong — ran against his nature.

"The bad thing about being honest and straightforward and doing that is, people know where you stand and they try to take advantage of you. They take advantage of your good nature. They take advantage of the fact that they know that you're a good guy, you are a straight shooter, and that you're not going to retaliate on them when they fuck you. Well, folks, most of the time I believe that's probably true. But God built me to be here to prove to you that what you have been doing, for God knows how many years, is wrong. You picked on the wrong man."

"I'm not tough. I'm not that strong," he thinks.

"But I am not afraid of death," he continues to think. "That was another one of those things, which a movie I watched said. There are a lot of things that will gnaw at a man's heart and soul a lot worse than death. And you know, this will gnaw at me for the rest of my life. And I'm not going to live with it. I may die with it, but I will not live with it."

Three weeks after the town meeting that sent Heemeyer on a new, secret course, an article appeared in the *Sky-Hi News* about Heemeyer's lawsuit against the town. The district judge had refused to dismiss the case outright, as the town had asked, which meant it would go to a full trial, but probably not for another nine months. This was good news for Heemeyer, giving him just enough hope to continue to pay his attorney and move forward in his resolve against the batch plant.

But that didn't change his mind about what he needed to do, what God had sanctioned already in his mind.

The planning commission approved the final PDO plan for the batch plant in early April of that year (2001) and the board unanimously approved the proposal in early May. Mayor Dick

Thompson had been sick and missed several meetings. Dick Broady had resigned in February and was replaced on the board by Joe Cross. Trustee Ted Wang abstained and the other board members all voted "yes." The Docheffs had complied with all the town requests and then some, making it difficult for the board to vote "no." The Docheffs could now get a building permit for their batch plant and start work.

The remaining potential glitch was the lawsuit that had been filed by Heemeyer. But the Docheffs acknowledged in a public meeting that they understood the risk of starting construction even though the lawsuit hadn't been settled.

"The town gave the approvals," Joe Docheff says. "That was us, on our own. We understood that (about the lawsuit risk)."

Of course there was a great risk that if the lawsuit went the wrong way, all their work on the plant would be stopped. Some board members shrugged, remembering Heemeyer's quiet new demeanor at the last board meeting, when nobody had shown up to back him. Perhaps Heemeyer knew something they didn't. Two trustees told the Docheffs that it was "their money. Go ahead. But don't blame us."

Mayor Dick Thompson, a longtime board member and longtime Granby resident, died June 21, 2001 after a lengthy illness. The official cause of death was a brain tumor. He had always aspired to be mayor during his years on the board. He had finally been elected to the post but he died before he could finish his term. Thompson owned and operated an excavating company with his three sons. He also had two daughters. His family had been in Granby a long time, first owning a motel in town that thrived during the days before Interstate 70 opened and took a lot of the motel business along its route to the south.

He was a talkative man who liked to emphasize a common sense approach toward government. When I first met him he could frequently be seen with an unlit cigar in his mouth, over to the side in the manner of Winston Churchill. One town wag used to say he looked like a bulldog with an old bone in his mouth. But he was a bulldog with a pussy cat's temperament. He genuinely believed that most conflicts could be resolved with heart-to-heart communication, a handshake and good intentions. He was out of his realm in the Heemeyer dispute.

And in many respects, so was the town of Granby.

10. An Offer Refused

It is easy to imagine the scene.

From the high front counter in his reception area in late June of 2001, Heemeyer could see where a backhoe, loader and dump truck were working in the area where the new batch plant building was proposed. They lurched back and forth in jerky motions like giant insects. Some were digging and another was hauling material. He would even have been able to hear the whine of their engines. It must have rankled him to be a daily witness to the work he so opposed, cementing his anger at the town, the Docheffs, the Thompsons, the newspaper and all the people in Granby who he was sure were snickering behind his back.

It was like he had explained to his friend Ian Daugherty, the town baker at Ian's Mountain Bakery. Heemeyer was a regular at the bakery and Ian had invited Heemeyer on a fishing trip to Alabama back in May. He told Ian multiple times that "they" were all conspiring to screw him out of success and happiness on this land right here at the muffler shop. Ian remembers that Marv was so obsessed about it all that he said he "would just bulldozer the whole town."

Ian ignored the comment at first but gave it a little bit more consideration when Heemeyer asked Daugherty to pitch in and pay 25 percent of the cost of his lawsuit against the town. After all, Ian had signed Heemeyer's first petition. But Ian refused kindly, explaining that "things had changed and it wasn't so bad anymore." Heemeyer barely spoke to Ian the rest of the trip and it was a long drive back to Granby. Heemeyer never patronized the bakery again. He never returned Ian's calls to borrow equipment for this or that job. He never spoke to Ian again.

The jangling phone would have interrupted Heemeyer's reverie. It was Joe Docheff, sounding friendly and eager all at the same time. It would have irked Heemeyer even more. He had called to tell Marv that he and his dad now owned Gus Harris's property south of the muffler shop and they were prepared to make an offer to Marv. He said they'd give, at no charge, an easement to the water and sewer mains that were now live through their property if he'd just drop his lawsuit against them and the town. This would have solved the water and sewer problem at his site that he had tried to solve so many years before in front of the sewer board.

Heemeyer hung up without saying a word.

A registered letter was sent to Heemeyer's address in which the offer was repeated. Heemeyer refused to pick it up. Heemeyer never said a word again about the offer made by the Docheffs.

The Docheffs proceeded full speed ahead on their project now that the final approvals of the town had been made and the utilities were approved. They signed a document with the town acknowledging the risk they were taking since there was a standing lawsuit in District Court challenging the project.

Major construction started in earnest that summer. It wasn't long before the miniature shapes and contours depicted in the diorama presented through the hearings began to take life-size, even bigger-than-life shape.

Heemeyer hoped and hoped they would have to tear it all down once the court ruled in his favor, saving him the trouble of having to do it himself.

By early August of 2001, six weeks after Joe Docheff had made his offer to Heemeyer, Granby Town Manager Tom Hale had a feeling of dread. He knew the town had been patient long enough with Heemeyer, looking the other way all those years on the water and sewer issues and the junk complaints, but now it was time to try and work it out. He wasn't looking forward to talking to Heemeyer about the fact that the water and sewer lines were active near his property. This meant Heemeyer was required by law to hook on, otherwise he'd be in violation. Needless to say, the phone call did not go well.

Heemeyer responded to it all in a letter he e-mailed to Hale in September.

Re: Notice and order dates July 19, 01

This letter is a request for documents or other information you referred to in our telephone conversation on 9"12"01 at approximately 1:30 p.m.

These documents or information will confirm that the well and septic on my property were installed before the ordinance you referred to in your letter was written.

You also indicated during the conversation that you would send me a copy of an easement for water and sewer, said easement lying to the west of my property.

You said you believed both water and sewer lines were active and I informed you I had earlier purchased a water tap that date being 12/27/96.

I indicated to you I would be willing to hook up to the sewer and pay the tap fee if the line was active.

I need the easement so I can take it to the sanitation department so they can confirm I can hook on.

This is also to confirm that I talked to you on 8/10/01 about my being grandfathered before the ordinance was written and you said you would have to check on that, that I talked to you on approximately 8/22/01 for confirmation of the grandfathering at which time you said you were waiting to hear from the town attorney, that I left a voice mail for a response on 8/31/01, that I finally was told on 9/12/01 that you did not believe I was grandfathered based on information you had in front of you.

This letter is also a request for leniency on the completion date as it took so long for you to determine the grandfather issue.

Please respond.

Marvin Heemeyer

The town waited, essentially giving Heemeyer the leniency he had requested. But some neighbors of Heemeyer wondered why the town was waiting so long and giving Heemeyer even more time.

One neighbor who was concerned was Steve Borda. He had been approached a few years prior by people from the Horn Ranch, a large spread located a half mile to the west of the Heemeyer and Borda properties. It was also located downstream, or, more to the point, down-ditch. An irrigation ditch, called Horn Ditch, ran through

Granby from east to west, carrying essential water from the Fraser River for the Horn Ranch. The ditch passed right behind the Borda, Heemeyer and now the Docheff properties on its way to the ranch's meadows on the west side of U.S. Highway 34.

Borda was surprised by the contact from the Horn Ranch.

"We came here to tell you to stop pumping your toilets into our ditch," Borda was told.

"But I'm not," he said. "I'm legally compliant with my septic and sewer. Come and look."

They inspected and realized Borda wasn't at fault. It was his down-ditch neighbor, Marv Heemeyer, who had been dumping his septic and toilet waste into the Horn Ditch. Apparently, he was simply running a pump from the buried tank into the ditch when the water was running high. The ditch didn't run year 'round.

They confronted Heemeyer but he angrily denied any wrongdoing despite the presence of a gasoline-powered pump and a wide hose that suggested Heemeyer had been pumping something behind his building.

Not surprisingly to Borda, it was shortly thereafter that he caught Heemeyer digging a ditch from the Heemeyer property to the Borda property in an attempt to illegally hook on to Borda's sewer service line. Borda told Heemeyer to quit and reported the problem to the sanitation district. Heemeyer filled in the ditch and said nothing of it ever again.

But these people were anxious for the water and sewer problems at the Heemeyer property to be fixed, once and for all.

Living through all this, after Heemeyer knew the immensity of what he had in mind, must have seemed like a whole lot of nothing to him — mere ripples of picayune harassment. And yet it was the sort of harassment that merely confirmed his worst suspicions about the conspiracy against him. And he knew, in his little dealings with neighbors and bureaucrats, that it was just a matter of time. He would see just how much he could get away with, how much he could dodge their tentative little maneuvers to ruin him. Maybe it would all work out. But he doubted it.

And there was that part of him that hoped and feared that nothing would be resolved.

11. Avalanche Hero

It would mark the pinnacle of Marv Heemeyer's life as the snowmobiling hero of Grand Lake.

A variety of pick-up trucks and their snowmobile trailers parked in the Idleglen parking lot. After a big breakfast at the Chuck Hole Café and stocking up on supplies at the Mountain Food Market, everyone agreed to meet at the parking lot and get their sleds ready. There were some hoots and hollers in the lot before the whines, screams and roars of revving snowmobile engines drowned out any natural sound. Already, a bluish-tinted smoke filled the air from the group of sleds. The fifteen riders who gathered that morning were serious riders who reveled in the extreme. They all had their hopes set on a great day of riding in the powder snow that had fallen in the last three days.

On this day John Linton of Grand Lake led the way, sharing the number one spot occasionally with Marv Heemeyer. John, a good friend of Heemeyer, was well known as an expert rider who knew the nooks and crannies of the snow-covered mountains for miles around Grand Lake. He was a longtime resident of the area and his local knowledge showed. He could ride and he could guide.

The entourage of sleds streamed in orderly but fast fashion up County Road 4, toward the high country. The group included riders and friends of Heemeyer such as Don Campbell, Anthony Sours, Clive Smith, Steve Holzworth, Scott Stephens, Brett Stanley and Garry Weaver. This was going to be a seriously fun day of riding.

An observer of this experienced group who didn't know better would have thought that the high speed at which they rode on the groomed forest service road was just for grins. But the truth was that they rode fast on that stretch because they simply wanted to get to the powder stashes, steep ridges and peaks as fast as they could. The groomed trail just made it easier to get to those thrilling locations faster.

From the roadway they headed uphill to the Gilsonite Trail and turned right on the top of the ridge so they were heading toward Bowen Mountain. The sun shone brightly. Linton led the crew to the backside of Bowen Mountain between Ruby and Fairview Mountains. It was time to start marking the bowls.

Linton headed out first, driving his screaming sled high up the virgin snow on the steep bowl until his momentum couldn't carry him any more and he turned gracefully to his left and downhill at the peak of his ride, flowing in the snow like it was a wave of luscious white water. Heemeyer followed and high-marked above Linton's tracks, taking advantage of the packed snow left by Linton's climb.

And so it continued, each rider taking advantage of the faster packed snow of the riders before, climbing higher and higher, marking the bowl with their sleds at increasingly higher points until it seemed as if the sleds were powering vertical to the sky near the top of the bowl's ridge, where a large frothy cornice beckoned. With fifteen riders, the entire bowl was quickly marked by the screaming sleds, riders below hollering and hooting futilely, unable to be heard above the din of whining engines.

With the snowmobiles now spread out in the bowl — some at the bottom, some at the north side, some at the south — Garry Weaver noticed an odd movement of the snow in the middle of the bowl. The snow was sliding. He shouted "Avalanche!" as the mass of snow headed right for the four riders at the bottom. All the riders who were lucky enough to be out of the way assumed the four riders would be buried. They revved their sleds and rode toward the bottom as fast as possible. Once the powdery and snowy mist that obscured their vision had cleared, they were relieved. The slide had miraculously stopped before hitting the riders. The four at the bottom hadn't known how close they were to being buried alive. Now the adrenaline was flowing after this brush with death.

The group headed to a flat spot and started a fire, cooking hot dogs and bratwurst, everyone talking excitedly about how they had missed a close call. It was a perfect day to be riding — cold and clear with lots of fresh snow. With the fire out, they then took turns riding each other's sleds, hoping to get a feel for how fast or slow the other sleds might be — a way to size up the competition. Then one rider pointed back over to the bowl. At some point, maybe while they had been eating or riding around in the meadow, the southern portion of the bowl had also slid.

All nodded their heads, helmets bobbing, as if to exclaim about their good fortune. They had been lucky again, which only invigorated them even more. In single file, the group headed up a steep ravine north of the first bowl. They were now in Jackson County and straddling the Continental Divide. The ravine opened up into an untouched open meadow. It was lined with stunted fir trees near its summit. Rounding out the meadow upward to the crest of the divide was a massive incline with a huge cornice at its top. It offered a temptation that none of the riders could resist. Weaver followed Tim Futter up the ravine. At different points, each became stuck and mired in the excellent deep snow.

While digging out, Marv Heemeyer and Linton had come back down along the line of riders and then headed back up the hill. At that moment a gust of wind blew across the mountains and a fine mist of snow, like white smoke, swirled in the air. Scott Swiefel, another rider, and Weaver looked at each other, knowing what this probably meant. The cornice had broken loose as part of a huge avalanche on that massive hillside. The riders were taken by surprise. The pitch of the hill wasn't very steep and, theoretically, the trees should have held the snow. No such luck. The entire hillside had suddenly broken loose and slid down, right onto several of the snowmobilers.

With Heemeyer and Linton in the lead, there was a mad dash to the debris field to try to find any buried snowmobilers. A quick head count, organized by Heemeyer and Linton, revealed that five sledders were missing and probably buried in the snow. They grabbed shovels and probes and started looking.

It was on odd scene. Chunks and piles of snow now were stacked in the meadow at least five to six feet deeper than what had been there just one minute prior. They could see disembodied sets of hands poking out through the snow. They saw two feet poking through to the sky in another spot. Four of the five sleds were completely buried.

This was truly a race against time. The ten other sledders all pitched in and started digging, working hard to uncover the victims' faces so they could breathe. Heemeyer, in between bouts of digging, helped to organize groups in the digging process. Heemeyer and Linton were working hard to efficiently use the manpower to free the faces of riders as fast as possible. Too long under this concrete-like avalanche run-off and a rider could die. This was a life and death situation.

"That's four," Heemeyer shouted. "Where's Steve?"

There was one boot sticking out from the snow amid a jumble of tree limbs and rocks a little bit further down the debris field. Four men rushed to the spot and worked hard to pull away the snow. They dug as fast as they could, running out of breath and trading places with each other for the best vantage point for this hard work. Heemeyer dug frantically. John Linton dug frantically, but this snow was heavy and compact. This was not like digging in the sand.

Marv knew the situation.

Most people buried in snow can be recovered alive if they are dug out within the first 15 minutes. Twelve minutes had already gone by. There wasn't much time.

They found Steve Holzworth's head four feet below the surface after they dug along his torso. His face was a mottled, water-color blue. His reddish, vein-streaked eyes blankly stared out at the white snow clumped around him, the pupils rolled back up into his skull. Weaver leaned in and noticed his nostrils quivered ever so slightly. There was hope and the digging and shouting started anew.

It was hard work and even more frenzied than before as they pulled and tore at the snow. People were swearing and sweating and finally Holzworth's slack but stiffening body was rolled up onto the surface. Heemeyer slapped his face and massaged Holzworth's cheeks. He slapped his face again, this time harder. He rubbed his shoulders and pushed on his chest. After a minute Holzworth coughed lightly and opened his eyes. He coughed again and the other riders smiled. Phlegm bubbled from his nose.

They now laughed, pounding Holzworth on the back after he awkwardly stood up two minutes later. After another 40 minutes, all the sleds were painstakingly freed from the rock-hard snow. The now-jovial group rode to another flat spot, started a huge fire and warmed up. The buried riders were frigid after being encased in snow while the rescuers shivered from sweating in the ice cold air. The warmth felt good and the stories started to circulate about how they had all survived the slide. Each story was a little different; each from a different perspective.

After the long but triumphant ride back to the parking lot, they all agreed to meet at the traditional spot, Pancho and Lefty's in Grand Lake, where they toasted their luck and regaled whoever would listen.

Heemeyer was as happy as he could be.

When it came to snowmobiling with his group of sledding friends, Heemeyer was not one to boast in the extreme about his accomplishments, especially when the ride and rescue that day had been a team effort. He and his friends had ridden into the distant wild fringes of the winter wilderness, marking high peaks and treading with their screaming machines through glorious, unmarked powder. They had faced and nearly succumbed to mortal danger in the slide, but they had triumphed and all had returned alive. The thrill of the adventure and the awe of facing down death left Heemeyer feeling content that night. He had helped to save lives, working with his friends, and now they could celebrate. It felt like victory.

And his reputation as the snowmobiling hero of Grand Lake was even more firmly established in the minds of the snowmobiling world of Grand Lake.

Perhaps, as he sat at the bar or some random friend's table in Pancho and Lefty's, his fights with the town of Granby and his neighbors were distant thoughts. In his triumph at that time he might have let himself think that there was still a chance he'd win his lawsuit, putting his foes in their places. He would have been so happy that he might have wondered why he even pondered his mission, but he tried to put all that out of his mind during that triumphant night.

12. Heemeyer Loses His Lawsuit

Grand County District Court had ruled to dismiss Heemeyer's lawsuit against the Town of Granby and the Docheffs on April 26, 2002. District Judge Richard Doucette disagreed with Heemeyer's claims on every count. The judge stated that the court "has concluded that the town has acted within the authority of its code and has not abused its discretion."

Heemeyer had lost.

I called him many times. Heemeyer finally responded.

"Talk to my lawyer," is all that Heemeyer said. He hung up abruptly.

"Marvin is disappointed in the outcome, and rightly so," Dietze said, his voice sounding apologetic. "This situation is difficult and the town is granted a lot of leeway in these cases."

Heemeyer was probably angry at himself at this point for ever holding out any hope that he might prevail in a lawsuit. But losing so definitively likely left him feeling angry and vindictive, but now in a way that was redeemed by his grandly malevolent plans for the town of Granby. Now he could seethe in secret and indulge his project.

Heemeyer expressed his disappointment in a letter he e-mailed to Dietze:

> *Still they approved the application in May 2001 but did not issue a building permit.*
>
> *At this point I thought you might be right with your "legally stopped" explanation until August of 2001 when the change to Granby's ordinance appeared in the local paper and construction resumed that same month. Again nothing has stopped. No injunctions, nothing.*

When you were notified of the construction you said something to the effect that some people just want to do it their way.

All after a lot of 'out of the box' thinking on our part to persuade Judge Doucette to hear your case while collecting an exorbitant and undeserved fee from me.

You placed an ace too early and tried to replace it with a joker disguised as an ace.

I fell for it although I didn't fully comprehend this until after Judge Doucette's decisions favoring the applicant and your complete reluctance to file an appeal.

Whatever happened to Dorothy Lockhart's favoring the applicant at the P and Z meeting? Why was the McDougal property favored with an easement and not me? You knew about this. Why a lot of favoring at many different times.

I always felt that if this was good enough to go to trial it had to be good enough to appeal. Wrong. Now we know why. Colorado Revised Statutes supersede local ordinances. You didn't know this?!!!!

And now the 15 to 20 thousand-dollar lawsuit which was the original reason you took me as a client will be laughed out of court according to your associates and now you agree.

You screwed me out of a reasonably assured victory and into an upwind concrete plant for a neighbor with nothing but future litigation on the horizon.

Additionally, now you imply that I'm supposed to be concerned about the outcome of future lawsuits you have pending in front of Judge Doucette if you ask him to set aside his decision. If Judge Doucette deserved to have a request to set aside his decision so be it. If not, why suggest it. I expect I will hear more eloquent rhetoric on this later.

This whole case was dead in July of 2000. But you wouldn't listen.

I now have a dismal future in many respects because of your incompetence. For these and many reasons I want an immediate complete and total refund of the 50,000 plus dollars that I have paid you since 3 July 2000.

Also, I think you owe the people of Granby an apology. Especially Pam Cornett who you called a very brave lady.

You have not represented my best interest since the day you told me the building permit and construction were illegal and had me take those pictures of the construction. You certainly did not stop this or make them follow it to the letter of the law, as was my initial request.

You know where to send the check.

Marvin Heemeyer

PS Retire.

Heemeyer's allegation of incompetence rings false because the work of Dietze resulted in concessions and then improvements in the concrete plant's design and operations. Dietze made it a better project in general, but he didn't stop it completely, which Heemeyer wanted.

In a pattern that was becoming typical for Heemeyer, Dietze, his one-time ally and chief confidante in the battle against the batch plant, became in his mind another enemy worthy of attack. And yet in his own words, Heemeyer refutes his own suggestion that Dietze was milking him for money and leading him on with an unwinnable case by stating that Dietze recommended against an appeal of the lawsuit ruling. If Dietze had been truly trying to "milk" Heemeyer, he surely would have recommended appeal after appeal, squeezing out every dollar he could. That didn't happen.

Heemeyer, who had now spent about $55,000 with Dietze, didn't feel the need to appeal in the courts.

He had another type of appeal in mind.

Heemeyer closed down Mountain View Muffler. He told people he was done with Granby. He was going to auction off all of his gear and get out of town.

This gave him time to attend auctions, drive his four-wheeler ATVs on the trails around Grand Lake and do as he pleased.

He loved equipment auctions. They were events where a man could find deals for pennies on the dollar. He bought old cars, loaders, lifts, all kinds of tools and other machinery at auctions. Now, he was looking for a particular item. It showed up at a Ritchie Brothers Auction in California. He drove out to look at it.

The dozer had been owned by Fresno Tractor for six years. The company had rented the machine to a variety of clients. Before that no one could say for sure where the dozer had been or what it had done. But that particular model had been built specifically for oil field and mineral prospecting work in Russia and China.

Heemeyer paid $16,000 for the Komatsu D355-A. It was a steal at that price, and he knew it. His Komatsu was slightly larger than a D-9 Caterpillar, the other bulldozer in that class of machine. He had it shipped to Granby on a specially made trailer, where it arrived in early July of 2002.

Marv Heemeyer's last advertisement in the *Sky-Hi News* ran October 3, 2002. In it, Roller and Associates, Inc., an auction company, announced the sale of almost all of the inventory at Mountain View Muffler. The auction was set for Saturday, October 12, with inspection taking place the day before.

The property and its buildings had a price listed at $450,000. Under construction equipment Heemeyer listed the Komatsu D355-A bulldozer, backhoes, trailers, graders and more. Lots of automotive and shop equipment was also for sale, including a BendPak Hydraulic Tubing Bender, lifts, air compressor, tools and other miscellaneous shop items. A total of seven snowmobiles and six jet skis were put on the block, along with a boat, motorcycles and snowmobile trailers. He was also getting rid of eight rebuildable cars, featuring a 1963 Impala. Engine blocks and car parts of all types were for sale.

The auction featured a loquacious and ebullient auctioneer. It was well-attended and Heemeyer sold almost everything he had for sale, with two notable exceptions. He hadn't gotten the asking price of $450,000 for the property and its buildings, although the current renter Travis Busse and his partner were interested.

And he hadn't sold the bulldozer.

Revealingly, he never put his welding tanks, tools and related welding hardware on the block. He also kept his best two snowmobiles.

"According to the Richie Brothers auction sales (in California) at that time that dozer was selling nationally for as much as $43,000.00," Heemeyer said. "OK I don't believe that any of the Komatsu D355s were in as good a shape as this one was . . . If any Komatsu D355 should have brought $54,000, which was what I had it at, that one should have. I was willing at the auction to take $33,000 for it. Couldn't get a bid. I got a $20,000 bid. That was the only real bid we got. Well, I had $24,000 in it. I'm not going to sell it for that, especially when Richie Brothers says it's worth $43,000. So I kept the dozer."

Was this the final sign Marv Heemeyer needed to end the push and pull of the complex morality play going on in his head?

13. Misguided Malice

"What good is our code if we don't enforce it?" Trustee Ed Raffety said after the July, 2002 meeting of the Granby Board of Trustees. He said people around town had "talked to him." Raffety, a former grocery store owner who had been a mediating influence on the board since the Heemeyer disputes began, was now at the end of his rope. He uttered these words in the same hot and stuffy meeting room where, two years earlier, Heemeyer appeared to be winning his case.

"I think he's taking advantage of us."

The town board's frustration was heightened by the fact that they felt they had been going out of their way to let Heemeyer resolve all the water and sewer issues on his own without any added expense or hassle. They had been giving him a chance to make it good, without angst. People in town had noticed, wondering why Heemeyer was being given such leeway. He'd been in clear violation for a full year and nothing had happened and many argued he had been in violation long before that. And now Heemeyer wasn't even willing to take advantage of the leeway he had been given.

It was frustrating.

Town Manager Tom Hale reported to the board that he thought Heemeyer had two problems at the Mountain View Muffler site. One was an ongoing junk complaint and the other was the fact that he still had not hooked on to the water or sewer. He told the board Heemeyer refused to attend a meeting with the Docheffs to negotiate easements for the water and sewer lines. He received no response on other correspondence and Heemeyer had simply stopped communicating. Heemeyer even hung up mid-conversation with Hale earlier in July.

Heemeyer refused to accept a citation hand-delivered to him in early August. Despite his refusal, Heemeyer appeared in Granby Municipal Court in November, and was found to be in contempt of town code by Judge Georgia Noriyuki. In essence, the court found that Heemeyer was indeed in violation and the court entered into a deferred judgment and sentence against Heemeyer. He was given a time frame in which to fix the problems with the water and sewer and he was ordered to remove the mixer-tank septic tank before July 28 of 2003.

It appeared that a local trash hauling company was using the property and he was told the property couldn't be used for anything other than storage and no water or sewage usage was allowed. Heemeyer agreed to sign the restrictive covenant that stated "the property shall not be used for human occupancy or habitation nor shall the property be opened for business unless and until the Property has been connected to the town of Granby water system and the Granby Sanitation District sewer system." It couldn't be released until the town did so. If he violated any of those terms he was to be fined as allowed by town law.

Heemeyer responded in writing:

To: Granby Planning commission, Granby Town Board,
Scotty Krob.

Subject: Misguided Malice

This is a letter of protest to be attached to legal instruments signed by me on 11/20/02 presented to me by an attorney named Ben McClelland.

Today I signed unjust and manipulative documents, as the lessor (sic) of two evils, to undeservedly appease what I believe to be a misguided, corrupt and unjustifiably malicious and vengeful group of people who have over the last 10 (TEN) years plus effectively, maliciously, willfully and perversely sought to impede my attempt to develop a property, earn an income and provide for my future . . .

Although I did not buy this property for myself I ended up being the owner. I had no plans or desire to be in Granby or stay in Grand County. God and only God put me here. I bought this property with no malice or anger toward the community or the group of people I refer to and only after talking to two prominent local Realtors. However, malice, anger, hatred and perversion is what I have received since . . .

The seeds of perversion that have been sown in this community affects (sic) your spineless actions and inaction's (sic) and both blinds and deceives you I can only hope as in the past you reap what you sow and that I will be close by to watch. Do not be dismayed. Your form of terrorism will survive.

For my future benefit the contents of this letter have been heavily edited. You just don't get it.

Yours respectfully,

Marvin John Heemeyer

The letter was brushed aside as a type of normal venting that takes place when people lose a legal battle.

After walking out of the courtroom when Heemeyer accepted the town's judgment, his attorney, Ben McClelland, heard Heemeyer mutter, under his breath, suppressed in anger, "I'm just gonna bulldozer this whole place to the ground."

Ben dismissed the comment. People were frequently angry and said such things after losing court cases.

The town waited and waited, hoping Heemeyer would do as promised and end the dispute. But reluctantly, after several months, the town imposed fines.

Despite the dispute with the town and the legal wrangling, Heemeyer continued to enjoy his favorite pastime. Matt Reed of Grand Lake remembers a trip he made with Heemeyer during the late winter of 2002-2003. Matt was the youngest of the group of avid snowmobilers who rode with Heemeyer on the famous Thursday rides. His mother, in fact, had asked Marv to keep an eye on Reed during the rides and Heemeyer had taken that request seriously. He watched over Matt and welcomed him into the group of seasoned and older riders. Reed remembers that Heemeyer was mysterious but clear. He spoke of "retribution" and drastic measures. Matt remembers that Heemeyer said "they" had taken from him and conspired against him.

Matt said little other than to acknowledge and to suggest that he understood. He remembers that Heemeyer said something that suggested he had the knowledge and the power to prevail. Matt Reed was one of many people who revered Marv Heemeyer as a master mechanic, an extremely skillful snowmobiler and an articulate spokesperson for a wide range of causes.

Mike Garrett, the auto dealership owner in Granby, had ridden with Heemeyer many times and became his friend. He said Marv was the best mechanic he knew. Marv was generous to him in many times of need, especially when it involved equipment. He especially remembers the time Heemeyer was baffled when Mike's sled beat his in an impromptu drag race on Rabbit Ears Pass.

Heemeyer asked to borrow the sled Mike had ridden. Heemeyer completely dismantled it, tore down the engine and then rebuilt it and returned it as new, all in a quest to see what mechanical advantage had given Mike the edge. Perhaps this obsessive track of mind, a compulsion to understand the slightest mechanical detail that gave advantage, is what drove Heemeyer to exaggerate his loss to the town. He had to know. He had to fix it. He had to make it right. Now was the time to act.

In March of 2003, Heemeyer (left) continued to enjoy the company of his snowmobiling friends on rides into the high country around Grand Lake.

14. The World in Black and White

Marv flared the cutting torch to life with one expert flick of the spark igniter. The loud, sharp pop meant his workday had started. This cut would be easy. It was for the exhaust line shield to be placed underneath the dozer's right front manifold. He had to protect those exhaust tubes because he knew cops would be shooting all around the machine and he knew a punctured manifold out-take tube, especially on a big diesel like this, would force too much intake and probably cause the big engine to rev too high and overheat. This was one detail of his planning, he thought, that would surely confound the Barney Fifes out there in copland.

He slowly brought the torch flame down the large sheet of steel, an eight foot slab, four feet wide, that he had driven up from Denver himself. God it was heavy. He had come in eight inches from the top corner, to his right, and dropped straight down for the cut, following the grease pencil line he had used to mark the steel. He cut down for three feet. He knew he had six more cuts like this to make, but he worked slowly and deliberately. With the slab leaning back in its cutting position, the steel chunk fell backward and down on a canvas floor covering he had in place, the bright smell of the molten steel filling the air.

He had only just begun to scratch the surface of the roughly 247 cuts that would be needed to complete the project. He had a long way to go, but he was already a far cry from where he had been two months ago when he wasn't even sure the dozer would fit into the steel shed.

Back then, when there was still snow on the ground, he had measured the opening but it was going to be tight. He had shoveled and scraped the snow off the machine and he had charged the massive batteries. He pre-heated some of the diesel fuel. All winter it had sat at the top of the small rise of the entrance driveway to his old muffler shop, the tall and wide blade of the machine facing out to the county road like a steel wall. A reinforced barbed wire gate in the same spot couldn't have done a better job of telling people they weren't welcome. And yet, he had taped a For Sale sign in the middle of the blade. He had taken the sign down before starting the dozer. It ran like a charm. It had been slow going when he eased the massive machine through the garage door on the shed, but it fit, just barely.

The close fit and the fact that he was in the building, out of sight from the world, let him know that it was all right, that he was right. That it was intended. That God really had wanted him to do this. This would be his new service to God. This was what God wanted, and now he knew it. On many Sundays in the past five years he had gone to services for the Christian Reformed Church in Denver. Not anymore. This was his church.

With no windows on the east side of the building, he knew he couldn't observe what was going on or protect himself from surprise visits. So he put in place a test run of what he wanted to do with the dozer.

He put two sneak-peek cameras he had bought for the dozer outside the building. He mounted them under the eaves, pointing down for just the right view. He hooked up the wire leads and fed them through pin-size holes he drilled into the steel siding. He then attached them to a computer monitor he had bought at a garage sale for $5. A splitter box, which cost only $12 on-line, allowed him to switch from camera to camera, or even have a split image of each camera's field of view on the screen. He now could observe what was happening right outside the building, in black and white on the monitor. It offered ghost-like profiles of the landscape outside.

It would do. He now had security cameras.

His plan was slowly falling in place. But this was taking longer than he wanted. The long drive back and forth from his house in Grand Lake to Granby was wasting time. He needed a solution to that problem.

He had a cot, television, DVD and cassette player, some old shelves and piles of canvas stored at home. There was a pile of old two by fours and an old cotton sleeping bag. This would be a start.

After hauling his supplies into the huge steel shed under cover of darkness, he began putting the two-by-fours in place. If he needed little bits of supplies, well, he could just sneak out the west door of the shed and walk over to the Country Ace Hardware, located nearby across a weed-saturated field. He could do this without anybody at the nearby trash company noticing.

He stapled tarps to the walls he had made, sealing in an area in the northeast corner of the shed and making the walls somewhat solid. When he was finished, he had his living quarters set up and ready to go. After acquiring a refrigerator, two lamps, a small burner and a microwave, he would have all the comforts of home. All he was lacking was a shitter and water. He could bring in water and he'd just piss and shit in a bucket and dump it in the Horn Ditch out back at night, when no one could see what he was up to.

Heemeyer also brought in a DVD player and a television set. This way he could entertain himself with his favorite movies while living in the shed. One film he enjoyed watching over and over was the Vin Diesel film *A Man Apart.* In this film, Diesel is something like an American Superhero. Playing the part of a DEA agent, Diesel faces a violent Mexican drug cartel that has murdered his wife in retaliation for his earlier arrest of a drug kingpin. In losing his wife he becomes the non-sexual and purified avenger.

Diesel quietly endures further provocation, then loses his badge and must face off against his enemies in an act of righteous revenge without the help of the DEA. He's alone, figuratively, as the Superhero must be. He is shot two or three times in the film and endures fights where he is outnumbered and the underdog, but he miraculously survives, as he must as a superhero. He then avenges it all by arresting the drug kingpin, ridding the world of another evil player. The film ends with him walking away, single, from the grave of his murdered wife.

Heemeyer also had the film *Independence Day* in his video library. This movie features another regular man as a sort of American Superhero. The hero avenges his initial unjust defeats through a form of violent vigilantism wherein he escapes sure death and then succeeds to save or purify the world again. As in the Vin Diesel film, the hero is the victim of some sort of governmental conspiracy.

Sitting in that steel shed, watching these films time and time again, Marv Heemeyer was painting himself into that mythic structure well. It only helped that government is depicted as either ineffectual or as the villain itself. The DEA takes Diesel's badge. In more than one Rambo film, the hero is betrayed by corrupt and indifferent military or government figures, leaving him on his own to avenge wrongs. For Heemeyer, Granby government (the town board and the sewer board) is not only ineffectual, it is corrupt and deliberately working against him through a conspiracy. It fits the mold well.

In this fashion, using his room in the shed with its Spartan amenities, he developed a pattern. People said they saw Marv rarely during this time. Maybe they'd see him on the road or in passing at the grocery store. But he wasn't out and about like he had been in the past. He probably had a pattern. Maybe he'd work four days in the shed, never leaving except at night to dump the slop bucket. He'd go in before dawn on a Sunday morning and leave at dusk on a Wednesday. On Fridays he'd make his trips to Denver to buy supplies. He'd go those four days a week without a shower, without meeting people and without going for a drive or recreating. He broke that pattern only when he needed to just drive and get away from it all. He'd go to South Dakota. He'd drive to California. He'd just drive.

One such trip was when he went back to his home state to pick-up the new firearm he had ordered the day before. It was a Barrett Firearms Manufacturing .50-caliber, semi-automatic rifle that featured a recoil-absorbing stock and flash suppressor. He had bought it from his favorite gun shop in the world, Gengerke Tactical Supply in Groten, S.D., located two hours away from his hometown. The store specializes in advanced weapon systems, such as assault rifles and class 3 weapons. It sells silencers and hosts machine gun shootouts every year.

The .50-caliber Barrett, valued at $7,000, is renowned for its impressive power, range and pure destructive energy. The rounds have an effective kill range of well over a mile and the weight of each round makes it something closer to a small cannon than a rifle. The rifle was designed for attacks on parked or landing aircraft, armored personnel carriers, rail tank cars, bulk fuel storage and concrete bunkers. The rifle is powerful enough to puncture armored limousines.

Heemeyer had a place for this weapon. It would go in the back of his firing area, facing the rear where he'd have the most room to maneuver the large gun inside his improvised tank. It would be his cannon.

After these trips Heemeyer returned to the shed. He had work to do.

This photo, probably taken in South Dakota during one of Heemeyer's final trips there, shows Heemeyer revealing the difference in size between a .50-caliber round held in his right hand (left side of picture) and what appears to be a .22-caliber round.

15. SOLD, at Last

Heemeyer had found a buyer for his Mountain View Muffler property. Travis Busse, who had been leasing the property to park his trucks and for a small office, was ready, with his partner Bob Martin, to buy the property.

Shortly thereafter Travis Busse approached the Granby Board and asked what could be done that would allow him to have water and sewer at Heemeyer's property if he bought it. The board and Busse worked it out and Busse and his new partner closed on the Mountain View Muffler land in October of 2003, paying Heemeyer $400,000, $50,000 short of what he had wanted at the auction a year before. The price was close to and even in excess of the amounts Heemeyer had demanded from the Docheffs for the property only four years before.

The next day Busse had permission for easements, and the day after he closed on the land, the water and sewer connections were completed.

Two weeks later, Heemeyer signed a lease agreement with Busse and The Trash Company that allowed him to rent the eastern portion of the metal building until June of 2004.

"Oh, I've got some work to finish, stuff to store, until then," he told Busse and Martin in front of the title company after the closing.

Heemeyer must have thought it was just typical how Busse had gotten those easements from the Docheffs so easily, how they hadn't let him cut across, singling him out, while others got their way. He couldn't see that his lawsuit was the main obstacle. He just saw that, once again, he was being excluded. He was the "outsider." It must have galled him to see how easily Busse got it all done.

Marv Heemeyer got a phone call from assistant town clerk Deb Hess telling him the check he had written to pay his fine for violating the court order was no good. They needed a new check written or he'd incur more fines.

That did it.

He walked out of his metal building on the property he used to own and jumped into his truck. His rear tires threw gravel as he whipped his truck out onto the county road. He was headed toward the Town Hall and he parked in front of the building at an awkward angle, taking two parking spaces.

Taking two steps at a time he climbed the stairs to the town offices. The Town Hall housed the Granby Library downstairs and the town offices upstairs. It was an old school building and it had the feel of an old school. Schools made Marv uneasy.

He walked into the town clerk's office, a frown on his face. He was dressed in work clothes and smelled of welding fumes.

"Did you call me about my check?"

He nearly shouted. Deb Hess was alarmed.

"Well your check . . . The bank wouldn't take your check."

Heemeyer stared down at Hess, talking through clenched teeth while he wagged his finger. She stood in a corner and she couldn't get around him.

"You have no right to bad mouth my reputation and my ability to pay by telling those gals at the bank that my check's no good. I've got hundreds of thousands in there!"

He leaned in even closer, his pointing finger now folded into something like a loose fist. His right arm gestured back and forth as he talked.

"All I've done is get abuse from this town and its lackey bureaucrats like you. You lie and cheat on me, you take my livelihood and then you spread rumors at the bank! It's true, you are all cowards and liars! I mean that!"

He was referring to the phrase he had written on the memo line of the check. He had scribbled: "Cowards and Liars Dept."

But that wasn't the problem. The bank, Liberty Savings Bank, had rejected the check because of the way he had written out the amount of the $3351 fine for violating the court's restrictive covenant. He had written "Thirty-three fifty-one" followed by two zeros over 100. This was not acceptable so they sent the check back to the town saying it had to be re-written.

For a moment, Hess didn't know exactly what to say. She hoped someone would come into the office and help her out. She felt threatened. He could beat her to a pulp and kill her, she thought, and all over a mere check.

"Mr. Heemeyer, I wasn't over at the bank and I wouldn't do that to you, sir," Hess said in response. "I have no reason to bad-mouth you. I just need a different check."

But for Heemeyer, it wasn't a mere check. It was the culminating insult and humiliation after a series of humiliations and losses in the eyes of the public. He was convinced that the town was out spreading rumors about him and "snickering at him in the post office." They were out to get him.

Hess handed Heemeyer the check. He scratched out the questionable amount line and hastily scribbled in "three thousand three hundred fifty one." He initialed the change mjh. He turned and walked out.

Hess photocopied the questionable check with Heemeyer's changes and filled out a deposit slip. She deposited the money. It cleared.

And now, Hess thought, perhaps it was all over with; all behind them. He had paid his fine. Travis Busse and The Trash Company had purchased the property and legally hooked up the water and sewer lines. And it appeared that Heemeyer was officially gone out of the town limits of Granby.

It was a false hope.

DEPOSIT TICKET

TOWN OF GRANBY
P.O. BOX 440 PH. 970-887-2501
GRANBY, CO 80446

DATE 11-21-03

DEPOSITS MAY NOT BE AVAILABLE FOR IMMEDIATE WITHDRAWAL

SIGN HERE FOR CASH RECEIVED (IF REQUIRED) ✱

LIBERTY SAVINGS BANK — A Federal Savings Bank, P.O. BOX 587, GRANBY, COLORADO 80446

CASH ▸	
23-7414/3020 0851003104 7010	3351.00
(OR TOTAL FROM OTHER SIDE)	
SUB TOTAL ▸	3351.00
✱ LESS CASH RECEIVED ▸	
$	3351.00

[redacted] 9998

MARVIN J. HEEMEYER
P.O. BOX 680 970-887-3130
GRANBY, CO 80446-0680

23-7414/3020 0854005072 No. 7010

Date 11/17/03

PAY TO THE ORDER OF Town of Granby $3351/00

three thousand three hundred fifty one & no/100 ~~thirty three fifty one & no/100~~ DOLLARS

LIBERTY SAVINGS BANK — A Federal Savings Bank, P.O. BOX 587, GRANBY, COLORADO 80446

Memo Cowards & Liars Dept — M Heemeyer

[redacted] 7010

Mr. Heemeyer rewrote check – will deposit 11/21/03 –

16. Spilling the Beans

The isolation would have finally been getting to Heemeyer. Winter was a time when he was usually out four or five times a week riding. Now he was limiting himself to one time a week for the Thursday rides. Being alone all the time allowed him to sulk and fume with anger. The solitude was getting the better of him and his mission to keep it all a big secret.

Heemeyer was with some of the riders and other friends. It was late afternoon in early February at the Sagebrush Grill in Grand Lake, a corner restaurant that served barbecue items and prided itself on the large tins of peanuts that sat, at no extra charge, on every table. When people walked the floor they'd invariably be crunching discarded peanut shells under their feet.

Across the table from Heemeyer sat a friend and snowmobiling partner Don Campbell, with his girlfriend, Antoinette "Tony" Beckley, also a good friend of Heemeyer. Secretly, Heemeyer was envious of their relationship. That's what he wanted. With them sat Bonnie Brown, a friend they all knew from her work in stores along the boardwalk in Grand Lake. She liked Marv and thought of him as a gentle teddy bear of a man, a friend to all and a renowned snowmobiler. He frequently bought her a beer or two, but it would never amount to much beyond socializing. In fact, the beer in front of her had been purchased by Heemeyer.

Most everyone had enjoyed a good meal. Heemeyer had consumed a few more beers than was normal.

Suddenly Heemeyer sat up, upright and rigid.

"That town has been undercutting me and fining me and scheming against me," he said. They all knew he was referring to the town of Granby. "Those good ol' boys have been conspiring to ruin me, the newcomer. The newspaper, the Thompsons, the Docheffs the town — all of them. I will get them, that's what."

This little outburst, seemingly out of nowhere, was surprising only in its severe and righteous tone. He had shared with his friends all the wrongs and slights from the town of Granby, but usually it was more lighthearted. Not this time.

"You see, because of them, I have nothing to live for. Not a damn thing."

Most of those present thought this was odd since for many Heemeyer had it made. He didn't have to work, he could snowmobile as he pleased, he owned his house and he had just made a bundle off the property in Granby. Why, it seemed like it was going OK for Marv.

The silence was awkward. The crunch of peanut shells echoed unusually loudly in the restaurant, magnified by the new tone of the conversation. People moved as if to get up to leave and pay the bill. Marv sat still.

"By God, I am going to bulldozer those businesses and all the businesses of the people who have done this to me. Who have ruined my life. I will show them."

Those at the table now looked at each other with quizzical glances. They shrugged their shoulders. They settled up.

Thirty minutes later Heemeyer joined the crew at Pancho and Lefty's. He was as jovial as usual. He bought a round of beers.

Marv talked to other people too, even people in Granby. People he spoke to were his perceived allies.

Ralf Lindenlaub owned and operated the Longbranch Restaurant on Granby's main street. He and his wife served good German food and were proud of their iconic location, name and covering over the Granby sidewalk. It set them apart. Ralf, who had escaped over the Berlin Wall to the west when he was a young man, came to America with steadfast views about freedom and the United States. He was not bashful about speaking his mind. When he had time, he'd come out into the dining room from the kitchen to talk to customers.

It was a slow Wednesday night in late February, which was normal for winter. Marv Heemeyer, who had come to the restaurant before, showed up. Ralf had been out front with his wife, Marlena. Ralf stood up.

"Hello Marv," Ralf said. Ralf was tall, like Marv, but he was thin, unlike Heemeyer.

"Hi Ralf. Here for dinner."

Ralf looked closely at Heemeyer and was amazed at how red his face looked, 'like a beet,' he thought.

Heemeyer ate, had a couple of beers and then ate some apple strudel.

When Ralf came out to help Marlena settle up the register, Marv, sitting in the booth behind the register, looked up.

"Hey Ralf," he said. He indicated with his hand that he wanted Lindenlaub to sit at the table. There were no other customers. Marlena counted out the cash quietly behind them, whispering the numbers in German.

"What do you want me to do with the trees," he said.

"What Marv? What are you talking about?"

"Oh, you know. The town's damn trees. Those picayune aspens the town planted right in your way."

Ralf now understood. It was about the fight he had with the town ten years ago when he complained that the new town aspen trees planted on Agate Avenue, Granby's main throughfare, as part of a beautification project, had grown up to block his sign. He told the town board those trees were hurting his business. He wanted them removed. The town refused.

"Oh, well, you know Marv, that's all settled."

"Nothing with this town is settled, ever."

Heemeyer and the entire town remembered well how Lindenlaub had reacted to the town's intransigence on the trees. He had called me up at the newspaper and told me to bring my camera. I showed up. Dressed in his best white cooking attire and white ballooning chef's hat, he stood by the aspen tree nearest the restaurant. It was a smallish tree, but big enough. He held a hand saw in his hand. 'Take these pictures now,' he told me.

I photographed the event. He deliberately sawed through the tree. It tumbled down toward the sidewalk. It looked much taller on the ground than standing.

'Now my business will be good,' he told me. 'I'll keep track. They will arrest me, too.'

He was arrested but the town relented on serious charges and Lindenlaub was allowed to replace the aspen he had chopped with a smaller, less obtrusive tree. The next winter Lindenlaub was happy to show me and any one else willing to listen the figures from the summer two years ago and the most recent summer, when he didn't have the aspen. The numbers purported to show a huge increase in sales, all because of the felled tree.

"No Marv. No. Everything is settled. I settled everything with the town."

"Oh, you know what's happened with me," Heemeyer said.

"No Marv. What's happened?"

"I know you know. Well, I got myself a bulldozer. And I will get them. I will really get them."

"What do you mean Marv?"

"Oh I got it at an auction. Then it didn't sell here. It was the only thing left at my auction that didn't sell. That means something, by God. God wanted it that way. So I built a tank."

"A tank? What are you going to do with it?"

"Oh, I will get those guys. I well get them all. I will get Casey. I will get the Thompsons. I will not kill anybody. But I will get them. I will get them all."

Ralf could see that maybe Heemeyer was a little drunk. His face was still red. Oblong, small white circles of salt, indicating dried beads of sweat, sat on his temples. Lines, as if from a mask, creased around his wide face.

"OK Marv, you do what you do," Lindenlaub said. He stood up from the booth. "Thanks Marv. You finished?"

Heemeyer nodded and he got the bill. It was the last time Heemeyer ate at the Longbranch.

17. Heavy Metal

He slipped on his coveralls, now stained with grease, steel wipe water and burn splotches from the welding. He flipped down the lid of his welding mask. He was back inside his realm, the realm of a master welder at the peak of his craft. This was a type of monastic denial, he told himself. He ate vitamins by the handful. And to keep his appetite in check, he'd down full glasses of Slim Fast, a weight control drink that he found to be very effective in curbing his appetite and keeping his weight down.

He had never been fat or even out of shape, but the image of his fat mother in the years before she died back in 2002 kept him constantly alert to the scourge of getting fat and letting himself go. He'd never let himself go like she had done. Never. He had always been fit, religiously so. He was the school champion half-miler, for Christ's sake. He knew fitness. He was no slob. It was a sin to let it go.

The work was now getting more difficult. And he was running out of time. The lease would expire at the end of May and he had some of the trickiest welds and adjustments ahead. The first layer on his cab consisted of three-eighths-inch thick panels of steel, carefully applied to the framework of the dozer. But now he was using half inch. This would be the second layer of steel. The two layers would leave a pocket nine inches wide on the sides and five inches thick on the top of the cab. Into these pockets he'd pour concrete, creating the best blast and bullet protection he could make. Not much of anything would be able to penetrate those three layers. He'd make sure they wouldn't get him. He'd show them by the work he was doing now. Careful, meticulous and inpenetrable.

And yet Marv Heemeyer was feeling rushed.

The side and bottom panels that would hold the concrete membrane between the panes of steel were difficult to align and then hold in place while he stitched the connecting points together. His lift, with two makeshift clamps on the far ends, held the bottom plate in the general area. Other wooden braces and c-clamps were used to brace the bottom sheet where it needed to be. Then, working first on the top side and then the bottom, he stitch-welded and then tacked along the seam. It would have to be airtight or fluids from the wet concrete would leak out after he poured it in. And any crack or fissure would leave seals vulnerable to any explosives that might be used against what he now affectionately called Marv's MK Dozer.

The positions he had to assume for these welds were not comfortable. They made his back and neck ache. But these were critical. He couldn't let up now.

About a week later, the cavities for the concrete were all in place and the cab was well-sealed. Outside, in the world of black and white, the snow was melting away. It was mud season, the worst time of year in the mountains. One day it could be clear, sunny and warm, like a true spring day, and the next it would be a blizzard, with heavy, wet snow piling up in drifts. The grass was grey or brown, no aspens or cottonwoods were green yet. People who could afford to get away at this time of year did so.

Mud season was a great time to be working hard indoors, and that suited Heemeyer just fine. He knew how he was going to build the embrasures or firing ports. Rather than sketch out the design, as he had done with other parts of the dozer, he would go step by step. Using the half-inch steel, he cut the first triangle and rounded the narrow end. He tacked the narrow end to the hole he had cut in the three-eighths steel plate on the outside layer. Cutting triangles like this, at just the right lengths, he put in place a firing port on the right side of his cab that would accommodate the barrel of the .223-caliber Ruger Mini-34 rifle. He wanted this port to be tight so he put the barrel of this sweet little weapon in place before setting the last two triangles. This would be the gun he'd use the most. It fired fast and it was powerful. And it had a great field of view. All those triangles angled down to that firing port, a funnel of steel.

Above, he cut the rectangular hole for his viewing port. Four inches tall and a foot wide, this port would allow him to see, a little bit. He finished the bottom and two sides and then slid in three layers of Lexan, that bulletproof glass. He had made notched pathways for the glass. Then, on the inside, he made a sliding steel door that he could open when wanting to look outside. No bullets would get through that arrangement.

And then he repeated this painstaking process for the front of the cab, working in cramped quarters where the smoke from his welds sent him into coughing fits and where the heat of his work left him sweating and dehydrated. In the front embrasure he placed the barrel of the .308 Fabrique Nationale Herstal semi-automatic rifle. This was another sweet rifle he had purchased from a hunter several years before. Like he had done with the Ruger, he elevated the scope placement on the barrel so it could be used to view the world outside the dozer cab through the port. This involved placing spacers to raise the scope. This gun allowed easy maneuverability to the front. The embrasure was perfect on this one, with hardly any light leaking in around the seal. The viewing port above had three layers of Lexan and the sliding steel plate.

He built another embrasure for the left side, but he left it covered. He hadn't purchased the rifle for that side yet. Maybe he could cram the barrel of his pistol through that hole and just start squeezing off rounds. It might be needed.

The rear embrasure was the most important for that was where he placed the .50-caliber. This would be the cannon for his MK Tank. He placed the barrel carefully in place and welded the triangular plates to the pinch-point. The gun rested easily in the firing port, suspended from the ceiling of the cab by a bungee cord. He left the sight on the rifle even though he knew he wouldn't be able to use it. His firing would be by open sighting through the viewing port above. This one, like the others, had the layers of Lexan and the sliding steel door. It was all done with care in the heat and smoky stench of the cab, where the odors of his own sweat mingled with the sharp tang of singed steel and charred clothing. It was a cab space that held smells and smoke and he finally placed a fan to blow it all out through his hatch.

The hatch would be his work of art. It would have an inner plate of half-inch steel and an outer layer of three-eighths. In between them, in the five-inch void like the rest of the roof, he'd pour the concrete. But it would have to fit perfectly. It would be the hatch they'd never find. He'd have a hatch that only he could use.

With the steel work for the cab finished, he returned to his house, ready for a break. There was a message from his brother on his phone.

His father had died.

This would delay it all, but it would give him a chance to see his family one last time and to give everything else away so that it couldn't be touched later on.

The photos show the open casket of John Heemeyer, the man who had trained Marv in the skills of farming, basic mechanics, shooting gophers and the joy of attending auctions. He was a patriot, and he had instilled in Marv a stern belief in the tenets of the Christian Reformed Church, where he was an elder. Marv loved and respected his father. He hated South Dakota. His father had suggested to Marv many times that the military could offer a way out of the rural backwaters of the upper Midwest. It was because of his father that he had joined the Air Force after two years of community college that was really nothing more than a trade school.

Heemeyer's nieces and nephews posed for photos in the funeral home and in front of the casket. It was an oddly joyous occasion, for this meant the estate of the father, his farm and all his wealth, would soon be doled out to the family members. Even better was the fact that Marv had come with an added gift. They wouldn't learn it until later but Marv Heemeyer had deposited into the estate of John Heemeyer, his father, almost all of his liquid assets, to be distributed through the estate. This included what was left from the sale of his business, the business assets and his land. It was a significant amount — almost half a million dollars.

Marv took a selfie before he left South Dakota after the funeral. He's standing by his pick-up truck, the door open. It shows cloudy skies, a thin stretch of leafless trees, not blooming yet with spring, and the edge of a barn. There's a snowmobile trailer hooked to the back of his truck with two snowmobiles on it.

A selfie snapped by Heemeyer at the family farm in South Dakota two months before the rampage.

Heemeyer's expression is not mournful. It reflects a stare into the camera that is blank but certainly joyless. It is rigid. A person could call it cold. But there is just the hint of sadness, of dour resignation.

This would be the last time he saw the farm in South Dakota where he grew up.

It was a long drive back to Colorado over roads and past landmarks that had become so very familiar to him. But this time he would take no solace from the expansive views and the solitary joy of driving in his finely tuned truck to his mountain home. He felt fear and resignation and a bitter resolve.

So he felt flat and emotionless when he drove up the driveway to his cabin in Grand Lake on that spring morning. Normally, he would have tried to get some sleep after the 18-hour drive from South Dakota. Then his emotions soared with a vindictive joy upon seeing the Thompson brothers working just down the road from his house. He couldn't believe his good luck and he didn't care at all what they might think. He turned from climbing his driveway and drove over where the red Thompson and Sons pickup was parked.

18. Letting the Thompsons Know While Hating Those Catholics

Heemeyer unrolled the window of his truck as he eased up toward where Larry and Gary Thompson were taking a shovel and pick-ax from the back of their red dump truck. The dump truck was hooked to a trailer that was carrying a large back-hoe. A snow-enshrouded Mt. Baldy loomed in the background and the town of Grand Lake spread below. The day looked to be an unusually warm and pleasant spring day. May could be an awful month in Grand Lake, but this day wasn't to be so. A vacant lot sloped downward from the street. Larry and Gary Thompson were preparing to dig for a new foundation. Marv felt anger well deeply within.

Heemeyer remembered this day well and he said so in his tapes. He quoted himself in his verbal altercation with the Thompsons. Larry and Gary remembered the encounter, but only vaguely.

'That family. That family has screwed me. I'll tell them,' Heemeyer must have thought at that moment.

Larry Thompson, the oldest of the still living Thompson sons, stood by his pick-up. Gary, who had been back by the bigger dump truck, was walking up with a shovel. A series of stakes and survey markers delineated a neatly rectangular space on the sloping lot next to Larry's truck. Marv pulled up and leaned out of his truck, his left arm draped to the side out the open window.

"You know what, Ron," Heemeyer said.

"Ron's dead," Larry said blankly, quickly. Ron was the Thompson boy who had served as head of the Granby Sanitation District, worked diligently for the fire department and seemed to be following in his father's town leadership role before he died of Leukemia six years earlier. It had been a blow to the Thompson family. And now with the patriarch, Dick Thompson, dead, it left just the two sons and two daughters.

"I'm sorry, Larry," Heemeyer smiled, pausing. Larry looked at Heemeyer as if to say 'What do you want?'

"But listen, maybe it's good that Ron's dead. Because you know," Heemeyer said.

"Hell no it isn't," Larry responded.

By now Gary was standing near the rear of the gleaming red pick-up. He leaned on the shovel next to the bed of the truck. He listened.

"You know," Heemeyer said, "about in 1992 your family made some decisions that financially affected my life for the rest of my life. And I can't afford it. It cost me at least a minimum of $300,000."

Now Gary, shorter than Larry and more quiet and reserved, stepped closer to Larry to hear more carefully.

"You need to pay me," Heemeyer said.

"What are you talking about?" Larry looked over at his brother and shrugged his shoulders in a loose and nonchalant way. He still leaned against the pick-up.

"Don't play ignorant with me." Heemeyer had raised his voice now. He wasn't leaning casually out of the door anymore. His elbow was now raised off the side of the door. It pointed at Larry.

"You know what I'm talking about. Your family made those decisions. And I'm referring to the ones where they kept me off, where Ron Thompson kept me off the sanitation district."

Now Heemeyer pointed at Larry.

"You know about that. You owe me."

Once again Larry looked over at Gary. He reached up to his mouth with his left hand and rubbed his chin.

"I want $300,000 from you," Heemeyer said.

"It'll never happen," Larry responded casually.

"Well, I guarantee you Larry, I'm going to collect. It's a duty I have. I basically can't call myself a man if I don't make this right."

Not a word from Gary or Larry. They watched Heemeyer.

"Ron died and I think of all the money that he got, and that you inherited, because he died, from your father's estate, that you had all inherited. I think that you all probably ought to pay me with that."

"Not going to happen," Larry said, standing erect now from where he was leaning against his truck. It was a motion that suggested it was time to get to work — to stop chatting.

"Well I am going to collect."

With that Heemeyer pushed on his gas pedal and drove away, fast enough to let some gravel fly and to let them know he was serious. He heard Larry shout something negative and he stopped the truck again, with gravel and dust rising from the sliding tires.

"That will never happen," Heemeyer shouted, laughing.

In his tapes, it's clear that Heemeyer was pleased he had elicited some response from Larry. He hated them, with their smug, downhome demeanor and their inherited wealth and their easy lives moving dirt and digging ditches. He saw them as the heir apparents of the Granby cabal that had worked so hard to hurt him and his effort to have wealth and standing in the Granby community. Heemeyer believed they just didn't want Marv the newcomer to challenge their position.

Now Marv drove casually onto the pavement of Grand Avenue in Grand Lake and then up onto U.S. Highway 34, heading toward his shed in Granby where a world of work awaited him. He didn't need any sleep now, not with the adrenaline rush he felt after confronting the Thompson boys. He felt good about telling them.

'He's a cowardly bastard,' Heemeyer thought to himself, his anger welling deep inside again. But the truck rolled casually along, right at the speed limit.

"He's a Catholic," Marv said to himself as if lecturing an imaginary passenger sitting next to him, reading his tapes aloud. "And I think they are some of the biggest cowards I have ever met. I've known it for years. They have a different idea. They read from a different Bible. And they believe, and I truly believe that they believe the only way that they can stay on top and give the Pope his money and all this stuff, is to keep their neighbor down. There is no building to the Catholics to their neighbors. They don't believe in encouraging their neighbor. And it's sad. That's so wrong. I never ran into anyone – rather in my small town when I was a kid where everyone's always backstabbing you. In a small community."

It was quiet in the truck. Lake Granby passed on the left.

'Yes,' Marv thought, 'those Thompsons are a big part of it all. Leaders. Granby lowlifes. Small-town crackers. Weird loners. Typical.'

He smiled to himself and his rage surged again. He remembered the slights of all the local Catholics. The Catholic Priest, Father Gottschalk, had spoken out against gambling to his flock, uniting them against him in the effort to bring gambling. Catholic rabble-rousing like a bunch of idiots, he remembered. And then there was the time Marv had asked Father Frank Gerber if he could use the St. Anne's Catholic Church for a wedding he wanted to perform as a certified minister of God. But the priest had said no, he couldn't use their little church, because they weren't Catholic. Couldn't share it. Typical Catholics.

Heemeyer remembered all the talk about the corrupt Catholics in his Christian Reformed Church as he grew up. That's why his church thrived; why it flourished since those days long ago when the Catholics ruined religion. It all fit. They were Catholic, small-town schemers out to get him. No wonder.

But they would see, for God had a mission in mind for Marvin Heemeyer. His truck droned on as Heemeyer headed toward Granby.

By then Gary was pushing a shovel into the ground making sure the survey marker was in place where it should have been. The metal clanked on the steel marker. He looked over at Larry and they shrugged their shoulders. They didn't know what was bothering Marv. They continued to work on the hillside overlooking Grand Lake.

If they could have heard Heemeyer's comments about Larry being a Catholic they would have shaken their heads in disbelief. Larry wasn't a Catholic and never had been. He wasn't much of a church-goer at all. But they knew Marv was an odd duck. That was just Marv.

As that incident with the Thompsons made clear, Heemeyer was in a confessional and confrontational mood that month. He would have a lot more to say, if only to himself, when he sat down in his cabin four days later.

19. Putting It All on Tape

Marv Heemeyer carefully pushes down the record and play buttons on the small cassette deck at the same time. He is deliberate about this, leaning over to look at the slowly spinning cassette deck spindles to make sure they turn. One rotates much faster than the other. He doesn't want to mess up his chance to tell the world his reasons. The red "record" light glows.

"Hello, my name is Marvin Heemeyer," he says, talking out over his cluttered kitchen table, out over his deck and to the stunning world below and beyond this rustic cabin perch where he has lived alone for 12 years. "Today is, let's see here, April 13, 2004. I am making this tape, and thought I should make it a year ago, made part of it, and didn't like it. I really didn't think it would make any difference if I didn't make it, but a good friend of mine said I should make it. And he said I should sit down in front of a video tape machine and do it."

The Columbine High School killers had used video tapes to explain their violent attacks only five years earlier. Marv wouldn't bother with video.

"You're just going to have to take my word that this is Marv Heemeyer, serial number 503-68-9471," he says to the tape recorder with its built-in microphone, referring to his social security number as if it were a number from a dog tag — as if he were a prisoner under some sort of official interrogation or deposition. "I'm living in Grand Lake, Colorado. This tape is about my life since I came up here to live in 1991."

He's by himself and he says he hopes the tape would soon be heard by a much larger audience, perhaps an audience that would praise the destructive series of events he is soon to initiate. He sets out to frame his persona in the context of conspiracies against him and as the lone vigilante setting out to redeem a corrupt town.

The day is relatively warm and clear and the view from his house is as stunning as always. There are large homes and rustic-looking cabins dotted in among the lodgepole pine trees that rim the lake. The lake water is thawing out with a white rim of snow on the edges fading to grey around a dark blue middle. It's a beautiful lake, rimmed by the mountains. The town looks like a story-book village, nestled as it is perfectly by the shores of the lake in the folds of green. But the beauty of that day is muddied by Heemeyer's angst over what he knows is the reality behind all this mountain beauty. The people are backstabbers, they are out to get him and they deprived of him of his right to prosper. It was a sham, all this post card beauty.

"I want to say that I believe that I am an American Patriot. I believe in the free enterprise system. I believe in a level playing field of competition. If you want to change that level playing field of competition to your advantage, basically you give me license to do that also when my opportunity comes around."

Heemeyer's cabin, three years after the rampage.

In mentioning that he is an American Patriot, Heemeyer nods toward a movement that came to fruition in the 1980s and 1990s that embraced conspiracy theories and espoused a profound and at times violent distrust of government in the United States. Echoes of Patriot movement ideals resound in the writings of Ted Kaszynski, the Unabomber, the Montana recluse who lashed out at government and society by killing people with mail bombs.

Mentioning that he is a Patriot evokes the cult of the Branch Davidians, whose resistance to local laws in Waco, Texas resulted in a tragic conflagration at the Davidian compound where 83 people and four ATF agents were killed after a siege by law enforcement. The Oklahoma City bombers Timothy McVeigh and Terry Nichols, who destroyed the federal center there and killed 168 people, were inspired in part by the loosely aligned Patriot movement.

Based on a near-rabid enthusiasm about a man's right to bear arms, the Patriot movement touted self-reliance and individualism against the intrusions of government. These Patriots liked guns and bombs. Like Kaszynski, Heemeyer planned his destruction while secluded in a rural environment. Like the Oklahoma City bombers and Kaszynski, Heemeyer was setting out to fix conspiracy-plagued government through uniquely violent methods. But Heemeyer would do so in a super-heroic way, making himself impervious to gunfire, like a new incarnation of Superman or Rambo. He would be immune to any efforts to stop him.

"You're the ones, you're the leaders of the community," Heemeyer says angrily to the tape recorder and to me, referring to the business leaders of Granby and the town government. I imagine that he's pointing his finger right at me. "And you set the example and you do the teaching, and you — by and through example, through your actions — you show the community how things are supposed to be done."

"You have given me license, through your example, to do what I need to do," he says, his voice serious yet matter-of-fact. "When I do this, that levels the playing field in my favor. So now we've got a lopsided playing field. Because when I come back at you, I'm going to destroy your side of the playing field. I'm going to destroy you. I'm going to destroy."

"Maybe what happens here this year of 2004 — the summer of 2004. Maybe you'll remember that." Looking back at a violent incident from Grand Lake's own history, Heemeyer elevates the significance of his mission. "Back in the early 1900s or late 1800s there were four people died up here in Grand Lake over where the county courthouse should be, should it be here in Grand Lake or in Hot Sulphur Springs," he says.

July 4, 1883, was the date of the renowned Fourth of July shooting when two county commissioners and an associate were ambushed by political foes near the western shores of Grand Lake. The two county commissioners who were ambushed died as a result of their wounds, as did the third county commissioner who helped to lead the ambush. Two others ultimately perished as a result of the shooting. It was the single most violent shooting incident in the history of Grand County, bringing to mind the lawless days of the Wild West when political differences and personal dislikes were settled with firearms.

"I don't know how many years people remembered that incident but they still talk about it today," Heemeyer says. "What the purpose of all those people dying, well, I really don't know. But it seems like this has to happen again and again and again. It is human nature: That we kill each other so that the next generation looks at things differently — (that) they open their mind and be open to other people's ideas. It's a cycle. As best as I can see it, God is saying it's a cycle — that God is saying it's time to happen again."

Heemeyer feels that it really is time. He had gone out of his way to give away his inheritance so it couldn't be touched. He had willed his house to his snowmobiling friend Bruno, so it couldn't be touched. Now he knows that he really is, virtually, penniless. So dying would make the most sense and even though there's a chance he will survive, he knows it's a small chance. He will be part of the cycle of destruction and death, even if it's his own death, as he moves forward. He has nothing to lose.

20. Scribbling in the Smoke and Mud

At this stage, only 20 days before the rampage, Marvin Heemeyer would have felt the trajectory of his mission was now inevitable. He would have written his last words and completed his last welding and engineering project like this, alone in the shed he had built and had once owned.

He embraces the finality and the self-destructive implications of his mission. He had always looked down upon cigarette smoking and yet now, as his health and trim physique didn't matter anymore, he goes ahead and indulges this habit. He pulls a pack of American Spirit "100% Natural" cigarettes out of the top pocket on his coveralls. It is a sin, and he knows it, to smoke. But he rationalizes that these cigarettes are natural. They have to be better than other types of cigarettes. He believes in physical fitness. And it's against his deeply held beliefs of life instilled by the Christian Reformed Church to smoke. Outwardly, he detests it in others.

He remembers how it was all a little tiff over cigarette smoking that caused him and Trish to break up. She had been a good girlfriend and they had had great fun. But once he caught her sneaking away to smoke to conceal it from her children and he had upbraided her. But she would have none of that hypocrisy, and she had pointed out that he, too, was a closet smoker. That incident was the beginning of the end with her, he thinks then, in the shed as he begins to work, that it was too bad because she was the best thing that ever had happened to him in all his years in Grand County.

And now he didn't care at all, for she was gone and he no longer harbored a fear of cancer or being unfit and the smokes were his incentive to move forward with pleasure and inspiration. The Indians used tobacco for sacred ceremonies and to draw their gods into their realm and these cigarettes had that Indian image on the pack of cigarettes. Is that why he had chosen this particular brand? He was preparing his own war party. For every bag of Sakrete he used up to fill the voids he allowed himself one celebratory cigarette. Not the peace pipe, but the war pipe to give the drudgery a series of goals and pleasurable rewards.

The MK Dozer sits enshrined in the fierce white glow of the spotlights, like a museum exhibition. In this he will show the world. It will be a statement. Even now, before the day, it is his accomplishment. He feels proud and powerful just looking at it.

He pokes open the first sack of Sakrete with the claw end of his hammer, grey dust floating upward. He picks up the heavy, awkward bag and dumps it into the mixer. He pours in a bucket of water and a shovelful of sand and he cranks it up, the drum turning slowly at first and then at pace, tumbling it all together. He had built stairs to get him to the top of the treads of the machine. Then, on the treads, balancing on a couple of two by six boards, there was another step stool. He steps up to it, bucket in hand, lifts the bucket and pours it into the gap at the top of the steel void. Heemeyer does this again and again, a job that would have challenged any man, bringing him to the brink of exhaustion.

And he cursed.

"Damn," he says. "Damn."

After three more trips the mixer is empty and it's time to dump in the next sack. Time for a cigarette, too, he thinks. The cigarettes are a reward, a guilty pleasure for desperate times. He sits down at the bench and puts a cigarette into his mouth. With no lighter or matches in the shed, Heemeyer uses his torch, leaning in, an American Spirit cigarette protruding from his lips, to light the end in the torch's hissing heat. He pulls into his lungs and the cigarette is lit. He takes his first drag a little tentatively and then shuts off his torch with a twist of the dials on the welder.

He feels better. Three drags later he feels bored and he looks over to see the For Sale by Owner sign he had taped to the big blade of the bulldozer. He had ripped the sign off just after driving the machine into the shed and leaned it against the wall 15 months ago. He looks and he thinks.

No sense in wasting time. Who knows what's going to happen with my tapes?

He builds a small desk next to the bucket and he begins to write on the For Sale sign with a felt-tipped pen. This way, they'd know for sure.

Had Cody paid me $66,000 on the day of the FDIC auction; I would not have to be so unreasonable.

Had the community not been so hateful toward the F.D.I.C., and me as a beneficiary of their actions; I would not have to be so unreasonable.

Had the san district let me into the district in the fall of 1992; I would not have to be so unreasonable.

Had the town told me they rezoned Harris prop; I would not have be so unreasonable.

Had Bud Wilson told me that I was allowed in the district at the next meeting of the san district in the fall of 92; I would not have to be so unreasonable.

Had it not taken me until the fall of 99 to find out; I would not have to be so unreasonable.

He scribbles quickly now, the sight of his thoughts on paper giving him inspiration and angering him more and more with each phrase, each idea. The cigarette by now has burned down to a nub. Ashes drop onto the sign. A bead of sweat drops from his forehead onto the sign, mixing with the ashes. He wipes the smudge off. He reads his scribblings and feels anger and vigor all over again. This they will see, he thinks.

He walks back to the mixer, pours in another bag of Sakrete, shovels in the sand and pours the water and starts mixing. His writing inspires him to work hard again, no matter the pain and the drudgery. He pours into the bucket, walks to the dozer, pours in the void, returns to the mixer, walks to the torch to light his cigarette, and he sits down again. He looks forward to writing. He reads his first jottings and feels angry and powerful again.

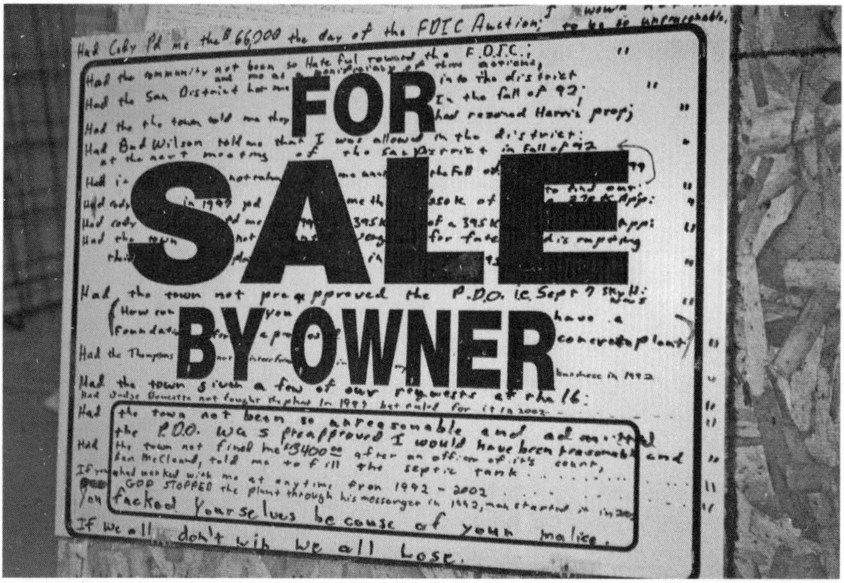

Heemeyer wrote down some of his last recorded thoughts on a For Sale sign he had in the shed. At one time he had that For Sale sign on the bulldozer when it sat outside before his work on the tank began.

Had Cody in 1997 paid me the $250 K of the $270 appraisal: I would not have to be so unreasonable.

Had Cody paid me in 99 the $395 K of a $395 K appraisal: I would not have to be so unreasonable.

Had the town not . . .   inf very fate . . . disrupting this plan(t) in 92: I would not have to be so unreasonable.

Had the town not pre-approved the P.D.O.; i.e. Sept. 7 Sky Hi News: I would not have to be so unreasonable. (How can you have a foundation for a portion of a concrete plant)

He writes and the writing of it and the remembering of it all in its literal form angers him beyond his own control. He finds himself muttering to himself, the cigarette smoke drifting up over his nose and across his face, making his eyes water as if he were crying. His tears mix with sweat. He has to stop again. The cigarette has died.

Had the Thompsons not interfered in my business in 1992: I would not have to be so unreasonable.

He reduces it now to a phrase or a thought at a time in between each sack. It's difficult writing this down and reliving it all. But it is all for this. These cigarettes are killing him, but he feels no guilt as he's a dead man anyway. He reminds himself again how much he hates these people, this town, these backstabbers. He writes and smokes. He dreads the work of filling the mixer again and the hauling, the pouring, the lifting.

Had the town given a few of our requests of the 16: I would not have to be so unreasonable.

The hypocritical judge and how he wouldn't want the plant in his yard but it's OK in my backyard. It galls him. The smoke rises. He jots, trying to get it all in. Back to the damn mixer and the dust and the mud. Awful work.

Had Judge Doucette not fought the plant in 1994(9) but ruled for it in 2002: I would not have to be so unreasonable.

He knows the town had planned it all out ahead of time. Just couldn't prove it. Bastards. My fault, he thinks. Get this mud work over with now. Go.

Had the town not been so unreasonable and admitted that the P.D.O. was pre-approved I would have been reasonable and: I would not have to be so unreasonable.

Had the town not fined me $3400 after an officer of it's (sic) court, Ben McClelland told me to fill the septic tank . . . I would not have to be so unreasonable.

They kicked me when I was down, he thinks. They sided with that fat ass lawyer and the bantam rooster Docheff. The Thompsons lined it out all ahead of time, how to get rid of me, the innocent newcomer. If only I had known. It was all to get back at me.

He inhales lightly now in little puffs. All these cigarettes leave him feeling numb. His right hand tingles in soreness from carrying those buckets.

Why couldn't they have done me better?

He scoffs at his own self-pity.

If you had worked with me anytime from 1992-2002: I would not have to be so unreasonable.

I know this is all out of the realm of man's paltry powers of reason, he thinks. I have to step out of being a mere man and fulfill my role. It's my duty.

Drugged on nicotine and sick from lack of water, he writes, furiously.

GOD STOPPED the plant through his messanger (sic) in 1992, man started it in 2002.

You fucked yourselves because of your malice.

If we all don't win we all lose.

He doesn't know if it is day or night outside. He doesn't know how long he has been working and writing. The glow in his work area comes only from the spotlight trained on his creation, his MK Tank. It is all so sickening to him, all that history of what had been, what they had done to him. He has run out of room on the sign, but he has more to say. He stands up to find more room to write.

Dizzy from the cigarettes, woozy from lack of moisture and now slightly nauseous from it all, like seasickness, he wonders what to do. But he has to finish this hellish task. He needs nourishment and liquid. But how? But what? He walks unsteadily to his living area. He pours water from a gallon milk jug directly into his mouth. It feels good. He needs food but he can't eat or he'd puke. He pours a packet of Slim Fast into a coffee cup and mixes in water. He drinks it. It calms his stomach. It kills his hunger.

He goes back out to the work area after grabbing a scrap of paper from the shelf in his little living area. It is a piece of 8.5 by 11 paper — originally a proof of loss document for an insurance claim. He places it on the sign and trudges back to the mixer for another load. After two more bags, after smoking two more cigarettes while pacing in the shed — he notes it is night after he looks in his monitor and sees a pool of black singed by white triangles from his spotlights — he sits down to write, calmer and now more tired.

Had Cody just one time come to me with a counter offer, I would not have to be so unreasonable.

At my auction in 2002, my minimum bid was $450,000.00, 10% of which would have gone to the auctioneer.

Had some one bid the $450,000 I would have walked away.

I netted $400,000 either way, at auction, or by selling it myself.

He stands and goes back to the mixer for another load, another series of trips back and forth, up and down, lugging the bucket, pouring the mud, working like a common laborer. But it is divine work, he reminds himself. He will tell the world it was divine work. He sits down to scribble, sweaty and nauseous.

It's interesting how the dozer was the only thing they did not sell at my auction. It was not until later I discovered it would just fit in the storage building.

It's interesting how I had until June of 2004 to complete the dozer.

It's interesting how a self-made single man who died at age 52 was send (sic) to buy the property in '92.

It's interesting to know that I did not buy the property for myself but for John Kleiner, Bill's brother.

It's interesting how he backed out of the deal.

It's interesting how I got stuck here as I only wanted to take a six-month vacation from Nov. '91-May '92.

It's interesting how I got Boulder Muffler back in 1996 and leased it out again only after someone came to me voluntarily.

Marv reaches out to his God. He nods his head. He rocks on his stool, back and forth back and forth. He slides down to his knees and puts his hands together in prayer. He doesn't look up. He looks down at the ground, his eyes closed. It is so obvious — God's hand in it all. He only wants to pity himself then and ask God why me? But he doesn't utter a word. He stands and goes back to the mixer and the awkward bags and the shovel and the bucket and the steps and the ladder and the pouring and lifting. And jotting it down.

It's interesting how sales taxes have not jumped significantly since the start of the plant (over)

He remembers the town made all those claims that were lies. The raw smoke of the cigarette burns his nostrils when he inhales. It's raining outside now and the roof above him begins to rattle gently at first and then it grows to a crescendo as the rain shower dumps onto the dust of the world and pounds the metal roof into a roar. It is a nighttime storm. There is no thunder that he hears, no lightning that he sees. He writes.

It's interesting how Dick Thompson died shortly after PDO approval

It's interesting how Ron Thompson died prematurely after PDO approval.

It's interesting how the Docheff girl died prematurely after PDO approval.

It's interesting how Marv Heemeyer died prematurely after PDO approval.

Is he the last to die prematurely?

Back and forth. Drink more water. Chug the Slim Fast. Drink. Don't eat. It's all divine coincidence which really isn't coincidence at all, is it? There is no coincidence. It's all pre-ordained and written to happen as adjudged by God. So I go. So they suffer. So we all suffer. Oh, the tobacco was a divine inspiration of death and destiny to move forward, as ordained, as predestined. Fate has chosen him, Marvin John Heemeyer. He stands, again, from his stool. More work. Scribbling.

It's interesting how Bob, Travis and the insurance guy did not suspect anything when they inspected the storage building in the fall of 2003. Especially with the 2000-lb lift fully exposed. Somehow their vision was clouded.

It's interesting how I never got caught. This was a part-time project over a 1-1/2 year time period.

It's exhausting rehashing it all like this and he leans down on that flimsy canvas stool and falls backward, catching himself, knocking the sign and paper to the ground. He gathers it all up. Now he knows he wanted Bob and Travis to walk in that door and point to him and tell him they caught him and that they knew and that the police had been called and they had saved him from his fate, from the only logical end to it all. And he believes in this moment of doubt that he would be saved not by his own volition but by others and he would still be redeemed and they would find it all and know if their awful ways without anyone paying the awful price that he would pay and he having to take it all back. It would be a redemption. A slap on the wrist and he would live. But no . . . He's here now, and he writes.

It's interesting how a town atty (Krob), Doucheff's (sic) atty (Daily), the planning commission the town board, Doucheff (sic) with all his years of planning and all his friends, "accidentally" screw up the PDO process (see judge's ruling spring of '02) and another (objective?) atty found out after just one of my visits to his office.

It's interesting how he milked me for over $51,000

He's down to two sacks of concrete now and he notices only two cigarettes remain. He takes them out, crumples up the empty cigarette pack and tosses it into the empty bucket. He fills that bucket with mud plopping over the bottom and the cigarette pack. He dumps this bucket, the second-to-last, into the void between the sheets of steel and the sloshing grey mass rises nearly to the top. He looks in and sees the cigarette pack and he wonders if it will ever be bathed in the light of day again and he laughs about wondering. He thinks of it as a clue. He wonders if anyone will care, but he shakes his head, knowing they will. They will learn.

He finishes as if in one sprint at the end of a marathon. He remembers all these people. Don't delay.

He thinks to himself with a smile that Ben has helped him.

It's interesting how Ben McCleand (sic) has never charged me for representing me on the septic tank issue.

He drinks the last drops of the water out of the jug. He pours the powder of the Slim Fast into his mouth. He gags. It's light outside. The computer monitor glows like day. He hears a trash truck drive past, its air brakes chugging with blasts of air. How would they learn, these people, this world? They are all so sick and corrupt. He writes to the new day:

It's interesting how everyone lost.

One thing the community should also learn: Don't let in-bred, window peeking perverts and bankrupt suicidals run everything.

Now do you have the courage to stand up.

You Granby have got to learn to listen. Can you hear me now?

II: The Rampage

2:01 p.m. Friday, June 4, 2004

21. "The ugliest looking damn machine"

If Marv Heemeyer had stood at a pulpit inside that metal shed in front of the throng of Granby, on a dais that was his homemade tank, this is what he would have said:

"God made me, given me a wide open path in building this to come up dead up against a brick wall. If I'm dead 30 seconds after I get out of this building . . . I'll accept that. But you're going to know what my intentions were. . . . You're going to know how intent I was on teaching you people that what you're doing is wrong . . . That you're going to understand, hopefully. And maybe that's all that needs to be done to stop you from the greed you have, the hate you have, the anger you have, the malice toward outsiders."

"It's not good, folks. I don't think that just knowing what I'm doing is enough . . . to do this stuff I have to do, up to a point, and then the machine will do one of two or three things . . . you're either going to blow me right off the fucking street, I'm going to have a heart attack and die, because I'm all pumped up, the machine's going to break, or maybe, maybe it'll go all day and I'll run out of fuel."

"Because it definitely is in God's hands. It is not in my hands . . . I know I'm going to be dead. There's no doubt about that in my mind. I am the co-captain of my life. God is first, I am second. OK?"

"This is where he's taking me."

He would point toward the town, weeping in anger.

"This is where you have tried to control my life. You have tried to be the captain of my life. You do not run my life. You do not determine my income. You do not determine what I desire. What I want. What I deserve. I determine that. And my God determines that. Not you people. No people can do that. If they do, then you are a slave to them. And I am not a slave to man. I am a slave to God. And I am a slave to what God tells me I should have. And that is why we are where we are."

But at that time on that early summer afternoon, Marv Heemeyer was not at a pulpit. He was finalizing his preparations. His last chore would be to cover the broad exposed ramparts of the tank's steel sides in grease.

He puts his scribblings of the last week in a conspicuous place, where they would be found.

He leans a ladder up against the recently greased side, its bottom resting on the treads. He climbs to the top of the cab and pushes the ladder away. He slides into the hatch. It closes in a perfect fit. He doesn't see any light until he switches on his interior illumination. He switches over the latch under the hatch so that no one would be able to get in. No one. He wouldn't make that stupid mistake. He laughs. He feels strong and proud. He will show the world. He cranks the starter and the diesel stutters, then hums to life with a guttural roar. He lets it warm up, getting the temperature just right. He drinks another Slim Fast. His lunch is in an ammo bucket. Two sandwiches.

The dozer pops forward in first gear, heading for the steel wall.

Two welding leads dangle from the back of the machine, dragging behind it like mooring ropes from a ship's bollards. The wall tears open with a slap and screech.

Sherry Dennis, the office manager and dispatcher for The Trash Company, which occupied the space where Heemeyer's muffler shop had been, was wrapping up her work 2:15 p.m. during a typical Friday.

Dennis was in The Trash Company office and garage building when she first saw the machine, from a distance. At first she thought Cody Docheff was testing some new equipment. She didn't know.

Just before Dennis saw the bulldozer-tank, Sammy Almaeza, an employee of Mountain Park Concrete who worked in the company's pre-fab building, heard a loud bang and a scraping noise. He and his fellow worker Juan, who were both outside tying rebar on forms in front of the pre-fab building, looked over toward the loud noise and saw the odd-looking bulldozer seconds after it crashed out of the steel building.

They watched the curious spectacle of the bulldozer as it trundled along through the parking lot in front of The Trash Company office and garage.

This was no ordinary bulldozer. The area where the operator sits was shrouded in grey steel, with what appeared to be small portholes. For Dennis and Almaeza, the sight of the odd-looking machine raised a lot of questions. They simply didn't know what was happening.

Steve Borda, who owned the property directly to the east of the old muffler shop, saw the same thing and he, too, wondered what was going on. He thought it could have been Cody driving some new piece of equipment. He noticed the welding leads trailing behind the machine.

Marv had driven his MK Tank right out through the east-facing wall of the metal building, creating a gaping and jagged hole.

Where the bulldozer-tank burst out of the steel shed.

The machine rumbled eastward, turning around to plod toward the large pre-cast building that belonged to Mountain Park Concrete where Almaeza and his co-worker Juan stood. Almaeza was nearby, but backing up, when the dozer slammed into the central panels in front the building. Almaeza remembers that it was like the sound of crash and ruin, like a roar of thunder, the scrape of steel-on-steel and the slam of falling walls exploding in the dust.. Juan ran to the office. What was happening?

Dennis thought the machine would stop before it pushed into the pre-cast building's concrete walls. It didn't and she called 911 in a panic.

The three workers looked on, stunned, as the machine methodically smashed into critical structural points, causing the massive concrete form roof to slam to the ground, crushing a truck and other equipment as it fell. There was a method. Rather than driving all the way into the building, the machine pushed in through the walls or beams to a distance of six to eight feet, then quickly backed out. In this manner the machine avoided becoming entangled in falling debris or being trapped inside a collapsed structure. After tearing into the front side of the building, the dozer worked its way around the building, crashing into the northeastern corner, causing more critical structural damage. Only the western and southern walls of the building were unscathed.

The pre-fab building was ruined. It looked like a bomb had exploded in the middle of the structure. Huge pre-cast concrete slabs that had been the roof had collapsed, as if pushed down from on high, stepped on by a giant. When the large slab which spanned the 100 feet of the building fell, it created a boom so loud that Almaeza thought he heard explosions. Walls had fallen in and pieces of concrete and equipment were scattered about, as if thrown into the air after a blast. That was to be the first piece of destructive mayhem caused by this menacing looking bulldozer.

The Mountain Park Concrete building was the first target.

Docheff and the others at the batch plant had the first experience of what it was like to see, hear and feel Heemeyer's MK Tank. The first sensation many people noted was the vibration of the ground under their feet as the machine approached. The sound was overwhelming. First there was the throttled and guttural roar of the diesel engine, like some sort of primeval growl. Then there was the impact of each individual heavy steel tread on the ground, slapping and clanking on pavement or thudding on the bare ground. The treads scraped on the metal linking them together, screeching through the air. To see it was to behold an enormous and anonymous steel marauder, dark and inscrutable. No person could be seen on, or in, the machine.

Docheff saw that this tank was now heading directly toward the batch plant building, where sand, gravel, chemicals and cement were stored and mixed before being poured into concrete mixer trucks. The walls were made of formed concrete panels. The south, or front wall, was 35 feet tall. The north wall was 31 feet high, allowing a slight grade to the roof. The east side had large garage doors to allow trucks to pass in and out for repairs. In front and to the south of the batch plant stood an 85-foot-tall silo, underneath which trucks parked while being loaded up. That silo sat taller than the building itself and was the defining landmark of the business. During the Christmas holidays the silo would be festooned with lights while a glowing, jolly image of Santa Claus would appear to be stepping into the tank as if it were a chimney.

The Christmas holidays were the last thing on the minds of people at the batch plant that afternoon as the dozer lumbered toward its next target.

Phil White, a driver for Mountain Park Concrete, was at the batch plant when the rampage started. He tried to stop the tank, with the help of Steve Borda and his family. They all tried to cram pieces of pipe and angle iron into the treads of the massive machine as it roared forward. But their efforts had no effect, the pipes and steel just popped out of the treads.

When that didn't work, Bob Howard, a longtime employee of Mountain Park Concrete, ran to his truck and grabbed his handgun, a .357 magnum.

"Be careful, it's loaded," he told Cody as he handed it to him. With gun in hand Docheff looked like someone out of the Wild West.

He walked carefully over to the back of the moving behemoth and fired twice toward what looked like some sort of window or porthole on the back of the cab. The two reports rang out loudly, even over the roar of the bulldozer, but had no effect at all, and Docheff handed the gun back to Howard, cocked and loaded.

Phil White then heard something whizz by over his head, probably a ricochet from the shots fired by Docheff. He left in a hurry at that point.

Docheff was now angry and determined to stop this machine that he was afraid would ruin his business. Gritting his teeth and acting with utter impulse, he decided he would jump up on the slow-moving machine and try to find some vulnerability. But he just slid off the sides, his hands covered in grease.

Out of options for the moment, Docheff ran into the main office of the batch plant and he told everyone inside to leave the building, fast, just before the dozer hit the southeastern corner of the building.

"It's Marv Heemeyer. Get out. Everybody get out! He's driving the ugliest damn machine you ever saw."

Marv Heemeyer's MK (Marv's Komatsu) Tank.

2:30 p.m.

22. Battle at the Batch Plant

Cody was on his own to battle Marv's MK tank and protect his property. He ran out into his loader and climbed in. The tank had already slammed into the southeast corner of the batch plant building, leaving crumpled concrete and a gaping hole. Sitting in the elevated cab of the front-end loader, Cody wasn't sure what he was going to do. He drove toward the tank as it was slamming into the east wall for the second time.

Wayne Miller of Granby snapped some photos of the battle of behemoths at the concrete batch plant. Here, Cody Docheff slams his front-end loader into the side of the bulldozer tank.

Docheff levered the big bucket of the loader into the track of the dozer, trapping it between the building and the loader. Borda and Smith were shouting at Docheff to lift up the dozer, but he couldn't. It was too heavy. When he tried, the loader rocked to the point where it had only one tire on the ground. He held the dozer for a few seconds, and then backed out. The big machine backed out right after him.

Seemingly unimpeded, the dozer was preparing for another run at the east wall when Deputy Jim Kraker of the Granby Police Department showed up. He was the first law enforcement officer at the scene, responding to two alerts over his police radio. Having spent time around heavy equipment, his first thought was that perhaps someone had passed out or had a heart attack at the controls of a bulldozer. As soon as he got out of his patrol car, people starting yelling at him to "do something." He grabbed his shotgun from his vehicle and ran up near the shrouded bulldozer as Docheff was maneuvering his loader in the battle against the huge machine. "Stop! Stop, or I'll shoot," he shouted, feeling a little bit foolish since he could barely hear himself think, much less shout, in all the noise from these heavy machines.

He told Docheff to back off, but Docheff wasn't about to stop attacking this machine that was clearly out to destroy his business.

The bulldozer was now out in the yard, in the open, and Docheff floored the gas in the loader, going straight toward the ripper, a large, slightly angled hook that descends downward from the back of the dozer. It's used to tear-up or rip soil and pavement. Heemeyer had the ripper raised to enable the dozer to maneuver easily. The impact jarred Docheff but also spun the dozer a little bit, now making the front face toward an old fuel truck on the property.

The bulldozer then headed straight toward the fuel truck. Docheff slammed into it again, forcing the dozer to spin back toward the batch plant. Unfazed, the dozer moved in the direction of a wall next to a large overhead door. The door area collapsed and then the dozer hit it again, and the header came down. This 36,000-pound chunk of concrete and re-bar fell squarely on the dozer's cab. Docheff thought this would finally stop the machine. It had no effect at all and the bulldozer just kept right on tearing into the building.

Docheff needed a different tactic.

He backed out, raised his bucket high enough so it would impact the highest point of the cab. He slammed his foot onto the gas and raced toward the side of dozer. A flat, metallic crash sounded out through the air. Docheff lurched forward, hard, slamming into his seat belt. The rear wheels of the loader lifted off the ground from the impact. He tipped one side of the dozer ever so slightly, about five inches off the ground. Cody had been knocked out from the impact of his loader against the dozer.

This was the moment Heemeyer decided to use his firepower, marking the first time anyone realized the machine was fully armed. At a new and higher speed, the bulldozer backed away from the building and then swiveled. A torrent of fire spat from the cab of the massive machine. Ten to twelve rounds slammed into the bucket of the loader, several of them piercing the steel. A plume of white dust rose from the bucket over the force of the shots. Docheff says it was pure luck that none of those rounds hit him.

Colorado State Patrol Trooper Dave Batura, who had pulled his cruiser into an area southwest of the batch plant, had seen Docheff slam into the bulldozer several times. He had taken his M-14 long rifle out of his trunk. Batura was a fit trooper who stood out because of his bald pate and imposing and direct demeanor. He walked toward the bulldozer tank.

As he approached the dozer, he saw it back up a little and turn. Suddenly, five blasts fired in his direction, right from the rear of the bulldozer-tank. He heard and felt the rounds whizz over his head. While the tank pulled forward again toward the east side of the building, Batura jogged to his cruiser with his head held low to report automatic weapons fire directed toward him was coming from the dozer. He said police should respond with that in mind. He thought to himself that the firing sounded and felt like it was coming from a large-caliber weapon.

Waiting by his cruiser, Batura continued to process what had just happened. After hearing the first calls on the radio about a bulldozer at the batch plant, he had expected to see a bulldozer haphazardly draped in sheet metal. But now he had a different thought: "We're going to need a bigger boat."

Batura watched the dozer slam into the building again, and he noticed what appeared to be small windows on the front and back of the steel shroud.

Dazed and still mystified over what was happening, Docheff roused himself enough to talk to Officer Kraker, who had run over to make sure Docheff was unharmed after the bullets had slammed into the bucket.

"I don't think nobody's in that dozer," he said to Kraker. "It's radio controlled. The way it's acting. It's Heemeyer controlling it."

"How do you know it's Heemeyer?"

"I know it is," Docheff said adamantly, looking around with his head crouched low. "He's got to be on one of these hills around here someplace."

The police still weren't sure who or what was controlling the dozer and if, in fact, there was anybody inside actually driving it. It was possible that it could have been remote-controlled. With its steel plating and its jerky, mechanized movements, it seemed like a robot; like an indifferent and ominous drone. That would have meant all the people standing around the batch plant were vulnerable to sniper fire from elsewhere, as well as from the dozer itself.

By then, the dozer was working its way around to the north side of the batch plant, pushing into the wall and poking large holes as it progressed. It was loud and dusty, between the sounds of the dozer's treads, the falling sheets of concrete and the roar of the engine. Another police officer asked Docheff to go after the machine once more. Docheff, although shaken, drove the loader around the side of the plant, where he found a belly-dump trailer that was being worked on. He picked it up with his loader and slammed it into the dozer. The sound was all screaming engines, the tear of shredded steel and thuds like the sound of impacts at a demolition derby. The machines battled each other like scorpions, carrying objects many times their weight.

The bulldozer was unfazed by the dump trailer and the loader, pushing both out of its way easily.

Trooper Batura and Deputy Kraker had been joined by other law enforcement officers. These included Colorado State Patrol Trooper

Jack DiSanti, and Lt. Walt Eldridge, Undersheriff Glen Trainor and Sgt. Rich Garner, all of the Grand County Sheriff's Department. They were trying to figure out how to stop the destruction.

Grand County Sheriff Rod Johnson was in Denver at the time, attending a sheriff's convention. So Trainor was in the lead position for the sheriff's department, working in tandem with the state patrol. Frustration was mounting as they watched the machine methodically crush the building right before their eyes.

Trainor had given Sgt. Rich Garner the order to do whatever it took to stop the bulldozer.

"Go ahead and fire," Trainor told Garner. "Let's try and skip a round in there, those portholes."

Trainor fired at the dozer. Garner took another position to the north and fired again.

From a protected position behind stacks of prefabricated concrete barriers and fences on the west side of the building, Batura then took another opportunity. He fired his M-14 at what appeared to be a front window port. He hit it several times, but the rounds merely created puffs of dust on the Plexiglas surface. The glass stayed in place.

The dozer plowed its blade into the natural gas piping and meter on the west wall. It slammed into the electrical service boxes. The next target was the electrical transformer mounted below the level of the paved driveway on the west side of the building. Fear filled Docheff as he realized that Heemeyer was trying to start a fire by causing the sparks from the ruptured electrical service boxes or power supply transformer to ignite the escaping natural gas.

Now the tank rotated around to get the ripper in place. The machine lurched forward, pulling the transformers out of the ground and scattering them into the nearby driveway. And then the .50-caliber rifle in the back of the cab started belching fire again, this time toward some concrete blocks, which crumbled under the force of the fire.

These were the concrete jersey barriers where sheriff's deputies and state troopers had been taking cover. The shots sent them running in the opposite direction.

The bulldozer dropped its ripper again into the depression where the power transformers were located, but it started to lean precariously under its own weight.

Docheff saw another opportunity to push the dozer over and he started to make a run toward the machine, but it maneuvered back upright quickly, and Docheff missed his chance.

Sgt. Garner, from his position to the north, heard lots of firing at this time, including the deeply concussive sounds from the .50-caliber.

After that firing incident — the third one with the .50-caliber — the bulldozer turned around so that it was now facing north again, along the west wall.

At this point it appeared safer for the law enforcement officers to start shooting at the dozer — any over shots would slam into the batch plant walls and not off in the direction of the town.

Batura opened fire at the dozer as Undersheriff Glen Trainor and Sgt. Garner moved into new positions.

The dozer slammed back into the northwest corner of the building. A large slab of concrete tipped over and slammed onto the bulldozer's cab. Garner saw it hit the barrel of a rifle that protruded from the right side.

Crouched in a firing position, Garner saw two puffs of smoke come out of the front portal, where the .308 was placed. He heard the zip of the rounds over his head. He fired back, in fear and self defense, at the front portal. The dozer hit the wall again and then turned and drove directly toward Garner's protected position, forcing him to flee toward some nearby trees to avoid the machine.

The state troopers and Lt. Walt Eldridge had taken up a covered position behind a six by eight foot rectangle stack of concrete blocks. Batura saw the dozer heading straight for the blocks and their firing position. He fired again, this time at the right side porthole, trying to divert the machine. No luck. It trundled without pause directly toward the stack of massive blocks. The officers fled their position just seconds before the machine pushed the blocks backward with heavy thumps, right where they had been standing.

Trainor saw it transpire, as if in slow motion, and it became clear to him that whoever was driving the dozer intended to take those guys out. The falling wall would have killed anyone who was behind it. It solidified in his mind a command decision that he relayed over the radio: "Use whatever force is necessary to stop this thing."

And strangely, it was at this point that most of the officers stopped firing at the dozer. They all knew that handguns and larger caliber rifles would probably be useless against the massive machine. Batura began to wonder if they could deploy larger, military-type weapons against it. He formed an image in his mind of A-10 attack planes, used with great effectiveness against tanks in the first Gulf war, zeroing in on the dozer.

The dozer rolled forward, relentless, heading east, toward Granby. People ran and darted away from the front and sides of the rumbling machine like insects scattering from a bright light.

Among themselves, the law enforcement types were now saying it was Heemeyer. They were forbidden to say so over the radio or to the media, but they knew it was him. They had hastily searched the metal building he had been leasing and the notes he left behind. Deputies were ordered to search his house.

Above all, they felt helpless and frustrated. They feared what was coming next.

It was the Wild West that afternoon at the batch plant. Heemeyer was the well-armed and invincible gunslinger on a steed of steel and brute force, impervious to bullets and heavy machines, masked and anonymous. All the others were the hapless townsfolk, their weapons useless, their steeds nothing more than insignificant contraptions. Most were on foot, unable to do much at all. It was confusing and chaotic.

But for the policemen and other witnesses at the scene, there was little doubt about Heemeyer's violent intent.

2:50 p.m.

23. The Ride of His Life

"I was reasonably sure I might die up there."
— Lt. Glen Trainor

Automobiles, even a large Ford Expedition, could not slow down the MK Tank.

Heemeyer rendered Grand County Undersheriff Glen Trainor's relatively new Ford Expedition into a virtual pancake as the bulldozer-tank left the batch plant. The big car was no impediment at all to the tank's forward progress into Granby past the precast building it had already demolished.

Seeing Trainor's Expedition a crumpled mess, police officers at the scene made a quick decision to tell county dispatch to initiate a reverse 911 phone call to the people of Granby. The town should be evacuated immediately.

Undersheriff Glen Trainor was now on foot.

Over the years I had gotten to know Glen Trainor fairly well. A knowing and sardonic relationship frequently forms between reporters and policemen since reporters need the news the police can give and police need the public affirmation a reporter can give. I had come to know Glen Trainor in that way, working on stories about garden variety local crime such as DUIs and car crashes or the more complex domestic crimes that required a sensitive but direct approach. Murders and high-dollar thefts were extremely rare.

Trainor isn't your typical law enforcement type. He does not reflect the macho image of the buff, weight-lifting policeman. He is a man of average build, average height and a friendly demeanor. A person encountering him out of uniform might mistake him for a manager at the hardware store or a Lutheran minister. He is more of a thinking-man's cop who worked his way up to the position of second-in-command of the entire Grand County Sheriff's Department through hard work in community policing and administrative acumen.

As the man who frequently represented Sheriff Rod Johnson at town or county meetings, he came across as conciliatory and diplomatic in dealing with an array of political matters. But there was an element of bluff cunning in his style, and he was capable of taking and giving heat when needed. That is what must have inspired him that afternoon in the battle with Marv's MK Tank.

With Sergeant Rich Garner, Trainor began to walk along beside the machine. It was moving forward only at four or five mph. They were looking for vulnerable areas, trotting up to the side and then back around behind it, aware the entire time of the gun barrels poking out, staying inside and below their fields of fire. The machine crossed through a field of sage brush and scrub, sending up a plume of grey dust behind it as it clanked forward toward U.S. Highway 40.

There wasn't much more Trainor could do by simply walking alongside the machine. He found a wedge of steel, stepped on it and tried to gain a handhold to pull himself up. All he got was a handful of grease. But back toward the ripper, he found another ledge and an angle of steel. He stepped on it and pulled himself on top of the dozer-tank as it turned toward town.

Glen Trainor searched for weak areas on the bulldozer's armor while he took the ride of his life on that June day. He is shown here on top of the machine just after the bulldozer damaged Mountain Parks Electric. Sgt. Rich Garner assisted Trainor from the ground. (Photo provided by Mountain Parks Electric)

Trainor and Garner tried firing into apparent weak areas of the armor, with no success. A stun grenade also failed to halt the progress of the machine. (Photo provided by Mountain Parks Electric)

Once on top, Trainor saw what looked like a cooling unit or radiator on top of the cab, which he thought might be a weak spot or vulnerable area in the shell. Gripping his .30-caliber KH handgun with both hands, and taking an angle so as to avoid ricochets, he fired several rounds into the cooling unit. The shots changed nothing. The tank continued forward, toward town.

Trainor crawled forward to the front of the cab, looked down and fired into the front porthole, breaking loose a big piece of Lexan. He thought if he kept firing, he could get through.

But before he could accomplish that task, the massive machine turned right into the new Mountain Parks Electric building, the customer-owned, rural electric utility company that supplies electricity to Grand and Jackson counties.

Tom Sifers, business manager at Mountain Parks Electric, was in the midst of a business meeting with local banker Sheri Lock when word of the first call from the police came in. Sifers is a slight man with a deep, resonant voice that is surprising for his size. From the Midwest, he's heavily involved in community activities and has served on the East Grand School Board and is a past president of the Rotary Club of Granby. He's a numbers man with a social aptitude.

At first Sifers thought it was a disgruntled employee creating problems for Cody Docheff. Then he looked out the window. He saw the odd-looking bulldozer, its cab shrouded in steel. Soon enough, a sheriff's deputy arrived and told them to get out of the building.

All the employees — women in dresses and linemen in work clothes — fled out the back, down into and across a 10-foot-deep irrigation ditch and caught a ride in a waiting ambulance to the nearby Polhamus Park where they would be out of harm's way.

With Trainor on top, Heemeyer started to destroy the garages at Mountain Parks Electric. Heemeyer deliberately drove the dozer into the masonry and brick walls that separated each garage door. He worked his way to the east and then headed for the front of the building, where administrative offices and reception were located.

While the bulldozer was slamming into the walls at the electrical co-op, Trainor and Sergeant Rich Garner worked together on another plan to try to disable it.

Garner tossed a flash-bang grenade up to Trainor, who then dropped it down one of the exhaust stacks. Nothing happened. A flash-bang grenade doesn't spew shrapnel upon detonation. It just makes a loud noise and a flash, as the name suggests.

Garner tossed him another gas grenade, but Trainor decided not to use it for fear it would compromise his position on top.

The dozer tank tore into the administrative offices in the front of the building. Trainor held on tight and crouched, trying to keep from falling off due to the jerky back-and-forth motions of the dozer. He decided here to call for a SWAT team and any other reinforcements he could muster.

The bulldozer screeched and clanked away from the electrical co-op, leaving behind huge gaping holes in the building's red brick facade. Ceiling tiles, electrical fixtures and pieces of drywall dangled from the upper parts of the jagged holes. Glass, insulation and masonry were fanned out in front of the building. If any person had still been sitting at their desks along that south wall they most certainly would have been either crushed to death or seriously injured.

Back on U.S. Highway 40, the dozer continued toward town. Trainor shouted to Garner that the Granby Town Hall should be evacuated. He knew that if Heemeyer went after Mountain Parks Concrete, then he'd be going after the Town Hall for sure.

Heemeyer inflicted serious damage to the administrative offices at Mountain Parks Electric.

Garner, who was trotting and walking along next to the dozer, fired more rounds from his handgun into openings he saw on the side of the machine. He saw some leaking hydraulics.

Suddenly the machine made an unexpected detour. It stopped and lurched to the left, straight toward the offices of Maple Street Builders, a small metal building off U.S. Highway 40. The front blade slammed into a pick-up truck parked in front and proceeded to push the truck into the building.

If anyone had been sitting at the front business office desk, they would surely have been killed. By pure chance, the office had closed early that day.

The machine then proceeded to climb the slight rise that takes the highway into the more congested part of town. It rumbled past the car wash, past the Frontier Motel, past Mesa Street and past Brooks Veterinary Clinic. And sure enough, true to the suspicions of Trainor, the dozer took a left turn on Zero Street toward the Granby Town Hall — the building in which Heemeyer had spent countless hours voicing his objections to the concrete batch plant.

Glen Trainor was on top of the bulldozer-tank when it took a sharp turn into the offices of Maple Street Builders in Granby. (Mountain Parks Electric photo)

24. Evacuate! Should I Go or Should I Stay?

"Everybody was in such a panic. I was just trying get everybody loaded into the car and make sure we didn't leave anybody."— Gary Hilton

At first, people in town didn't know whether they should flee their buildings or hunker down inside.

The Town Hall building housed the Granby Library in the basement with the town offices upstairs. Not only had town employees and library staff been in the building at the start of the rampage, but a group of children, ages seven to 12 years old, was present for the first week of the summer library season. It was time for the children's story hour.

Sharon Spurlin, who had just finished a long tenure as the Granby Town Clerk and was now the financial director, was in the process of backing up her computer to a tape drive when the first calls came in that somebody was driving a tank and shooting guns in the western part of town. Sharon could, in fact, hear shooting in the background.

For the town staff, the confusion over whether to stay put or evacuate played a role in their initial moments. The first phone calls to the town said nothing about evacuation. But it wasn't long before they got calls that told them to evacuate. Spurlin knew it had to be Heemeyer right from the start. She had been the town clerk during the hearings on the batch plant.

Then a call came in from Spurlin's friend Sherry Dennis at The Trash Company.

"Sharon, it's Marv! Get the Hell out of there!"

She started to worry that Heemeyer would not only attack the Town Hall, but could go after her family, too.

Granby Town Clerk Pro-Tem Cindy Seader had gone, in a hurry, to evacuate the library. She knew there were children there.

In the Granby library, there was certainly some confusion about what to do.

Vickie Born worked as a clerk in the library. It was the first day after school had let out, and there were five children there who were "just hanging out." With a spare, no-nonsense demeanor, she was the perfect woman for herding children in a hectic situation.

When she first heard of what was happening — that there was a tank with guns — she thought the most prudent course of action would be to remain indoors, where there could be no random gunfire. She thought they could all hide under desks and tables.

Then there was a second call and a town employee — Cindy Seader — came down to say "you have to get out, now." Born didn't know what was really happening.

Tess Riley was the children's librarian for the Granby library. With a soft demeanor and a warm, empathetic smile, Riley was frequently concerned about a child's well-being in ways that went beyond her job. Potential violence at the library startled her. When it all started, she had been eating lunch in her car near the elementary school. She thought the sounds of gunfire and the sirens were all part of a training exercise. Then she realized that though her husband, an investigator with the district attorney's office, was in Denver, he would have known about any such exercise and probably would have told her. She rushed back to the library.

Just as the dozer came into view about half a block from the Granby Town Hall, the last person inside the building had finally been evacuated. That would have been nine-year-old Dannie Broady, who left in the car of Children's Librarian Tess Riley.

It had only been a little over an hour since the rampage began.

The dozer headed north on Zero Street, clanking, creaking and rumbling. It passed the Granby Post Office and crossed the intersection at Jasper before taking a sharp turn to the right.

Once the menacing machine was on the lawn next to the Town Hall, Undersheriff Trainor jumped and slid off the machine. Trainor had fired 37 rounds from his handgun into various places on the bulldozer with no effect whatsoever. Nevertheless, as soon as Trainor was safely out of the way, police officers decided it was time to try slowing the machine down with their firearms again.

The dozer struck the Town Hall for the first time, pushing the large blade into the west side of the building. Bricks tumbled, glass shattered and a gaping hole was exposed. It backed out and then roared forward again, knocking down the brick walls and masonry, and shattering more windows. Witnesses to this stage of the rampage say the sound of it all was different now because the heavy bulldozer was driving over the soft lawn outside the town hall. This reduced the clanking of the treads on the ground. But it amplified, somehow, the squealing of steel scraping against steel in the treads. The engine howled ominously, insistently.

There, looking naked and exposed to the world, was the office of Granby Town Manager Tom Hale. His desk hung precariously with an angled pitch to the west. A photo from a fly-fishing exploit in South America sat tilted on the wall. Pink batts of insulation were exposed for the first time in years while two-by-four studs cracked and tipped as the cinder blocks behind the brick exterior walls fell. Lights dangled from the crumpled ceilings, held in the air by electrical wiring. The screaming machine backed out onto the lawn once more, turning to face the northwest corner of the building. The treads dug into the sod, creating churned-up furrows. The machine hit the corner, destabilizing more structural elements in the old building and sending the second floor slipping downward as more bricks, mortar and cinder blocks fell toward the earth. The west side of the town hall was a shambles.

The dozer systematically traveled around the town hall, avoiding the large concrete steps by plowing over and destroying the children's playground behind the town hall.

Gary Hilton of Granby, an erstwhile snowmobiling partner of Heemeyer's, watched the dozer as it did its work. He had been three blocks away at his brother's house when he started to hear shots being fired. He drove down to see what was up and saw the bulldozer smashing up the playground. That angered him since he had played there as a child. The sod in the playground that had been so carefully planted by the Granby Rotary Club 10 years earlier was now a jumbled, tangled mess. The jungle gym was smashed and swing sets were crushed and twisted about like limp spaghetti.

The machine turned from the playground area and headed back into the building, creating a large hole that exposed the town's public meeting room. It was the same room where Marv had pleaded his case in numerous public meetings.

Now that the town meeting room had been demolished, Heemeyer worked his way into the parking lot on the east side of the building, where he attacked three town cars. First he slammed into a Jeep Cherokee, then a Crown Victoria and then a Taurus. The vehicles were totally destroyed. In the course of smashing up the cars, he also drove right into the east side wall of the town hall. In three thrusts with the slow-moving machine he was able to create a wide hole in the library. Bricks and mortar, cinder blocks and wooden studs, light fixtures and ceiling panels all fell into the library's children's reading area. The second floor, the ceiling for the library, began to crack, unaccustomed to the load from above that was now unsupported by the bearing walls on the eastern side of the building.

All the while, the police had been concentrating their fire on what appeared to be cameras mounted low on the bulldozer and facing to the rear. But despite the fact that Sergeant Norm Rimmer of the Grand County Sheriff's Department had special rounds in his shotgun, they had no effect on the cameras, which they later discovered were shrouded in bullet-proof Lexan. The dozer moved on as if mocking the futile efforts of the law enforcement officers.

Gary Hilton had watched the dozer tear away at the Town Hall and it dawned on him: There were children at a private day care center only a block-and-a-half away. He had to help. Hilton, a state patrol trooper and Wayne Miller, a Granby resident, arrived at the day care center at the same time. Seven children piled into their cars and were driven away from the firing and commotion.

Just two blocks away, in a residential neighborhood, others were facing their own terror. Blake Mills was six years old when the rampage occurred. He lived with his mother and father, Deb and Dennis Mills, and three-year-old sister Rachel on Jasper Street. Deb was outside doing yard work, as Rachel and Blake played nearby. Blake had just finished kindergarten the day before.

A teenager came running up to the fence, panicked.

"Lady, get your kids in the house! There's a man down the street with a gun."

Deb and her two children ran inside. She locked the back door. Blake ran and locked the front door. Peeking through the blinds hanging on a front window, they saw people in panic. People were running this way and that, parking their cars wherever. It scared them.

Deb didn't really know what was happening, when she received the reverse 911 call and was told to get out of the house and go east.

She felt confused and extremely worried. She called the police department back, but the person who answered the phone wouldn't tell her if the problem was a person walking or driving with a gun. Perhaps they didn't know

So the plan was that they'd drive to the Granby Medical Center, just four blocks away. Yet every time she'd open her front door, the women at the library administration building across the street would scream at her: "Don't leave. Go in your basement."

"I don't have a basement," she screamed back.

Now she panicked. She could hear gun shots. She didn't think she could make it from her front door to the car, with her children in tow. She thought to herself: 'Oh my God, if I go out there, is there going to be a stray bullet?'

They finally ran to the car, crouching in fear but glancing up to see all the people running this way and that. Everybody was shouting different instructions, different orders. The fear was contagious.

Once in the car, she drove to the Granby Medical Center on Granby's main street. She couldn't have known that she was driving her family right back to the general path of the dozer.

Blake doesn't talk about the events of June 4, 2004. In his mother's eyes, he's the boy who was drastically changed by the rampaging bulldozer.

3:30 p.m.

25. Taking Swipes at Town Pride

Because I have reported on so much of Granby town politics over the years, I viewed the next stage of the rampage as a particularly symbolic stretch of violence. Heemeyer knew town issues, past conflicts and many aspects of the town's pride. I think Heemeyer knew exactly what he was doing in choosing what at first might have seemed like random, insignificant targets.

At the intersection of First Street and Jasper, Heemeyer angled his machine toward Liberty Savings Bank. The bank had recently completed a new building at the intersection of U.S. Highway 40 — Granby's Agate Avenue — and First Street, which was the only intersection in town with a traffic light. Still plodding implacably at four or five mph, the tank set a relentless course. This time Heemeyer was going to make a point about Granby town pride.

The Granby branch of Liberty Savings Bank was, ironically, a product of the very savings and loan crisis that ended up putting Heemeyer's business in Granby.

For Liberty, an Ohio-based savings bank company, the opportunity to be in Granby arose when Colorado Savings and Loan got into trouble in the late '80s. In a quiet move orchestrated by federal regulators after a crisis in local banking that had seen a run on a neighboring bank three years prior, the savings and loan was purchased by Liberty in February of 1990. Liberty built a brand new structure right on U.S. Highway 40 in 2002. In a small town like Granby, this new building was an impressive addition.

Engine roaring, its tracks squealing and clanking, the dozer pushed right up over the sidewalk on First Street and slammed into the northwest corner of the bank. With the massive blade turned toward the bank's front doors, the dozer essentially drove right through the building. Large gaps, shattered glass, loosely scattered masonry and an awkwardly tilting brick wall were all that was left behind.

Police officers stood watching, still trying to find weaknesses in the Brobdingnagian beast. Now Heemeyer drove right into the metal post that supported the new traffic light in downtown Granby. The new traffic lights, cables and electrical wires stretched across U.S. Highway 40 jiggled and bounced in the air as if a giant were shaking the poles, but remarkably, the pole didn't come down.

In trying to knock over the traffic light Heemeyer was jabbing his blade right in the eye of Granby town pride — a pride that small-town residents across the region could appreciate. Fraser and Winter Park, in the ski-resort region of the county, each got traffic lights before Granby. Even Kremmling, the ranching town to the west, got a traffic light before Granby. While the town fathers had campaigned for the traffic light for several years based on the safety concerns at that busy intersection, it also didn't hurt that the light symbolized something else as well: that Granby was growing and busy — that it now needed such a light. Heemeyer slammed into it again and again. For some, this seemed to provide a gut-level rationale to cheer on the otherwise ominous progress of Heemeyer's creation.

Soon, Heemeyer gave up and headed south toward R&J Liquors, hitting a fire hydrant in the process. Water flooded the intersection.

Lt. Walt Eldridge once again gave some serious thought to knocking out the viewing camera they had discovered.

"As he pulled back out on U.S. 40, and started up the hill, we thought taking that rear camera out would be a good thing," he says. He moved up behind the bulldozer. He shot at the camera with his .45, firing a full magazine. Still, the bulldozer clinked and rumbled forward. It seemed more than ever like the embodiment of brute force of steel, the inevitability of momentum and the epitome of power. The police were flummoxed.

State Patrol cruisers were now following either to the rear or alongside the dozer. It was almost as if Heemeyer was being escorted through town, but it was Heemeyer who was in control.

The dozer continued east, passing by Middle Park Insurance on the south side of the highway. It seemed to be sparing Bill Hertel's

Western Guncraft gun shop next door to the insurance office. Soon the Longbranch Restaurant, a Granby mainstay with the only covered sidewalks in the town, would be on the left of the dozer. Then something unexpected happened. Heemeyer braked the right-hand treads of the machine, steering the dozer directly toward Alpine West Office Supply, but once the tread crushed the curb and rolled up onto the sidewalk, he jerked the machine to a straight trajectory. He was aiming for an aspen tree. He hit the first one and it fell as if it was made of balsa wood. Then one of the town's street lamps took a direct hit from the big blade, falling quickly with a dull clatter before it was crushed. Then another small aspen tree fell with a swaying and bowing convulsion. It was smashed and uprooted.

But before hitting the next tree — a small, well-trimmed cherry tree in front of the Blue Spruce Motel — the dozer swerved back onto the highway and proceeded east again toward its next target.

This little detour of the dozer left some people scratching their heads, thinking it was merely another random jab by Heemeyer at the town, its civic pride and a controversial aspect of its recent past. Keith Klingbail, who owned the Blue Spruce Motel with his wife Kendra, saw it from a more personal perspective. He thinks Marv was trying to do him a favor.

Klingbail remembers that he had been talking to Heemeyer before the rampage when he asked him to complete a small welding job. The conversation ended up being about Klingbail's grievances concerning the aspen trees on Granby's main street. Klingbail told the town board that the trees, planted as part of a civic-improvement project years before, had grown to the point where they obstructed the view of his motel's sign from the highway. He had asked if the town would cut or replace the trees in front of his neighbor, Alpine West Office Supply, with smaller cherry trees like his. But the town and his neighbors resisted. So, Klingbail was stuck with aspen trees, which he felt hurt his business.

The issue of the aspen trees was no small matter to the town board. The trees had been planted to improve the appearance of Granby's main street and to make the town seem like more of a pedestrian-oriented place where passing motorists would want to stop and shop. This was, at least, the idealistic reasoning behind the planting of the aspen trees and the installation of new curbs and gutters when they were agreed upon by the town in 1984. It was the start of an attempt to re-make Granby into something more like a resort town in the Rockies, like the more prosperous towns of Steamboat Springs and Breckenridge. But as the trees grew, so did disenchantment among some members of the main street business community.

Running over those trees had significance.

Klingbail's motel sign was now clearly visible to motorists approaching from the west.

Police cars and town vehicles were particularly hard hit by the force of the bulldozer. (Photo by Jean Landess)

3:45 p.m.

26. The Assault on the Newspaper Building

Heemeyer had taken out five buildings in under two hours. Now, the rampage was becoming a spectacle. This is when the radio station started broadcasting its blow-by-blow narrative of the event. A producer and announcer were sitting on a bluff above Granby, watching it all and relating what they saw. Many people who had their radios tuned to the local AM station were starting to get an idea of what was happening.

KRKY reporter Gary Redfield did his best to convey what he and his son, Sam, 16, saw from the mesa overlooking the town. The station also managed to air comments from Bonnie Brown, a friend of Heemeyer's who said that she had a hard time believing it would be Marv Heemeyer in the bulldozer-tank since he was such a nice and gentle guy — such a big Teddy Bear of a man. She hinted that if he was doing this, then he must have been pushed, as if the enormity of his rampage somehow justified it all. The insinuation was that it was the town's fault, not his, and that he was somehow noble in his actions. In her on-air comments, Brown initiated a large part of the public myth surrounding Heemeyer. With the rampage in progress, Heemeyer was already being cast as the trod-upon gentle giant — a hero pushed to extreme measures.

At the intersection of Fourth Street the bulldozer continued implacably forward, passing by the Mad Munchies Sub Shop and Spirits-N-Things liquor store. Here Heemeyer took a sharp turn to the right and crashed over the street's south sidewalk and into the *Sky-Hi News* building.

This is a photo that was taken by Patrick Brower just moments before the Killdozer slammed into the Sky-Hi News building. Here, the Killdozer is heading east on U.S. Highway 40, only one block from the newspaper building.

Another battle with law enforcement officers ensued.

Heemeyer rammed the machine into the front of our offices, pushing in about six or seven feet, then backed out, repeating the methodical process he had used on other buildings that day: slam into the wall, back out, proceed further down the wall then slam in again. It seemed as if Heemeyer was particularly intent on damaging the northeast corner of the building, where my office sat. Heemeyer had met with me three times in that very office to discuss letters to the editor he had submitted. Within minutes, he had compromised the structural integrity of the building and the front third of the roof caved in with a terrific crash.

Luckily, the dozer could not reach in far enough to directly hit the six-unit Goss Community printing press that sat on the east side of the press room. After one last devastating jab into the pressroom, Heemeyer turned the bulldozer around and headed out of the parking lot, hitting cars and trucks left parked there. Cinder blocks, large slivers of wood and insulation covered the dozer. A strand of insulation draped awkwardly over the blade.

Video shot by Lt. Leo Piechocki of the Grand County Sheriff's Department captured many moments of the rampage. Here, the bulldozer slams into the Sky-Hi News offices.

Sheriff's Deputies were beginning to show up in even greater numbers. Some, like Deputy Roy Ybarra, had been working out in a local gym when he got the call. He showed up at the *Sky-Hi News* building with a shotgun in hand, dressed informally in his workout clothes.

"I decided to shoot at the portals," Ybarra says, using his shotgun, which was loaded with buckshot. But, of course, his shots had no effect. I snapped photos of Deputy RoyYbarra standing by the rumbling machine.

Deputy Roy Ybarra was summoned from a workout at a local gym when news of the rampage spread. (Photo by the author)

Deputy Sean Curran also arrived after following the wake of the dozer from the town hall. At the newspaper building he and another deputy attempted to cram a large bar of steel into the tracks of the machine as it was slamming into the building. But the steel popped out like the pipes and steel angle iron that had been shoved into the treads at the batch plant. Curran proceeded to fire 18 times at the perceived weak spots in the dozer to no avail.

Sgt. Norm Rimmer of the Sheriff's Department, after trying to shoot at radiator hoses on the bulldozer when it was near Liberty Savings Bank, took a position on the balcony of the 440 Apartments next door to the *Sky-Hi News* building. He fired his .223 Bushmaster a total of 11 times at the impervious machine.

Deputy Ryan Phillips arrived on the scene and told Sgt. Garner, who had followed the bulldozer all the way from the concrete batch plant, that he had a .300 ultra mag sniper rifle. Garner gave Phillips his M-14 in exchange for the more powerful sniper rifle.

"I took four or five shots at the back portal," Garner said. "I reloaded and moved down below the balcony of the (apartment) building. And I took a couple of shots at the side portal, which would be the driver's left side. And several more at the back portal again. He (Heemeyer) started backing up pushing the pickup towards me and we displaced out of there."

Police continued to fire at the bulldozer-tank at the Sky-Hi News building in Granby. (Video footage by Lt. Leo Piechocki of the Grand County Sheriff's Dept.)

When Deputy Bus Wurm of the sheriff's department arrived at the *Sky-Hi News*, he was armed with his Bushmaster, a .223-caliber rifle with extra velocity and power. He fired rounds from his weapon, continuing to fire a total of 27 times at the ports in the front and rear of the protective armor on the cab. It made no difference.

This one-sided exchange of gunfire confirmed again that there wasn't much that could be done against this home-made tank — at least not with conventional firearms. Undersheriff Trainor said they felt resigned to fighting a losing battle until bigger weapons would arrive. When the machine pushed out onto U.S. Highway 40 again, it left behind a completely destroyed newspaper building. It looked like photos from the London Blitz.

The dozer rolled on relentlessly.

"It was well-enveloped in steel," Ybarra says. He was trotting alongside the machine as it passed in front of the medical center. "After all that looking around, I don't think there was any way to get into it. When it was going down Agate (U.S. Highway 40), myself and a few other guys we got right there, crawling, looking under it to see if there was anything wide, anything that we could cut, to get at anything and there was nothing. It was completely enveloped . . . We were looking for any little crack. Everything was welded. There were no creases of any kind."

As the bulldozer headed east again on U.S. Highway 40 Sergeant Rich Garner had reason for renewed hope. Scott Spade of the Kremmling Police Department had just shown up on the scene near the *Sky-Hi News* with a humongous bolt action .50-caliber rifle. Garner took the weapon and started to plan how he would use it against the bulldozer-tank.

3:55 p.m.

27. Getting Back at the Thompsons

Now that the rampage had been going on for one and a half hours, there was an air of absurdity about it.

The homemade tank clanked along in the wide open, surrounded by jogging police officers. The tracks of the machine dented warm stretches of the asphalt pavement with a series of ladder-like troughs, punctuating the air with a metallic clatter of steel against steel. Many people, despite the danger, were mesmerized by what was happening right before their eyes. Guns, a front-end loader, pipes, angle iron and cars couldn't stop it. It was as if the world were helpless against this menacing, Rube Goldberg invention.

Still, the fight against the homemade tank hadn't stopped. Two more challenges would be thrown into the path of the machine.

But first, Heemeyer had his work to do: Get the Thompsons.

The long-established Thompson family had been mainstays of Granby affairs for years. Dick Thompson, the patriarch of the current generation, had been mayor of Granby and served on the town board faithfully, presiding over affairs during Heemeyer's concrete batch plant fight. But he had recused himself from voting because he owned land leased by the Docheff's. He died in 2001, but his legacy continued.

His son Ron (who had died earlier from leukemia) had served on the Granby Fire Department and had been on the board for the Granby Sanitation District when Heemeyer had gone to that board on sewer issues. Ron and his two brothers, Larry and Gary, were skilled heavy equipment operators and truck drivers. They were the crew that kept Thompson and Sons Excavating operating with their spotless and brightly painted red and white trucks. Daughters Linda and Brenda were well-known in the town through their various jobs as clerks at prominent local businesses. None of them had married. They lived at home. Thelma, Dick's widow, kept the books and helped to run the business. She presided over the clan with a quiet calm.

Over the years Dick Thompson and his parents had managed to acquire property in the Granby area. Some of it was income-producing, such as the land up on the bluff near the concrete batch plant, where gravel and earth provided the materials for growth and development and road-building. They owned a strip of buildings in town next to their home. They leased out two of these buildings, one to Xcel Energy, the natural gas utility provider for the area, and the other to a tile company. They also owned other lots in town.

Adjacent to their home, where Thelma lived with her grown children, sat the shop for the excavation company. It was a large steel building bordered on the east by a large parking lot where trucks, backhoes and other heavy equipment were stored. Another lot behind Wrangler Tire at the intersection of Sixth Street and Jasper Court housed beat-up old trailers, pipe and piles of material. The site of that lot over the years had prompted occasional complaints about its appearance to the town board, but the land was zoned for a wide variety of uses, so no action had been taken.

Heemeyer was headed straight for the shop of Thompson and Sons Excavation.

He passed by the town laundromat. He ignored Granby Heating and Sheet metal. He was intent on the garage and property of Thompson and Sons. The machine lurched over to its right and to the south along the road. Here it took out trees, a small back portion of the Xcel Energy building and part of the back of the Thompson family home.

Brent Scowcroft, an employee of Independent Propane located nearby, had been trying to stop the dozer in a unique way. He had a tank of oxygen in his hand with a release hose. Trotting alongside the dozer and around it he was trying to find a place where the pure oxygen could be sucked into the engine and therefore high rev or stall it. Despite numerous attempts, he failed to stop the continued destruction.

It had been yet one more heroic effort thwarted by the bulldozer-tank.

Thelma Thompson had been napping here, in the Thompson home, only moments before Heemeyer started to attack the Thompson properties. (Sky-Hi News photo by Jean Landess)

Larry Thompson, the oldest of the living Thompson boys, had just arrived from a job site in Grand Lake to witness the attack on his family's property. He's tall and slight with a thinning pate. He has a knack for throwing a skeptical glance to the side while nursing a toothpick in his mouth, sharing opinions about local government and construction work guided by common sense and a no-fooling-around air.

He watched as Heemeyer's machine knocked over trees, slammed into the back of the family house, shoved a trailer in the work yard up on top of a dumpster, and then pushed a lowboy trailer into the side of the shop.

The large shop building now had a gaping hole in its side. Equipment had capsized and vehicles were damaged. The back of the Thompson home looked like it had been hit by a bomb. But Heemeyer wasn't finished with the Thompsons.

The dozer turned and headed straight back over the tracks he had just made. This time he was heading for a storage lot owned by the Thompsons.

Backtracking as he did gave people added time to ponder the dozer and some new defensive efforts were being considered. Clark Branstetter, who was the head of Grand County Road and Bridge, was driving into Granby from an outlying county property when he heard confusing calls on the radio, asking for county help. It wasn't very clear what he would be facing. Police waved him past their roadblocks into town. He decided to call for the Caterpillar D-8A scraper that was at the airport north of Granby. There was another similar scraper at the county landfill three miles west of Granby. They were the biggest machines the county had nearby, weighing 40 tons. He briefly conferred with police at the scene and they said to bring those in to town to tussle with the dozer.

At the same time Sgt. Rich Garner had received the .50-caliber rifle from Kremmling police officer Scott Spade.

Garner ran north of the dozer, lugging the 49-lbs. gun, and took a position from where he fired one shot.

His shot had no effect.

Heemeyer proceeded right into the storage yard for Thompson and Sons, pushing a storage trailer into parked vehicles and piles of pipe and spare parts for heavy equipment. Heemeyer then turned the bulldozer around.

The bulldozer hit the Xcel Energy building again, but this time from the front, pushing an Xcel Energy pick-up into the building, totaling the vehicle and crumbling the building with one brutal shove.

Tenants of the Thompson properties paid the price as Heemeyer was intent on getting back at the longtime Granby family. (Sky-Hi News photo by Jean Landess)

Then he went back to the Thompson home, this time from the front, where Thelma Thompson, 82, the matriarch of the Thompson family, had been taking a nap only 30 minutes earlier. Luckily, she had been called ahead of time and had driven to safety under her own power. Heemeyer drove the dozer right into the front yard, taking out two large spruce trees before lunging at the house, leaving it a crumpled shell. Combined with the earlier attack on the back of the Thompson family home, Heemeyer had done some serious damage to the residence. It had been totaled. If Thelma had been in the house at the time, there's little doubt that she would have been killed.

Here is where Sgt. Garner found an opportunity for better shots from the unwieldy .50-caliber rifle. He aimed for what he thought was the area where the radiator was located and fired three times.

But the machine continued forward. Apparently, the shots had not hit the radiator.

At this moment yet another tool from the meager arsenal of the local populace arrived on the scene. Branstetter was driving one of the massive county scrapers. He was going to try and stop the bulldozer, or at least slow it down.

It was something like a cat-and-mouse game as Branstetter tried to block the forward progress of the machine. But at each blocking move the bulldozer plodded forward, unfazed by the massive scraper. Heemeyer simply pushed the scraper sideways. Finally, in what Branstetter thinks was an unintentional move on the part of Heemeyer, the dozer angled into one of the large tires on the scraper and burst it. With one flat tire, the scraper was even more useless than before. Branstetter parked it nearby. Heemeyer drove his machine backwards in front of the building he had damaged and then passed over a lawn next to a massive spruce tree back onto County Road 60. The machine turned right again and headed west, as if going back into downtown.

Heemeyer had hit the Thompson properties 14 times.

Heemeyer's next target was a propane gas storage yard.

4:15 p.m.

28. To Blow Up the Town

The .50-caliber rifle used by Sgt. Garner hadn't worked against Heemeyer's creation. At least not yet.

The massive Caterpillar scraper used by Clark Branstetter to try to stop the dozer hadn't worked either. It sat immobile in the parking lot in front of the Xcel Energy office where it had lost its fight with the bulldozer. Branstetter's actions revealed him as one of the courageous players during the rampage. In hindsight, Branstetter says if he had known what he was going to be up against perhaps he would have filled the scraper's bed with the tons of soil those machines could haul. Then, maybe, he could have really slowed it down. As the dozer drove out of the parking lot there was still another scraper on the scene. But its bed was empty, making it less than half the weight of Heemeyer's machine.

There was hope, as dim as it was, that Heemeyer's homemade tank could still be stopped before more damage could occur.

Heemeyer had churned his way out of the Xcel Energy parking lot. This time the dozer was heading downhill on a spur to the south of County Road 60 that served a low-lying semi-industrial part of town that housed apartments, contracting offices, a crane business, a propane fueling yard and a sawmill.

The first reaction of law enforcement officers when they saw the tank heading down toward the lower properties of County Road 60 was concern for the people and employees who lived and worked in the area. A call went out from Colorado State Patrol officers and sheriff's deputies to evacuate people in apartments and businesses as quickly as possible. It was feared he was heading for the apartments down below. They had no idea what Heemeyer really had in mind.

But the fight against the dozer had not ceased, with another scraper and more rounds from the .50-caliber ready for use.

Nervously and helplessly, law enforcement officers watched as the machine clanked down the hill. By now, the audience of the rampage was growing rapidly because news helicopters from Denver TV stations were circling overhead.

Heemeyer ignored the apartments. He ignored The Sky Crane shop, also on his right. A tall bluff covered by sagebrush and weeds rose 40 feet to his left off County Road 60. My house was 400 yards beyond. On the north side of County Road 60, above the dozer's route, sat houses in a tranquil Granby neighborhood and the Grand Living Solar Senior Homes, a cluster of 40 senior residences made distinctive by then-inactive hot water solar collectors perched on the roofs.

Almost directly south of the homes, and about 50 yards away, sat the propane bulk plant for Independent Propane. A bank of five 3,000-gallon tanks sat close to the road near the senior housing complex. Two massive 30,000-gallon tanks sat further to the south, closer to the railroad tracks. A few delivery trucks were parked at the site and a mobile home used as an office flanked the western side of the property. Directly to the east of the propane storage yard sat the Granby Sawmill, a rough-cut sawmill operation that stored thousands of board feet of dry, ready-to-burn timber.

It was, under the right conditions, a massive conflagration waiting to happen. Suddenly it dawned on law enforcement officers: Heemeyer's next target was the propane storage yard. But he wasn't going to drive over to them and knock them over as he had done in other attacks earlier that day. His designs were even more ambitious. He drove the bulldozer to a spot about 100 yards to the west of the propane tanks on the dirt road down below. Then he spun the machine around so that the rear of the machine, where the .50-caliber was perched, faced the propane tanks. He stopped.

This was when Cpl. Dave Batura urged Grand County dispatch to tell all people to evacuate at least 1,000 yards away from the Independent Propane bulk plant. Deputies were sent to hurriedly make sure that seniors and other residents of the senior housing complex, located well within 1,000 yards of the propane tanks, were evacuated. There was a real chance now for major carnage.

The dozer sat idle for a moment. Then Heemeyer opened fire with his .50-caliber rifle, shooting at the propane tanks. Tellingly, the blasts of the rifle raised fields of dust around the ripper and plating on the rear of the tank.

Heemeyer then spun the machine around and drove about 25 yards toward the propane tanks. He stopped the machine and spun it around again. But now, it wasn't clear what he was going to shoot.

It took about a minute for Heemeyer to position the bulldozer as he wanted, apparently in an effort to get a good shot at what turned out to be electrical transformers mounted on power poles to the south and east of the propane tanks. Sparks generated by rounds impacting the transformers could have caused a fire that would ignite the escaping propane gas, causing a massive explosion.

Heemeyer drove the machine forward into the embankment to the north of the road. Because of the front blade, which he raised as high as he could, he couldn't inch the nose of the dozer very high up the bluff. The design of the rear firing port proved to be flawed, as steel plating welded to the back of the machine and on the ripper limited the degree at which Heemeyer could fire the weapon below a level plane. Shots downward, in other words, hit the armor on the dozer. Getting a better angle of fire from the tank toward either of the transformers required angling the bulldozer so that the back was low enough to allow shooting over the armor on the ripper.

It took almost two minutes for Heemeyer to position the machine just right for accurate shots from its most powerful piece of weaponry. Heemeyer tried to sight the rifle, saw it was not oriented correctly, then tried to maneuver the machine again until it had the most opportune angle possible. Then he fired off four more rounds from the .50-caliber in the direction of the transformers. Plumes of dust billowed from the rear of the dozer at the force of the .50-caliber rounds. He managed to hit the transformers at least once. Three other rounds missed, and Sgt. Garner reported that he saw the rounds impact a large hillside a mile to the southeast.

Joe Swisher, the manager of the Independent Propane plant at the time, says none of the rounds hit the tanks. There was no sign of any impact. The tanks that were in place at the time were still in use six years later.

Heemeyer spun the dozer around so that he could have clear shots at propane tanks in eastern Granby. (Clipping from KCNC helicopter news footage that was provided to the sheriff's department)

Nothing happened. There was no cathartic explosion and there were no dramatic leaping flames, which seemed to be what Heemeyer wanted, like the fabulous violent climaxes of James Bond films or superhero dramas. This apparent attempt to blow up the town, burn down the senior housing and create a potentially tragic and lasting impression, had failed. Or, perhaps, it would just take a few moments for escaping propane gas to drift to the area of the potentially sparking transformers. Heemeyer didn't wait long to see and he lurched the bulldozer around so it was facing west again and he proceeded toward his next engagement, against another one of the Grand County scrapers.

Heading up that hill Heemeyer had to suspect that he had failed to cause a huge explosion. But he knew he had already made his mark and he still had plenty of work to do. The dozer had 10 hours of fuel left and they couldn't stop him. He would have brushed off the failure at the batch plant. Perhaps he would have smiled or laughed at his invincibility and power, knowing that the world was now watching a hero at work while he carried out his mission of righteous destruction and revenge. It was all OK, he would have thought, and they deserved it. The world would know.

"Can you hear me now?" he would have thought, smiling grimly to himself.

A sliver of fear would have preoccupied Heemeyer too. A glance at the temperature gauge of the dozer showed it resting in the red. He'd have to hurry.

Branstetter had positioned the second scraper near the top of the hill on the County Road 60 spur road, blocking the way into town. Heemeyer drove the bulldozer up the hill as fast, seemingly, as it could go. He slammed directly into the back of the scraper. Branstetter gunned the engine, trying to push back against the dozer. The two pieces of heavy equipment battled it out for 10 seconds, like giant, soulless robots, with their twitching and massive motions, fighting to the death. The scraper was no match for the dozer. It easily pushed the scraper out of its way, making the scraper jackknife under the force.

Clark Branstetter thought the second county scraper would have been much more effective against the bulldozer if it had been full of tons of soil, making it more of an obstacle. (KCNC TV helicopter video clip)

The scraper was no match for 85-ton Komatsu bulldozer. (KCNC TV helicopter video clip)

The bulldozer progressed, solitary in its mission, back into downtown Granby. The group of law enforcement officers was no longer trotting alongside. Fewer cars were following. There was an air of resignation on the part of law enforcement. Or, perhaps, an air of anticipation. They knew that SWAT teams from Jefferson and Summit counties in Colorado were on their way. Also, a broadcast by Grand County dispatch revealed that the "peace-keeper," a small cannon, was en route on a flatbed from Federal Heights, a city near Denver. Local law enforcement reiterated the need for bigger firepower, a comment that had been made right at the start of the rampage at Mountain Park Concrete nearly two hours ago.

Unimpeded, free as a lark and still as menacing as ever, the bulldozer/tank headed west on U.S. Highway 40, covering ground it had already traveled earlier. The main street of Granby was empty, except for cars and debris left by the bulldozer on its first pass.

Maneuvering back to U.S. Highway 40 for a better vantage point, Sgt. Rich Garner was exhausted. He had fired nine rounds at the machine from the awkward .50-caliber bolt action rifle. The weapon was heavy. It was difficult to aim. And he had accidentally hit Deputy Roy Ybarra in the head with the barrel of the weapon while he was trying to maneuver the gun.

It was clear to Undersheriff Glen Trainor that Garner was fatigued. Emergency Medical Services was called to make sure Garner was OK. He was given water and told to relax, a difficult thing to do under the circumstances. He thought that he had gotten a round into the engine compartment or radiator, but he wasn't sure. Sheriff's deputies were watching from a distance, some taking cover behind a former gas station building on the north and the medical center on the south of the highway.

State patrol cruisers took positions to block traffic, provide watchful eyes and help coordinate new law enforcement arrivals at the scene. The scraper that was still capable of operating sat idle in front of Xcel energy, waiting for another opportunity. It was obvious by now that it couldn't stop or even slow Heemeyer, but Branstetter thought maybe there was another way it could be used to help.

Law enforcement officers used a variety of weapons in futile attempts to stop the dozer. (Clip from video footage shot by Lt. Leo Piechocki of the Grand County Sheriff's Department)

The bulldozer plodded along past 7-Eleven, a store that was usually bustling with business on a Friday afternoon. When the machine passed there was no activity at the convenience store. Bystanders had cleared out. It's as if after the shooting incident at the propane plant people were suddenly reminded anew of the killing power of the tank.

Television news helicopters hovered overhead.

Heemeyer turned right, veering toward Kopy Kat Graphics and Printing. The Gambles store sat next door to the west. The machine pushed right over the curb, taking out a lamp post on the way. Just as the machine climbed up over the curb and onto the sidewalk a massive plume of white steam and smoke billowed out from underneath. The dozer's blade ripped out the corner of the wooden-sided Kopy Kat building. Another one of the aspen trees that lined the main drag fell with a bowing lurch under the force of the blade.

A large plume of steam and vaporized coolant suggested that the dozer was overheating prior to the attack on Gambles. (KCNC TV helicopter video clip)

The dozer pushed forward, seemingly unfazed by the plume of escaping white mist and smoke rising from underneath. But as the machine worked its way west on the sidewalk and smashed the steps and deck in the front of the store, it left a trail of steaming water and anti-freeze. This was the first evidence that something serious had happened to the massive machine. Yet another aspen tree jerked upon impact with the dozer blade and fell prostrate, crushed.

The dozer rumbled and lurched into position in front of the Gambles Store, owned by Casey and Rhonda Farrell. Casey had served on the Granby Town Board during the batch plant hearings. The Farrells had been eating lunch at a nearby restaurant when they heard that something bizarre was happening with a bulldozer. They were told they should evacuate the store and leave the area. So they went to the store, told everyone to leave, and locked up. One out-of-town couple asked if they could remain in the store in the back office until the excitement passed. It was fortunate that Casey and Rhonda told them no.

The Gambles store was the final victim of the bulldozer's rampage. (KCNC TV helicopter video clip)

Heemeyer took his time maneuvering the dozer into place, turning it around so the massive blade faced Gambles. He revved the engine once and then slammed into the corner of Gambles, taking out another lamp post in the process. He backed out, letting a large wall section fall off the blade and onto the street. Then he drove right into the middle of the façade of the building. The store that had been a fixture of Granby's main street for 40 years was being slowly demolished in full view of television helicopter camera crews and the townspeople looking on. The dozer backed out again, laden with another layer of debris, and positioned itself for a straight charge right down the west wall of Gambles.

The dozer smashed its way down the west wall of Gambles. (KCNC TV helicopter video clip)

The behemoth pushed through the wall with ease, taking the building down as it went. The bowed-truss roof of Gambles tilted and fell to the ground, detritus piled beneath it. Quickly then, as the machine proceeded forward, the remaining county scraper was driven in to block the driveway access behind the dozer. The dozer rolled forward through the Gambles masonry building and then continued into a steel storage building in the rear. The steel walls and roof crumpled and bent like cardboard and paper. The tank pushed halfway through the steel building and then stopped moving forward. Here, Heemeyer angled the dozer a little bit to the right and a little to the left, but that was all. He was able to move forward only a few inches, with its left track grinding into the earth and the crumpled steel roof resting on top of its cab.

Sheriff's Deputies stood watching from cover behind a neighboring house just 20 feet to the west. Suddenly, the dozer sat still, a little bit of steam escaping from its engine compartment.

A metal storage building behind Gambles crumpled under the force of the bulldozer. (KCNC TV helicopter video clip)

Lt. Walt Eldridge and another deputy cautiously approached the motionless machine. They found another camera and covered it. The engine of the bulldozer whirred to a stop. They walked around the dozer, worried that firing could start again at any minute. They carefully avoided the rifle barrels. Then Eldridge and the deputies heard a pop from inside the cab of the dozer. It sounded like the report of a handgun, but they couldn't be sure.

Why had the bulldozer stopped? Inside the Gambles back building there was a small, little-known half-basement used for storage. When the treads of the machine passed into that building, the inside tread dropped down into this depression, preventing the bulldozer from getting any traction. It was stuck.

With the dozer finally motionless, police carefully started to examine the machine, fearful of booby traps on the outside shell of the tank. (KCNC TV helicopter video clip)

Another factor played into Heemeyer's plight at that point. That huge plume of white and grey steam and smoke billowing out from beneath the behemoth was the result of the main radiator hose bursting. Although some had been speculating that a bullet from Garner's .50-caliber rifle or another weapon had managed to penetrate the engine's armor and pierce the radiator, no bullets entered the engine compartment. The machine, simply, had gotten too hot. When the hose burst, most of the fluid leaked out in a paroxysm of mist and smoke. With no coolant, the dozer would not have been able to operate much longer.

Heemeyer had over-designed and over-engineered the MK Tank. It was too heavy. And the overheating problem was compounded by the armor restricting the flow of air over the radiator. Heemeyer had added another 25 tons of weight to the machine with the armor and concrete. That was a lot of extra weight to be carrying around. Even the extra fans Heemeyer had placed inside the armor in an apparent attempt to circulate more air into the engine compartment and create better cooling capabilities had failed. The radiator line burst due to the pressure of too much undissipated heat.

Twenty minutes later another bulldozer, owned by the county, was brought in as quickly as possible. This bulldozer, a Caterpillar D-8, also from the landfill, was parked with its blade pushed up against the blade of the dozer-tank, just in case it started again and attempted to move forward. At this stage, local officials didn't want to take any chances. Blocked in front by the D-8 and behind by the scraper, if Heemeyer managed to push free, there would be a colossal showdown among the three pieces of heavy equipment.

Now satisfied that the dozer was trapped, a whole new set of fears crossed the minds of officials on the scene. What if Heemeyer were to exit the machine through some hidden hatch, guns blazing? What if the machine was booby-trapped to explode? What else could Heemeyer have dreamed up, even with the dozer immobile, that could cause more damage? After the last two harrowing hours, most anything was imaginable. Many assumed the worst.

Gambles was left in ruins. Here, the bulldozer-tank sits where it stalled after demolishing the longtime Granby business. (Colorado Bureau of Investigation photo)

Law enforcement officers surrounded and crawled up on the immobile machine. Some had M-14 rifles at the ready. Deputy Roy Ybarra brandished a shotgun, the same one he had fired earlier at the machine. On top of the machine, moving debris aside, Lt. Walt Eldridge held his handgun at the ready.

The scene was bizarre. Gambles was completely destroyed. Pots and pans were scattered under the collapsed roof along with smashed up barbecue grills, cans of paint and gardening supplies and tools. Lounge chairs were smashed and twisted. Piles of bricks and mortar and shattered wooden trusses, splintered and ragged, towered among piles of bricks and mortar in the place that had once been a Granby landmark.

I saw all this while watching a Denver news channel at a friend's house in Hot Sulphur Springs. The police had warned me that the machine could be heading to my house. I had run home from my destroyed offices as fast as I could. I woke my sleeping and pregnant wife and our son and, in a panic, pushed them into our station wagon. From my house, where I could hear the reports of rifle fire only four blocks away, I sped out of town the back way, away from the dozer. I looked back at my house wondering if it would be the last time I'd see it intact.

Seeing the bulldozer-tank sitting in the wreckage at Gambles, although somehow a sad sight, filled me with relief. Only then did I know for sure that Heemeyer was not going to destroy my house. Only then did I know that my family was truly safe from the menace of that tank.

But my relief was followed by dread. I had a sinking feeling about the work that loomed ahead of me.

At least we were safe and alive.

29. Heemeyer Resurrected to the Sky

I arrived back in Granby at about 6 p.m., roughly an hour after the dozer stopped moving in the rubble at Gambles. My family was safely settled back at home. What I saw was best described by Mike Beasley, the director of the Colorado Department of Local Affairs. He had flown by helicopter into Granby from Denver with Colorado Governor Bill Owens.

He said it looked like a tornado had touched down on Granby's main street.

Equally as unbelievable at that point was the news from Undersheriff Glen Trainor that it appeared no one had been killed or even seriously injured during the rampage.

By then I had called family members and friends to reassure them that although the newspaper building was completely destroyed, I was OK. Many of them had seen glimpses of the rampage on TV news that evening.

That night, the mainstream media and the blogosphere were fascinated with the wild events that had taken place in Granby. Evening television news shows were broadcasting video clips of the marauding bulldozer. The world was falling under the spell of Heemeyer's act. He was already gaining a following. Images of the rampage were even broadcast in small villages in northern Italy, where my in-laws lived during the summer months. A fascination with this extreme act was taking hold already, not just in the U.S., but around the world.

Marv's MK Tank, the dozer-tank, the bulldozer, slowly but surely started to earn a new name: Killdozer. It would be difficult to say exactly when that term was first applied to Heemeyer's exploit, but it probably started on-line where media-savvy bloggers remembered an off-color, poorly produced 1974 TV movie called *Killdozer!* That awkwardly acted movie became something of a cult classic. It was about a D-9 Caterpillar bulldozer possessed by alien spirits that wreaked havoc all on its own, without human intervention. The name Killdozer had also been used by a hard-rock band in Wisconsin, playing off the name of the TV movie. Those were the origins of the term Killdozer. And that evening, after Marv's exploits became known, his machine took on a whole new identity.

This new identity for Heemeyer's dozer-tank reflected well the multi-faceted aspects of Heemeyer's accomplishment. It was at once something frightening and yet hard to believe. It was something that people across the country could see as funny and that could be mocked, yet the reality of its destructive power and potential for harm gave it added gravity. Maybe it didn't kill anyone, but it could have.

And it was, well, strange, and hard to believe, like science fiction itself.

The Killdozer had been sitting silent for only an hour, just about 50 yards from the *Sky-Hi News* building. Gambles was, essentially, just across the street from our offices. Police officials didn't know if the machine had been rigged to explode at some designated time after it stopped moving. They didn't know if there were booby traps concealed in the armor that would detonate if people tampered with the machine. They didn't know if Heemeyer was going to finish his heroic act by popping right out of a secret hatch with guns blazing. Even when the machine sat perfectly still, clearly disabled, it projected a menace that instilled fear in observers.

That evening, while the new image for Marv's machine began to take hold, I was back on the job, both as an editor and as a manager of a business that had been demolished. But fire officials and law enforcement would not let me get near the mostly flattened *Sky-Hi News* building.

So I couldn't go to look at our building. It was cordoned off. All I could see from about two blocks away was that the newspaper building was crushed. I remember being speechless and worried.

The Sky-Hi News building was a total loss. (Colorado Bureau of Investigation photo)

Fire department officials were concerned about letting anyone near the building since there was a good chance that the cinder block walls that remained standing could easily fall over, hurting or killing anyone in the area. There was also a danger of explosions from ruptured gas mains and severed electrical lines. This was despite the fact that utility officials had shut off gas and electricity to the damaged buildings.

The view down the highway to the west, toward our building, was revealing. My car had been pushed out into the highway so that it sat broadside to the normal east-west traffic flow. Another car sat next to it, poking diagonally out from the driveway next to our offices. Whole cinder blocks, broken bits of cinder blocks, shreds of wood and drywall chunks sat in the highway, all left there by the Killdozer just after it had left the *Sky-Hi News*.

Shell casings from sheriff's department weapons sat at random angles on the pavement. Over toward Gambles, Grand County Sheriff's Deputies armed with what looked like M-16 rifles crouched behind the wheels and steel sides of the county scraper that had been parked parallel to the highway to block the Killdozer in place. Firemen decked out in full bunker gear were working their way up U.S. Highway 40, checking for flames and sparks. It looked like a war zone.

During the standoff after the bulldozer stopped moving sheriff's deputies and SWAT team members from across the state assumed the worst could happen. Here, Deputy Jim Kraker, standing, and Deputy Jon Skelly prepare for the worst. A sniper from Summit County is prone near the two deputies. They were taking cover near the scraper that was used to block the exit of the dozer from the Gambles lot. (Sky-Hi News photo by Jean Landess)

That feeling was accentuated by what was happening on my side of the cordon. The parking lot in front of the 7-Eleven was the unofficial mustering place for SWAT teams, firemen and other law enforcement personnel. The SWAT teams, from Jefferson and Summit County, were garbed in black and were armed with automatic weapons and bulging clips of ammunition. The place bristled with firepower and nervous energy.

Then the helicopter arrived with Gov. Bill Owens on board. He stepped out, surrounded by aides, to view the scene. I photographed him as he promised aid and assistance for the town in its rebuilding efforts. He helicoptered out of the area after talking to local officials and some of the victims. The sun set in a slowly fading globe of orange, accentuated perhaps by the dust that lingered in the air. The wind did not blow that night.

It had been decided that everyone should proceed as if Heemeyer were still alive in the Killdozer. With that in mind, people were kept well behind the cordon and activity around the Killdozer was limited.

The next step would be to try to blast into the Killdozer to either kill or capture Heemeyer and to find out for good what was happening with this massive and deadly weapon. Officials still didn't know the extent to which Heemeyer had fortified the machine with armor and concrete.

Sheriff Rod Johnson was back in town. One of the first things he wanted done was to clear off the top of the Killdozer to see if there was a way inside. It appeared there was no hatch. Immediately the word spread, first in whispers, then in awe-filled exclamations, then in phone calls, e-mails and messages across the country.

Heemeyer had welded himself inside the cab of the Killdozer. He had set out on his destructive mission sealed for good inside his own tomb, his own self-made coffin of steel.

This elevated the intrigue and appeal of Heemeyer's rampage another notch. It seemed heroic. It seemed brave. It was inconceivable.

But it then forced the question in many people's minds: What had Granby done to Heemeyer to warrant this desperate and extreme act?

By then, knowing that the SWAT team planned to use explosives to breach the Killdozer, the cordon keeping people away was pushed even farther to the east, past the 7-Eleven and all the way to the intersection of Sixth Street and U.S. Highway 40. But the sheriff's deputies let me remain at the 7-Eleven.

The bomb expert with Jefferson County placed his first charge on the track of the Killdozer.

There was a countdown to the first detonation. A sharp blast pierced the night air. I crouched reflexively. Aside from the sound of the blast, it seemed nothing at all had happened. It was 9:39 p.m. The track was untouched. It was difficult, even, to tell where the explosive charge had been placed.

But the explosives technician was undaunted. He had another idea.

In the white neon light of the 7-Eleven, on the sidewalk in front, I watched the explosives expert build a shaped charge of plastic explosives that would be used on the Killdozer. On a sheet of plywood he rolled out chunks of a substance that looked like silly putty. He built this material in a rectangular shape about two feet wide and four feet long. This, he explained, would be placed on the side of the Killdozer's cab in the hope that it would penetrate the steel. It would be detonated from a distance several hundred feet away. If Heemeyer were still alive, the sheer force of this blast would kill him, regardless. The explosives expert worked patiently and carefully. I was afraid to sneeze. I stepped sideways away from him even though he assured me it was perfectly safe.

At that point all neighboring residences were evacuated. Windows were taped and covered with sheets of plywood in the vicinity and police carried out another careful search of the area to make sure people were not too close to the blast zone. Collateral damage from the explosion greatly concerned the officials at the scene. They were also concerned that if the machine had been booby trapped somehow, this detonation would probably set off those other explosives.

Uncertainty, tainted by fear, was once again the dominant sentiment. The Killdozer and Heemeyer still held sway. A loudspeaker was used to announce into the Killdozer that a high explosive was about to be detonated, just in case Heemeyer was alive inside. Was this a warning intended to convince him to exit the machine voluntarily, if he was still alive? Was it just a warning that he was about to be blasted into mush? No matter, they were going to let him know. I was ordered away from the 7-Eleven and was told to stand behind the cordon with most everyone else.

A little after 10 p.m., a second blast ripped through the night.

As Sheriff Johnson explains it: "He popped that baby off — we broke a lot of windows, by the way — and looked at that side of (the machine), and, didn't even (dent it)."

All that remained of the rectangular plastic explosive was a smudge-like grey perimeter on the steel, resembling exactly the shape of the charge I had watched the explosives expert build. No hole. Nothing.

The explosives expert, apparently, had no idea what he was up against. Heemeyer had built an extremely well-fortified tank. Little could be done to break the impressive armor casing.

One other blast was tried that night around the hinges that appeared to have been placed for a hatch around an air conditioning unit on top of the Killdozer. That blast succeeded in loosening the hinges but the hatch was so tightly placed the explosives still couldn't effectively breach the armor.

Finally, a cutting torch was used around the air conditioning unit on the top of the cab. At 1:28 a.m. on the morning of Saturday, June 5, a hole had been made in the armored shell of the Killdozer. It took 45 minutes to complete the cut, pull out the concrete and make a second cut.

In that long wait the rumors swirled and the speculation mounted. The Killdozer was invincible and impregnable. The police couldn't get in. Heemeyer had welded himself in. The sense of awe and fear, enhanced the image of Heemeyer in the crowd and community. This Killdozer was an astounding piece of work. Its creator was an ingenious and courageous man.

Still fearful of booby-traps and other bombs, police worked cautiously and slowly once the cab had been breached. They still weren't positive about whether Heemeyer was dead or alive, or just wounded. It was the safe way to go about this uncertain operation. Soon, after laboriously lifting away the steel and concrete, it was possible to shine a flashlight into the inscrutable, unyielding black of the cab's interior. A few wires and twists of copper tubing obstructed the view at the opening. More cutting and chopping made the hole larger and beyond, barely discernible in the cone of glowing smoke cast by a handheld flashlight, was the slumped figure of Marvin Heemeyer.

Leaning forward in the seat of the bulldozer, with his hands on his thighs, palms down, sat the man who had caused so much damage in the town of Granby. A small black hole in the upper back of his skull marked the exit wound of the shot from the .357-caliber hand gun that now lay between Heemeyer's feet. His hair was cut short, military style. He had fired into the roof of his mouth. Blood had trickled out of his right ear. The front of his blue, Hawaiian style print shirt, which he wore over a blue, long-sleeved T-shirt, had a large brown stain covering the front, a result of hemorrhaging from the gunshot. A gush of blood from his nose had coagulated in place. Heemeyer was dead.

Yet once a member of the extraction team was able to look inside the cab, he found something unexpected. The hatch hadn't been welded in at all. Rather, it was such a tight-fitting hatch that the welding seam was invisible from the outside. Examining the hatch from the inside, while leaning in through the small air-conditioner hole cut by the torch, they could see that Heemeyer had rigged two large latch springs inside the hatch so it could be pushed open with relative ease. Lifting the hatch from the outside would have been nearly impossible, but he wasn't welded in. He could have exited the shell if he had wanted.

One extraction team member wormed his way into the cab through the air conditioning unit opening. He easily opened the hatch.

Fear and caution were still the operating guidelines that night and it was decided that not much more should be done until Grand County Coroner Dave Schoenfeld arrived at the scene. He was scheduled to arrive later that morning, when there was daylight. Until then, a vigil of sorts would be maintained. Police would keep an eye on the Killdozer, just in case, and a growing number of locals and other onlookers began to gather, most on the bluff just north of the Killdozer that provided a good view of the machine. Bright spotlights illuminated the hulking machine, casting it in an eerie glow, like a museum display or the center of a circus ring. Dust from the easily disturbed debris and thick, meandering strands of smoke from the cutting torch lingered in the air.

After a few hours of sleep, I awoke at 6 a.m. and headed back into town. It was a clear Colorado day with a stunning blue sky. There wasn't a cloud to be seen. The air was cool. After interviews with television stations near the damaged Town Hall, with a smashed-in wall as a backdrop, I returned to the Killdozer.

It was clear to me then that the story of the rampage was taking shape in the eyes of the media. Heemeyer had had numerous disputes with the town over zoning issues and had not gotten his way. A possible insinuation of this line of reasoning was that he had been "pushed" to this extreme action because of the disputes. That was the easy-to-grasp and most sensible story line. But I was already beginning to have different fears about this story and how it could be framed to appear that Heemeyer was a sort of folk hero who had gone to extreme measures to get back at government, society, the media and the corrupt world of the establishment.

An air of apprehension still lingered near the hulking machine. The inspection inside the cab, from the hole cut into the top and the hatch, didn't reveal any obvious signs of rigged explosives, although explosives experts worried about the steel, pressurized tank inside the cab. What looked like a tank used to charge an acetylene torch turned out to be compressed air.

The inspection of the cab from the hatch did reveal that there were three monitors placed in the front of the cab for remote viewing of activities outside the cab. Well-labeled ammunition boxes, nearly full, were placed strategically near the corresponding weapons. Clips had been carefully loaded and placed in the boxes. Empty Slim Fast containers littered the floor and two hand-held radios used to scan police radio frequencies sat at awkward angles near Heemeyer's feet. Switches were labeled. The key sat in the ignition.

Once the cab of the bulldozer-tank was breached, investigators found a complex and ingenious system devised by Heemeyer to allow him to see what was happening outside the completely enclosed cab. (Sky-Hi News photo by Jean Landess)

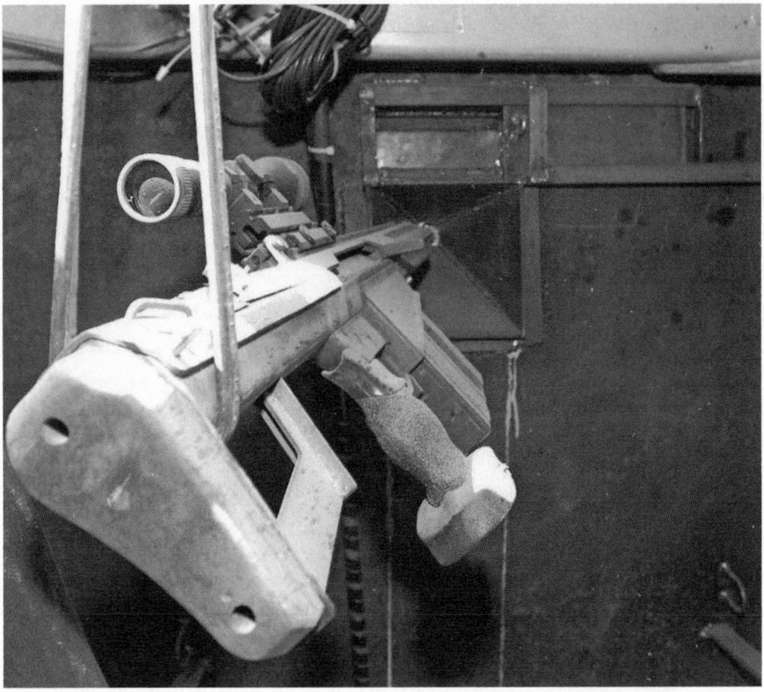

Inside the cab of the Killdozer, Heemeyer installed his .50-caliber rifle on a sling ready to fire. (Photo by the CBI)

Grand County Coroner Dave Schoenfeld arrived to confirm that Heemeyer was dead. Then the difficult task of extracting the body began. Using the help of Paul MacDonald's Sky Crane, the corpse was lifted gingerly through the hatch. EMS technicians and law enforcement officers guided the body upward in an upright position so that it would fit through the small opening in the top of the cab, as MacDonald, also a member of the Granby Fire Department, maneuvered carefully.

The top of the Killdozer's shell was shielded from public view by other firefighters and emergency medical services personnel who held up plastic tarps. TV stations representing the major U.S. networks had crews stationed around the Killdozer, filming the extraction. Photographers from the Denver newspapers were taking photos of the scene. Commentators intoned into their microphones. The world, at that point, was watching. Once out of the hole, Heemeyer's body was wrapped and then zipped into a blue body bag.

I was one of the many news photographers who captured the moment when the body of Marv Heemeyer was levitated high above the scene of his final act of destruction, high above the town he despised, and high above his MK Tank, the newly christened Killdozer. One image of that eerie scene ran in our newspaper, the *Sky-Hi News*. It showed the arm of the crane angled high into the clear blue Colorado sky with a taut cable jutting down to the earth. At the end of the cable was a stretcher upon which Heemeyer's body had been placed.

That image, even though it earned us at least one negative letter to the editor, summed up the moment. Here was proof that Heemeyer was dead. Proof for all to see. And here he was, being lifted solitary into the sky, as if he were an offering to the Gods of heroism, hate, anger, politics, destruction, revenge and contradiction. And here he was, the sad remains of a tortured and anguished man who couldn't reconcile his seemingly happy life to his predicament. It was the body of a man who relished and reviled in the designs of his vindication; yet it was the body of a man well-liked by many for his friendliness and acts of kindness. For victims of the rampage, law enforcement officers and curious onlookers, their faces looking up blank and white to the sky, it was blunt testimony.

The body was then placed in a waiting ambulance and transferred to the mortuary. No lights flashed on the slow-moving emergency vehicle.

There was no triumph. There were no smiles. Except for the whine of the crane and its rumbling engine, that moment was quiet. There was no air of victory. But now, for certain, the Killdozer's rampage was over.

Heemeyer's body was lifted away from the Killdozer on a clear Saturday morning, with Byers Peak and snow-covered peaks glistening in the distance. A similar yet more graphic photo, showing parts of Heemeyer's torso, ran in the prominent Denver daily newspaper *The Denver Post*. Those images prompted some complaints from readers of both papers. (Sky-Hi News photo)

III: The Second Rampage

30. On the Wrong Side of the Story

"You should be proud of yourself."

It was less than 24 hours after the attack. Will Bublitz, the police reporter for our papers, slapped me on the back. I gave him a tired look. It was a clear-blue-sky Saturday morning and I could see the snow-capped Indian Peaks marking the Continental Divide to the east. How I wished at that moment that I could have been at the top of one of those peaks. Here in town, I could see down Granby's main street.

The *Sky-Hi News* offices were in ruins. The coroner and the county emergency medical crew had just driven Heemeyer's body off to the morgue. I watched helplessly as Casey and Rhonda Farrell, the owners of the Gambles store that had been demolished by the Killdozer, hugged in quiet sadness in the middle of U.S. Highway 40 in front of their ruined business. I told them I was sorry. I turned back to Will.

"Why should I be so proud?"

"Well, you made the list twice."

Bublitz was already working on the rampage story.

"What list?" I asked.

"Marv's list. Marv had lists that he left. They found them at the shed. In his house."

"Well, that'll make the story more interesting. Can you get the lists?"

"Probably. He left more. He left some sort of manifesto up there too, in the shed. The cops have it now. I guess he sort of explains himself. Says you and the town caused it. Tonya (Tonya Bina, the

Grand Lake reporter for the newspaper) says half of Grand Lake believes it."

Even though Heemeyer had left behind some notes in the shed explaining himself, it was the lists found by the police that got the most attention. The lists had no explanations attached — no headings to give a hint about their meaning.

The first list had local names:

Randy Schmuck
Steph Plater
Gus Harris
Ted Kellner
KC Farrell
Thompsons
Doucette
Bud Wilson
Douceff (sic) Littler
Doucheff other
Wang/Hale
Brower Pat

The second list was more like a compendium of potential targets, although names were mixed in too:

Concrete plant
Electricity
Main Street
Public Buildings
Thompsons
Catholic Church
Mntn Parks Elec
Thompson Bros
Doucheff (sic) etc
Patruck Brower (sic)
KC Ferrell
Gus Harris
(Undecipherable word)
Randy Schmuck
Josh Peterson
Kellner

Lockhart
Doucette / Dietz

They were just lists, compilations prepared by Heemeyer that were open to a wide range of interpretations. And already, people started to take sides.

Tonya Bina was our Grand Lake reporter and she had been interviewing friends and acquaintances of Heemeyer in Grand Lake in an effort to build a story about how people in Grand Lake felt about their neighbor and fellow citizen.

But it wasn't exactly going as I had expected or hoped. Already I was beginning to feel like the victim who was being attacked and assailed for being on the wrong side of the now-dead Marvin Heemeyer. Could this really be?

Orange cordon tape was draped across U.S. Highway 40. Yellow evidence tags with black numbers on them, like the flowers of weeds, decorated the highway in odd spots where spent shell casings littered the road. I wondered about the lists and what Marv had left behind. This would begin the process of learning Heemeyer's narrative about why he carried out the rampage. We would start to understand Marv.

But I couldn't help but stand there in the midst of ruin and sorrow and wonder how I could possibly have angered Heemeyer so much.

I felt anxious all over again. I had that sinking feeling again that I was not going to be the hero of this narrative.

Granby Mayor Ted Wang, who had presided over many of the Heemeyer hearings of the past five years as interim town manager, board trustee and town mayor, set up an improvised press conference with the crumpled town hall as a dramatic backdrop. As I ambled away from my interviews I looked over at the throng of microphone- and notebook-wielding journalists huddled around Wang. I walked back over to listen in. With cameras and microphones present, he was asked about his impression of Marv Heemeyer. Wang said Heemeyer was an "unpleasant man, full of bluster and rage." He added: "I'm trying to be politically correct, but this guy was a nasty son of a bitch . . . He had the maturity level of a 5-year-old."

Heemeyer's body was now in the morgue in Hot Sulphur Springs and the physical recuperation for the community was already underway while the virtual rampage raged with increasing intensity in the media world.

For me and my staff, I knew we had to do a good job of covering the rampage so as to clear the air of rumors that had started. Yet I also had to figure out how I was going to publish our newspapers and save what was left in our destroyed building. We would begin covering our own, and the town's, resurrection.

That Saturday morning police officers weren't allowing me near the newspaper building, mainly for safety reasons. Most of Granby's main street, in fact, was still closed. Traffic was being routed around town on a dirt road that passed south of town near the railroad tracks. By 11 a.m. I was finally allowed to walk near the damaged structure but was told not to enter the building as the remaining upright walls were at risk of tumbling over. I got as close as possible and looked in to see what could be saved. My office was completely crushed and I gave up hope of saving my computer, laptop or camera. File cabinets in my office looked like crumpled, twisted beer cans.

The bookkeeping computer containing our financial records looked like it was smashed under the splintered credenza. The main server computer containing all our ads, stories and layouts appeared to be in pretty good shape but I was worried about a broken water line nearby. That water was casting a rainbow-colored, fine spray over bound back editions of the *Sky-Hi News*, issues dating back to when the paper was founded in 1945. I panicked over the thought of those ruined back editions and pleaded with the town to turn off the water to the building, which it did later that day.

While the front of the structure where our news, production and administrative offices were located was destroyed, the press room in the back half of the building had fared much better. The press was dented but in good shape even though the raised ceiling had collapsed on it. The 40 rolls (20 tons) of newsprint stored in the press room were in good shape.

I knew we could probably save the press and the newsprint, but it wouldn't be easy. And we had to do so before high winds, rain or passing trains destabilized the cinder block walls to the point where they'd cave in onto the press and the paper. I could actually see the walls vibrate when trains passed only 150 feet to the south of the building. And when the wind blew, cracks in the wall widened, pieces of masonry tumbled to the ground. It was a precarious situation. We were in a race against the clock. I prayed for dry and windless days.

Others in Granby were frantically working to stay in business. Joe, Cody and Susie Docheff planned their recovery right away, despite the fact that the covered area of the batch plant was ruined and a severe hazard. Mountain Parks Electric cordoned off the damaged parts of its building and employees were working away that Saturday morning in an effort to continue providing service. Not one second of electric power had been lost as a result of the rampage. George Davis at Maple Street Builders was already busy at work restoring his crushed building where Heemeyer had pushed a truck right into his offices. The truck may have been a complete loss, but the offices weren't.

Our little drama that surrounded getting back on our feet was repeated in its own way at most of the businesses that had been attacked by Heemeyer. The Docheffs were extremely resourceful in getting back up and running, but they had a year or two of rebuilding ahead of them. The town had to replace a town hall and the library district had a library to replace. These dramas would unfold in the coming year or two. The Thompsons had a home and shop to rebuild and a garage to repair. Mountain Parks Electric had to decide what to do with its crushed façade and damaged garages. Liberty Savings Bank had a crushed west entrance.

And Casey and Rhonda at Gambles general store didn't know what they were going to do.

With the help of our hardworking staff, we managed to get newspapers out that week after the rampage. The papers were full of news about the event. But by far the most controversial and interesting aspect of the coverage that week, and for years to come, centered on assertions about Marvin Heemeyer. His intent, his reasons for his rampage and his character were all put under the spotlight of our news coverage. And the fight over his image as a hero, and whether he was right or wrong, was well on its way.

The Town of Granby scheduled meetings Saturday morning and convened an emergency session of the board. For Granby Town Manager Tom Hale, financial administrator Sharon Spurlin, and Granby Town Clerk Deb Hess, this was a period of frantic work over long hours. They quickly found temporary offices, ordered furniture and were moving full speed ahead with getting the town back to normal. The town staff struggled to make sure they had an office with its doors open for the citizens Monday morning, June 7. This was no small task. Recreation Director Julie Martin, Cindy Seader, Spurlin and Hess did whatever was necessary to be ready. Some town work was even done on people's personal computers, in their homes, just to make sure the process moved forward. Spurlin did payroll for the town staff on her personal computer at her house.

Town crews were also out working overtime to make certain that roads were usable, utilities operating and, in general, people could work and live in the town of Granby immediately after the rampage.

The town hall and the library, in the same building, were completely destroyed and were a safety hazard. No one was allowed in until engineers could assess the damage. Liberty Savings Bank assessed the damage and realized the bank could be open Monday, despite the gaping hole by the western doorway. Thompson and Sons Excavation could do their work without their garage and house. They were hard at work, helping clean up the mess created by Heemeyer in town, as early as Sunday morning. Xcel Energy could do its work without offices and minus a truck.

But the saddest and most unfortunate situation centered on what Heemeyer had done to the Gambles general store. Since it was a retail operation with its inventory located right where Heemeyer had bulldozed, it wasn't so easy for Casey and Rhonda Farrell to get back in business. The store and their inventory were completely ruined. They couldn't go elsewhere and find a good retail location. And even if they could, what would they put in it?

Bill Johnson, the owner of the newspapers and owner of the real estate in which the newspaper offices had been housed, arrived on the scene Saturday afternoon from Wisconsin. Although he had a home in Grand Lake, he had been out of town when the rampage started.

I already had a plan in mind for the operation of the newspaper business. We would relocate all of our operations, except for printing, to our small office in Winter Park, where we housed the *Winter Park Manifest* editorial and sales offices. We had the Internet connections to make it work there although we'd be hard-pressed for adequate space.

I had already placed an emergency phone call to Intermountain Color, a web press printing company in Denver, to see if they could make room for printing our papers five days a week.

Many other papers in the region had called to offer helping hands with computers and printing.

Later that afternoon, after many of the firemen and policemen were concentrating on moving the Killdozer out of the rubble at Gambles, I decided to take a risk. Five-thousand copies of our Monday, June 7 *Daily Tribune*s were sitting neatly stacked by the back door of the press room, ready for delivery. We had printed them Friday afternoon only minutes before the rampage began.

Head Pressman Mike Garcia, *Middle Park Times* Editor Larry Banman and I all agreed we should take the risk of entering the building to grab the newspapers so they could be distributed. Distributed, that is, without any news of the rampage. I tested the back door, watching for any sign the wall might tumble, and we scrambled in, grabbed the bundles, and scurried out, looking back over our heads as if we expected the building to fall. It didn't.

That foolish little act of derring-do allowed us to say truthfully that we never missed one edition of our papers because of the rampage. That was our little Pyrrhic victory in the face of near-total destruction by Heemeyer.

31. Salvaging Our Businesses, Salvaging Marv's Reputation

On Sunday morning, the second Killdozer rampage was taking off with full steam in the Denver newspapers. Despite the death of President Ronald Reagan on Saturday, June 5, the Colorado papers still treated the rampage prominently. But in the rest of the nation, our story had already vanished off the front page.

But reactions to the coverage and to the event in general were already coming my way.

"What your damn mayor said about Marv just isn't right," one angry Grand Lake merchant said to me Sunday afternoon.

He was referring to Wang's comments that Heemeyer was an "unpleasant man" and a "nasty son of a bitch." Those comments appeared in a *Denver Post* story Sunday morning, the result of the frantic interview that took place Saturday.

When I read that quote in the *Post* that day (in a story that was picked up by the *AP* wire and sent around the country, if not the world) I was dismayed, as were many other people closely connected to the rampage, both victims and bystanders.

While at that moment I wasn't exactly feeling love and happiness when I thought of Marv, I was feeling some pity for the man. It felt to me that maligning the suicidal Heemeyer, who was freshly dead, was sort of like kicking someone when he was already down. This was doubly unfortunate since one of the big pro-Heemeyer beliefs already floating around was that the town had *already* kicked him when he was down, where he appeared to lose at every turn. It was like piling on.

Wang's comment also reinforced an idea that Heemeyer had touted, which was that the town and the community had been nasty toward him and out to get him. He claimed it was something personal against him — a conspiracy against "newcomers." The mayor's comments were living proof of Heemeyer's worst suspicions.

I know that Wang's comment inflamed the tone and vehemence of the people who were inclined to defend Marv, intensifying the pro-Heemeyer point of view with a sort of reactionary anger. It also put Heemeyer on an even higher pedestal than before, making him look like the heroic martyr he wanted to portray. Wang had lashed out at Heemeyer, and quickly Marv's friends and allies — and many people across the country who never knew Heemeyer but were inclined to rally around his plight — lashed out in return, in letters to the editor and on the Internet.

Not only that, a sort of regional and in some cases national fascination with the Killdozer itself, aside from Heemeyer's motives and persona, had been gaining traction.

Stories in the *Denver Post* and *Rocky Mountain News* Sunday got across people's comments that he was a good guy and a bad guy, fueling the tension about the Killdozer rampage.

Bonnie Brown of Grand Lake waxed on about how Marv was a Teddy Bear of a man who would lash out at people only if he himself had been threatened.

"He's a real lovable, soft, sweet guy. I didn't think he would hurt them intentionally — but that he would go after their businesses and hurt them financially, the way he thinks they hurt him," Brown told the *Rocky Mountain News.*

There was Marv's brother, interviewed in the *Denver Post*, who referred to Marv as a nice guy who was almost perfect. In his eyes Marv was a good ol' country boy who grew up on the farm and held a school track record.

But articles also hit on the negative side.

Heemeyer could be menacing to people, particularly when it came to business dealings. Many say he was easy-going and fair at his muffler shop. But two days after the rampage, in the Sunday *Denver Post*, Christie Baker of Granby was paraphrased as saying she and her husband had a run-in with Heemeyer.

She told the *Denver Post* that Heemeyer threatened her husband's life over a muffler. She said she and her husband, Doug, had taken a truck to Heemeyer's shop and Marv had installed the wrong type of muffler. They refused to pay, and Christie Baker said they soon heard about Heemeyer's threat. Through an intermediary they paid the $124 in cash to Heemeyer.

Or there's the story of Cliff Eudy, a former business partner of Heemeyer in the late 1970s, as reported in the *Rocky Mountain News* the Sunday after the rampage. They ran Scotty Mufflers before the two had a falling out in 1980, when they fell into debt to a supplier.

Eudy said he and Heemeyer agreed between themselves to raise money to pay off the debt. Eudy borrowed $10,000 from his ex-wife's family and put it in a bank. Heemeyer didn't contribute his share, Eudy says, and tried to withdraw money from Eudy's account.

"I told him that's not fair to me," Eudy said to the newspaper. "We sat down and talked for three or four weeks, and I thought by talking to him I thought I had an understanding that we could do things together."

But it didn't work out and they went their separate ways. Heemeyer took over a shop on South Broadway in Englewood and renamed it the Mid-State Muffler Shop, while Eudy took control of a shop on West Colfax. They got rid of their two other muffler shops in Commerce City and East Colfax Avenue because they were losing money.

Eudy told the *News* that he was later forced to go into bankruptcy. Heemeyer, he said, sold his muffler shop on South Broadway and opened up a new one in Boulder. Eudy didn't see or hear from Heemeyer much afterward. While Eudy said he didn't think Heemeyer had a short temper, he thought Heemeyer was a shady businessman.

"He was a very friendly personable type of guy until you really got involved with him," Eudy said. "In my mind and in my opinion, he's a backstabber. He was real nice when he could get what he could out of you. When he got to the point where he couldn't get what he could out of you, he would get nasty."

Ron Brynoff of Granby, who knew Heemeyer on a friendly basis through the muffler shop and a snowmobiling trip together, told his story about Heemeyer. One day Brynoff saw that Heemeyer was selling a Polaris 1992 wide track snowmobile. Brynoff bought it for $1200. He put oil in the machine, took it out for a run and after one mile the engine blew because the transmission had a leak. He found a crack in the case after taking it apart. He speculated that somehow water had gotten into the transmission case, causing it to crack in cold temperatures.

He went back to Heemeyer, told him about the problem and offered to return the sled if Heemeyer would give him back $1100.

"I thought he'd try to be nice and work with me on it," Brynoff says, letting Heemeyer keep $100 and the sled.

"Heemeyer simply said 'Nope. That was sold as is.' He wouldn't work with me at all. I never talked to him again."

Because the Killdozer rampage wasn't front page national and international news for long due to President Reagan's death, Americans and the world had gotten just a taste of the Heemeyer rampage in Granby. Only the bare essentials of the story were left embedded in the mind of the public — that a man had gone nuts in a bulldozer because the town had done him wrong. The world wasn't given a chance to hear and see the rest of the story. It was just a sensational blip.

While Heemeyer's victims — victims like me — struggled to get our businesses and lives together, a new virtual rampage began. With just the sparsest notion of what had transpired in Granby on June 4, 2004 and before, people began to run with the romantic version of the story. This virtual Killdozer rampage would continue long after the Killdozer itself had stalled in the rubble at Gambles. I remember feeling confounded and stupefied, really, over the way Heemeyer was being mythologized in this way after the damage he had just inflicted on our community.

32. The Ascent of Marv as Victimized Hero

The local Lutheran minister planned a *Healing in the Park* event for Monday afternoon, three days after the rampage. All the community, and especially the victims, were invited to attend. It was intended to be a unifying and cleansing event that would present a show of solidarity in the town after the rampage. I wouldn't be able to attend because I had a rush of news to cover and I was overwhelmed by the logistical details of getting back into business.

But I heard about what happened during the event. It sent tremors of worry and doubt through my whole being.

Polhamus Park sits a block off Granby's main street just west of the town hall and post office. It has tennis courts, a large grassy field, a gazebo I had helped to build with the local Rotary Club, and an old log church where the recently deceased Mayor Dick Thompson had been married 40 years before the church had been relocated to the town park. One basketball court and a frequently vandalized set of bathrooms made the town complete along with the performance shell that faces out to the large field.

But that day, what set the park off more than the green grass and old fashioned church was the fact that one narrow street — Zero Street — separated the park from the crumpled Town Hall. As people showed up to attend the Healing in the Park, most of them took the time to wander over to the chain link fence surrounding the Town Hall and peer in at the caved-in brick walls, the twisted playground equipment behind the building and churned up lawn, furrowed by the heavy treads of the Killdozer. It reminded the attendees of why the town needed some healing.

The concrete performance shell, made with materials and labor donated to the town by Cody Docheff and his family 15 years prior, sat perched on a grass-covered knoll. A total of 200 people stood in front of the shell where several ministers were solemnly gathered in a row along the back wall. At the agreed-upon time they all bowed their heads in prayer and a moment of silence. Aside from a few cries from babies and impatient murmurings of children, a somber silence fell over the gathering.

Improvised prayers tailored to the town's disaster were muttered. They were along the lines of how the gathering showed solidarity, hope and healing for the community, and especially for the victims. There were the predictable comments about how the community would triumph over adversity. There were many comments about the importance of healing and community spirit.

Casey Farrell, who was attending the event with his wife Rhonda, also addressed the crowd, although reluctantly. He thanked the people for their support. He looked worried. He had become, that day, not the cheerful and helpful shop owner anxious to lend a helping hand, as so many people knew him, but a troubled and worried businessman and civic leader who had served on the school board and the town board. He quickly left the platform as if he didn't want to be cajoled into saying much more.

A call for more comments got an unintended response. A man with dark hair and a mustache strode through the crowd and took the stage.

He shouted loudly that Marvin Heemeyer was a hero and that the town had gotten what it deserved. He said something along the lines of the town being corrupt and that "there would be more," and "it's happening again."

He loudly shouted that the town had taken his family's land and that the government was a bunch of liars.

The crowd was stunned. There were reports of a few boos from the back of the crowd. But mostly, people said it was just awkward. The man, Roque Morales, 64, of Granby and Denver, was hurriedly escorted off the stage.

Morales came from a well-known family in Granby who had managed to successfully continue as the only clan farming the land north of town. His parents had worked the old lettuce fields, creating a farming dynasty that was now run by his brother Joe. Roque (known as Rockie) had returned to the county and the Denver area after serving in the military and Vietnam. He had a range of real estate investments and one was a piece of land his mother owned near a new town subdivision and park. Roque had claimed in meetings that the town had deliberately "stolen" a portion of his mother's land in that subdivision process. He also was involved in land disputes in Denver and Winter Park. He had insisted many times in public meetings that the town and "the government" were out to steal his family's land, despite the county claims of the town attorney and its surveyors.

The next day, after the *Healing in the Park*, he stormed over to the house of Jo Moore in Granby and insisted to her that Heemeyer was a hero and that the town was stealing from him. She disagreed.

He even went so far as to call the office of the attorney general in Denver and rave that what Heemeyer did "was going to happen again." The chief deputy of the office of the Attorney General in Denver, Don Quick, forwarded an e-mail reporting the rant of Morales to Grand County authorities.

When I learned there had been rumors of "it happening again," it sparked real fear in me, the town and others.

Roque, it seemed, was part of a growing chorus in the public coming to the defense of Heemeyer and praising him as a hero. And the letters to the editor were pouring in, many in defense of Heemeyer, many attacking our newspaper and the town.

But there was another sort of healing taking place. Sharon Brenner, director of the Granby Chamber of Commerce, had formed a board and started the Granby Community Relief Fund. The fund managed to raise money from across the county and the state, bringing in close to $1 million in both cash and in-kind donations. There were small contributions from lemonade and bake sales and large contributions from state emergency relief funds, the Winter Park Resort, Colorado towns and others.

All the money was redistributed back to the victims on an as-needed basis. This fund was a big help for those whose insurance was lacking and for innocent bystanders who lost property such as cars and even jobs because of the rampage. This sort of healing was welcomed and appreciated and it really did show solidarity across the county and region for Granby.

With the expressions of sentiment that somehow Heemeyer must have been justified, and that the town and the community were at fault, many people were indirectly putting the blame for the rampage squarely on the shoulders of the town and its citizens. The community was also subjected to ridicule because of the bizarre nature of the rampage itself. So the concrete way in which people and communities reached out to help was immensely reassuring to the victims.

A letter to the editor in the June 10 *Sky-Hi News* by Noelle Pineau of La Quinta, California, came to Heemeyer's defense. It was one of several. I was hearing more and more, both from friends and from strangers, that Heemeyer was being hailed as a hero. These comments were discouraging. But I was firm in my resolve to get all the points of view out in front of the public.

She states she read about the incident on the Internet. "How could you and everyone else concerned in Granby let that happen?" She questions why Heemeyer never got his way, agreeing that no one would want a concrete plant's "eyesore" and "stink" right next to their building. "Instead of working to find a compromise as the city should have, he was let down, forced to endure this awful nuisance and ultimately lost his business."

She states that from what she read Mr. Heemeyer "did not seem like a vicious man: he had no record of past aggressions, during the rampage he was careful not to hurt anybody, only their property. It also appears that he was a very ingenious and skillful man to have been able to design and build his makeshift tank, and it seems to me the community has lost a valuable member . . . Now that you drove that poor, lonely 52-year-old man to despair and ultimately death, humiliating and dragging him down a little bit more every day, are you happy? For whatever damage he has caused to property, ultimately you are all alive, and he is dead. You have finally won. Your pride must be satisfied. What about your conscience? Shame on you, Granby city."

A page-one story by Tonya Bina ran that week. She interviewed people in Grand Lake about Marv and most people came out saying he was a good guy who must have been "wronged" by the town of Granby.

Grand Lake Mayor Judy Burke, in Bina's *Sky-Hi News* story, continued with the notion that Heemeyer wasn't out to hurt people. Burke is quoted as saying: "I always thought he was OK. Think about somebody so alone, with no one to talk to to the point he had to do something like this. But he didn't plan to hurt anyone. He had it planned so everyone saw him coming and could get out of the way in time. The only one he ended up hurting, besides financially, was himself."

This was not what I was expecting, especially from a civic leader who could have easily been the victim of such a rampage. People were saying that he hadn't intended to hurt anyone, that perhaps his actions were justified and that he was just a "Gentle giant," as one fellow snowmobiler said to Bina.

We wrote stories summing up the nature of Heemeyer's tiffs with the town and the newspaper in the past, stating that in general Heemeyer seldom agreed with the newspaper or the town on a variety of issues, many of them stretching back to well before the concrete batch plant fight. Retired columnist Cece Krewson, who had covered the gambling fights in Grand Lake 11 years prior, remembered in a guest column he had sent from Pennsylvania how Heemeyer had accosted and threatened him during the seemingly ancient gambling debate.

We re-capped all the old debates about the batch plant and the water and sewer hook-ups. We painted a picture of a town and community that were reluctantly at odds with Heemeyer and that feared him far more than it conspired in any way against him.

33. Setting the Record Straight, to no Avail

I took a photo of Cody Docheff crouched in the bucket of his front-end loader. He's pointing at one of the nine holes in the bucket where rounds fired by Heemeyer pierced the thick steel, showing discs of daylight in a random pattern. I was amazed that the rounds could have passed through such a thick layer of steel. Heemeyer had used armor-piercing ammunition. The photo ran above a story that addressed the questions raised by many people about Heemeyer's violent intent. Two weeks after it all, many people thought Heemeyer had "good intentions" and didn't want to hurt anyone. He just wanted to damage property.

A web page called "No B.S. News and Commentary" by Russell S. Bingman called mainstream media outlets "lying liars" in their coverage of the rampage and it made this blatantly false claim: "Certain facts remain indisputable: No weapons or guns have been produced, least of all any kind of a .50-caliber weapon, and no one was hurt or injured during the 2 to 3 hour melee, save for Marvin Heemeyer." He goes on to suggest that police shot Heemeyer and claimed it was a suicide. He says Heemeyer wasn't out to hurt anyone. Rather, he was a hero of the common man, out to send a message to meddlesome government and back-stabbing small-town society.

But the fact is that there was a .50-caliber weapon, as well as two other rifles and handguns. No one was injured, that's true. But Heemeyer was not shot by law enforcement officials. He did shoot at people.

Heemeyer fired anywhere from 9 to 11 times at Cody Docheff during the battle at the batch plant. (Photo by the author)

Comments in Denver newspapers, on a variety of Internet sites and in letters and comments in the *Sky-Hi News* all stated that Heemeyer hadn't intended to hurt people during his rampage. They contended he had set out only to damage property, thus creating an out-of-control myth machine about the rampage.

Not all the letters and phone calls I received followed this line of reasoning in defense of Heemeyer. In fact, the majority of comments assailed Heemeyer's actions. But a vocal minority was rushing to his defense.

A rare press release from the Grand County Sheriff's Department proclaimed: "A significant amount of information has been circulating regarding what many people believe was Mr. Heemeyer's lack of intent to harm anyone during this incident. Statements of both witnesses and the physical evidence recovered contradict that belief."

My column that week summed it up by stating that the evidence clearly demonstrated that, at the least, Heemeyer didn't care if he killed people during the rampage.

One of the charges that would have been filed against Heemeyer, had he lived, would have been attempted second degree murder. The district attorney also, apparently, agreed that Heemeyer harbored violent intent against human life.

At that time, it was clear that Heemeyer might have succeeded at killing people and causing a great deal more damage if the design of his Killdozer had allowed clearer lines of fire from the weapons he had installed. The Colorado Bureau of Investigation and local investigators had been crawling all over the massive machine, stored in Fraser, looking for added information about the event.

When I was given a tour of the dozer that week it was pointed out that there were obvious marks where Heemeyer's own rounds had slammed into his own armor. I saw and touched the ragged holes and crude indentations that the .50-caliber rifle made in the Killdozer's armor. The evidence shows that when he fired at the propane tanks, the armor on the ripper blocked and deflected his shots. What if the armor hadn't blocked those shots? The video footage of the shooting at the propane tanks clearly shows Heemeyer trying to position the Killdozer for a better angle at the tanks.

Leo Piechocki, the investigator for the Grand County Sheriff's Department who was in the mid-point of preparing his final report on the rampage, harbored no doubt about Heemeyer's intentions. At the propane plant, Piechocki told me flaws in Heemeyer's design helped save lives.

"He was shooting his own armor, which was a very lucky thing," he said, standing by the massive dozer. "If it wasn't for that one design flaw, he would have been hitting the propane tanks. And there would have been a whole different ending to this thing."

"I'm convinced he didn't care if he killed anyone," Piechocki said. "I'm convinced he would have been happy if he had killed people. Obviously, he would have been happy if he'd killed Docheff. He wouldn't have cared if he killed a cop. And by attempting to blow up the propane tanks, to me that means he intended to take as many people who were around him out. So, the bleeding hearts that say he planned it so he wouldn't hurt anybody, that's BS."

In general, the design of the firing ports and viewing ports didn't allow for direct aiming of the weapons. What if he had been able aim clearly? And because the Killdozer was so tall and the firing ports were so high, with armor plating extending out a fair distance below the weapons, it was difficult, if not impossible, for rounds to go low enough to hit pedestrians close to the Killdozer. Corporal Dave Batura and Sgt. Rich Garner might have been killed on the spot at the concrete plant had Heemeyer been able to shoot lower.

Did the rounds go over their heads because he aimed over their heads? Did they pass over their heads because Heemeyer couldn't shoot any lower? Or did they go high because the rounds bounced off armor on the tank that blocked the straight trajectory at Batura and Garner? We'll probably never know the answers to those questions. But it's clear he fired in their direction.

Batura, in assessing Heemeyer's intentions, takes an almost philosophical, detached point of view. This is despite the fact that he was an apparent target of Heemeyer's.

"My reaction is, A, he was armed," Batura says. "B, he fired the rounds, no matter where they went, or what their intention was. C, he did it in the afternoon, on a Friday afternoon. Which if you're trying to do something at 2:30 or 3 o'clock business . . . I mean if he had gone out on a Sunday morning at 2 a.m. unarmed, and just started taking buildings down, I would have said maybe he wasn't trying to (hurt anyone). But I mean he's going . . . He went for Thelma's house, the newspaper, the town hall. I mean, if we hadn't gotten those kids out of the library . . ."

Then there's the question of the .223 Ruger semi-automatic rifle that was projecting out of the right side of the tank. Its barrel was bent early in the rampage. Sheriff Rod Johnson said there was one spent round in the .223, suggesting that Heemeyer tried to fire the weapon but realized the barrel was bent, blocking the rounds.

What if that barrel hadn't been bent?

I interviewed the sheriff about it all that week. Had Heemeyer deliberately tried to avoid hurting people or had he just missed? We looked at photos and reviewed the videos.

Sheriff Johnson said there were other problems with the tank's design that hindered firing the weapons effectively. The large plate of steel in front of the tank that covered the engine in front of the firing port for the .308 rifle created a natural catchment area for debris to gather. After the Mountain Park Concrete rampage and the Mountain Parks Electric incident, concrete blocks and other materials settled on that deck, blocking a clear line of fire for the .308.

Heemeyer could have welded a piece of protective steel above the firing port for the .223 to protect it, but he didn't. And the steel on the ripper on the back of the Killdozer severely limited the effectiveness of the .50-caliber.

"He did a couple of dumb things," Johnson says, despite his alleged genius in designing and building the Killdozer. "He did a couple of things that would have been common sense" not to do.

So the offensive capabilities of the Killdozer's guns were limited by design flaws and luck. But the defensive capabilities were impressive. Of the estimated 1,000 rounds or so fired at the Killdozer by law enforcement, Johnson thinks only one round made it in.

"In my examination of that cab we actually had one round from law enforcement that got inside that cab," he says. "It came from the right side above the .223. There was a window. It was made up of layers of Plexiglas. When he cut that Plexiglas, he had about a quarter inch or so that didn't fill that window up and that bullet went through there." It hit a metal flange inside the window, leaving a dent, and it ricocheted from there. "It hit the .50 on the side, bounced off the .50 and hit the top of the cab he made."

"And that's the only round that I believe we got in."

"I think it's narrow-minded to say he didn't try to kill anyone," Sheriff Johnson says. "I guarantee you he was trying to kill Cody when he was ramming him with that loader."

Or, maybe the better question is this: Did he care?

Former Granby Trustee Dick Broady says it's just nonsense when people try to say he didn't want to kill or hurt anybody.

"How was he to know that he didn't kill anybody by bringing those places down?" Broady asks. "He wouldn't have known that those children were evacuated (from the town library). They could have all been still in the basement of that building and he could have killed several of them. So don't give me this shit about he wasn't out to kill anyone. He didn't care. He didn't care, not in the least."

The Real Reason No One Was Killed

Our editorial that week pointed out the real reason no one was killed or even seriously injured during the rampage.

The main reason for this minor miracle has been clearly ascribed to the law enforcement effort that took place in the midst of the rampage, even though the initial efforts to stop the Killdozer were confused and ineffective. Officials with the law enforcement agencies involved, mainly the Grand County Sheriff's Department and the Colorado State Patrol, realized that it would be nearly impossible to stop the Killdozer. And as early as the first altercation at the concrete batch plant the decision was made to start evacuating the town of Granby.

Colorado State Patrol Corporal Dave Batura and Lt. Mike McGinley, along with Grand County Undersheriff Glen Trainor, all agreed that the town would need to be cleared out. The best way to do that was by utilizing the county's 911 system that allowed a "reverse" way of communicating so that messages from the county's dispatch center could be sent out to homes, businesses and others in the 911 database, which was almost everyone with a phone line.

While a great deal of the attention of police officers was focused on trying to stop the Killdozer itself, the majority of the law enforcement and rescue effort was centered on keeping people out of harm's way in Granby. Police officers spent considerable time knocking on doors and herding people out of town. This was critically important. A perfect example of this response was the way officers hustled into the Grand Living Solar Senior Homes, near the propane tanks targeted by Heemeyer, to make sure no one was left inside. These people would clearly have been in danger if the tanks had exploded. They were all evacuated safely.

In addition, law enforcement, with the help of the U.S. Forest Service, Grand County Emergency Medical Services and the numerous county fire departments set up barricades to keep people from coming into town during the worst moments of the rampage. This, too, played a critical role in preventing injuries or death.

Gadflies and pundits who have commented randomly on the Internet about the rampage at times mocked the public efforts, mainly because law enforcement was unable to stop the Killdozer with its weapons or other tactics. But the truth is that law enforcement in Grand County was extremely effective in helping people dodge the lethal damage threatened by the Killdozer. Officers did a good job of protecting people, not by stopping the Killdozer, but by getting everyone out of harm's way.

In the long run, this was surely the best way of making sure Heemeyer didn't kill or hurt anyone other than himself.

While we worked to "set the record straight" about Heemeyer's violent intentions, it was as if the world wasn't listening.

A letter to the editor in the *Sky-Hi News* that week set the tone of the soon-to-be ongoing debate that would rage. Scott L. Stephens of Broomfield was a snowmobiler and good friend of Heemeyer's. He praises Heemeyer as a do-gooder and a man his children would refer to as "mayor" Marv when they'd go to Grand Lake. He continues: "I do not condone his actions of June 4, 2004, but I cannot condemn his actions without also condemning the actions of others that led up to the events of June 4, 2004. It is my hope that there will be an investigation into the business dealings of the officials of the town of Granby. While what they did might have been technically legal, I don't believe what they did was right, neither morally nor ethically, and I don't believe that good, honest people would push a man as far as the town of Granby pushed my friend Marv Heemeyer." He also suggests that the town did not treat Heemeyer with "respect."

Out of one side of his mouth he's condemning Heemeyer's actions while at the same time saying it was the town's fault. Another letter writer put Heemeyer up on a pedestal.

Aranka Matolscsy, after attacking the newspaper in general (assailing its layout, grammar, syntax and use of a photo showing Heemeyer's covered body being lifted from the bulldozer) states the rampage "is a very sad reflection on the state and direction of human cultural evolution, in general, and within our community." Citing the need to balance private property rights with governmental and societal concerns, she states: "If the community at large isn't already beginning to understand, Marv was just one of many people in this area who feel the same way but for individual reasons. These sentiments have been brewing here for years and years — perhaps why so many are now considering Marv a hero and a champion for the common man."

And then there was the interview I conducted with a friend of Heemeyer's.

This friend told me that Granby should be happy about how Marv had gotten the town huge amounts of free publicity that most towns would die for.

Because of the rampage "Granby's infinite," he says. "It will never die now. All around the world now people know of the bulldozer guy. Shoot, I was just in Mexico this June and we were talking to this like, you know, taxi driver or somebody. 'Did you ever hear about that bulldozer thing?' 'Oh yeah, yeah, the bulldozer that tore up the town?' 'Yeah, that's where we're from!'

"So it's a world-wide deal, now, that Granby, now Granby's on the map."

All I could think at that moment was this was just the sort of publicity the town could do without. And once again I was being told Granby was better off because of Heemeyer. I could see that this Heemeyer friend truly believed what he was saying. He wasn't being ironic or jocular. Heemeyer, he said, had helped Granby.

At this time, an enduring mystery about the actual rampage was uncovered shortly after the dust had settled. A van that was found in the metal building where Heemeyer built the Killdozer had been rented from a rental agency at the airport in Omaha, Nebraska. The rental slip confirmed that it had been rented by Heemeyer for seven days, starting May 27. It was due back the day of the rampage. Heemeyer paid $492.99 for the rental.

The Grand County Sheriff's Department asked the Omaha police to check things out. Sure enough, a day later, police there had found Heemeyer's pickup truck, a red 2002 GMC Sierra, parked in the lot at Eppley Field. With a search warrant they were able to inventory the interior.

The car had a wide variety of items in it, including a Kodak disposable camera in the driver's door, two check books, three magazines for a .45-caliber handgun, pages from a phone book, a .22-caliber revolver behind the seat, two bags of Winchester .22-250 bullets, one .50-caliber bullet and one for a .223-caliber weapon.

Why had Heemeyer bothered to park his truck in Omaha? Why had he rented a van there? People theorized that Heemeyer got the rental van so he could case the Killdozer's targets ahead of time incognito. But if that's the case, it would have been just as easy to do so by renting a van in Denver. There's some significance to the Omaha airport that has escaped people otherwise familiar with Heemeyer and the rampage.

The film inside the camera was developed and it revealed photos taken at the funeral for Heemeyer's father. One self-portrait of Heemeyer from that roll of film offers a sad look in his eyes.

Sheriff Johnson speculates that maybe Heemeyer had stopped at the airport in Omaha on the way back from his hometown where he may have confided with friends and family before that last week. But that's just a theory. And besides, Omaha isn't exactly on the way back from Heemeyer's hometown in South Dakota.

Other people thought that maybe Heemeyer had devised a way to escape from the Killdozer after the rampage and flee, somehow, to Omaha, where he'd retrieve his truck. That theory, they admit, was far-fetched. But people were grasping at straws trying to figure out why.

Yet, to date, perhaps except for an inner circle of friends and family, no one knows why Heemeyer left his truck and rented a van at the airport in Omaha, Nebraska.

While that mystery remained, another mystery was resolved in those first two weeks after the rampage. Grand County Coroner Dave

Schoenfeld issued his autopsy report, addressing two rumors that had circulated. One was that Heemeyer must have been under the influence of drugs or alcohol when he set out on the rampage. Another was that Heemeyer had terminal cancer, or some other life-threatening illness, that must have prompted his actions.

Schoenfeld said he found no evidence of drugs or alcohol in Heemeyer's blood. Also, he found no signs of cancer or any other fatal illness. Heemeyer was sober and healthy during the rampage.

Schoenfeld also presented to the public a statement from Heemeyer's siblings, which they wanted published in the local paper. We ran their statement with the obituary. The statement they gave read: "With the citizens of Grand County, the Heemeyer family is saddened by the actions of our brother, Marv. We pray that out of this tragic event will come God's peace, possible through forgiveness and grace." It was signed "The Heemeyer Family."

Schoenfeld said he felt that the attitude of the family, as he perceived it in the dealings over Heemeyer's body, was that Heemeyer's rampage was the fault of Grand County. The family told Schoenfeld to let Marv's local friends figure out what they wanted to do with Heemeyer's cremated remains.

34. The Cult of the Killdozer

While I spent time and effort trying to "set the record straight" about Heemeyer and his actions with story after story about the facts of the rampage, another counter trend was emerging in the world of public opinion. Marv Heemeyer, his rampage and his creation were becoming objects and events of veneration. If people couldn't worship at the feet of Heemeyer himself, they could worship the Killdozer and its rampage. The Cult of the Killdozer, as revealed in many letters and public comments, wanted to have its ritual and its shrine, all celebrating Marv Heemeyer.

People started calling for a Dozer Days celebration to commemorate the rampage. While some had different ideas about how such a "Dozer Days" celebration should take place, many others didn't even agree that there should be such an event in the first place.

The idea of some sort of celebration started when Boulder, Colorado, resident, Steve Mertz wrote a letter to the editor in the *Sky-Hi News*. He suggested that the town host the world's first tank rodeo. *"People from all over the world could build home-made tanks and bring them to your town on the anniversary of the rampage. I would suggest starting the rodeo off with a parade. Events could include races and an obstacle course. The festival would culminate with a demolition derby. Like 'Battle Bots' on a much larger scale. In evenings you could host a small folk and country music festival."*

Mertz goes on to write, *"This might also be a good way for the town to 'heal' both economically as well psychologically.*

"I hope this doesn't seem too insensitive. All the best to each of you."

He also urged saving and displaying the Killdozer, a theme that would continue to crop up.

Then there was the letter to the editor from J. Hanlon of Denver.

> *"Having spent 10 years marketing my lodging business in the mountains, I can't help but be intrigued by the marketing possibilities the Dozer Disaster presents for the Town of Granby. Leadville has its Burro races; Nederland has its Frozen Dead Man Days and Boulder has its Kinetic water race."*
>
> *"So why not an annual 'Dozer Days' weekend for Granby? Owners and operators of bulldozers would be invited from around the world to an international Dozer Meet that would include: Contests for the Biggest Dozer, Smallest Dozer, Best Paint Job, Best 'Tricked out' Dozer, most Unique Dozer, Oldest Dozer, Best Foreign Dozer, Best Handmade Model Dozer (separate kids and adult contest) and a Concourse of Elegance."*

Hanlon then suggests that the Killdozer itself be put on display for all to see and marvel at year-round.

> *"As for the infamous Dozer? It can be on display year around at the local visitors bureau or historic society, but open for interior 'climb in' inspections only on Dozer Days (contributions welcome)."*

These letters started the serious discussion on whether the town and the county should celebrate the Killdozer rampage with a Dozer Days event and enshrine the Killdozer itself as if it were a museum piece.

Yes, there were those who spoke out against such celebrations and shrines, but the debate didn't die. Rather, it got more intense. People wanted to make Heemeyer, his rampage and his dozer into bigger celebrities than they already were.

I felt discouraged. Kenny Be's satirical cartoon in *Westword*, the alternative news weekly in Denver, only heightened my angst over how public opinion was proceeding in celebration of the Killdozer and the rampage. It was a funny take on all these ideas, but for me, it hit painfully close to home.

His cartoon was headed "Reinventing Granby." Then, in a subhead: "Marvin Heemeyer's Bulldozer Rampage may just be the best thing that ever happened to Granby. In 90 minutes, he turned Colorado's least interesting mountain town into what could be its #1 attraction."

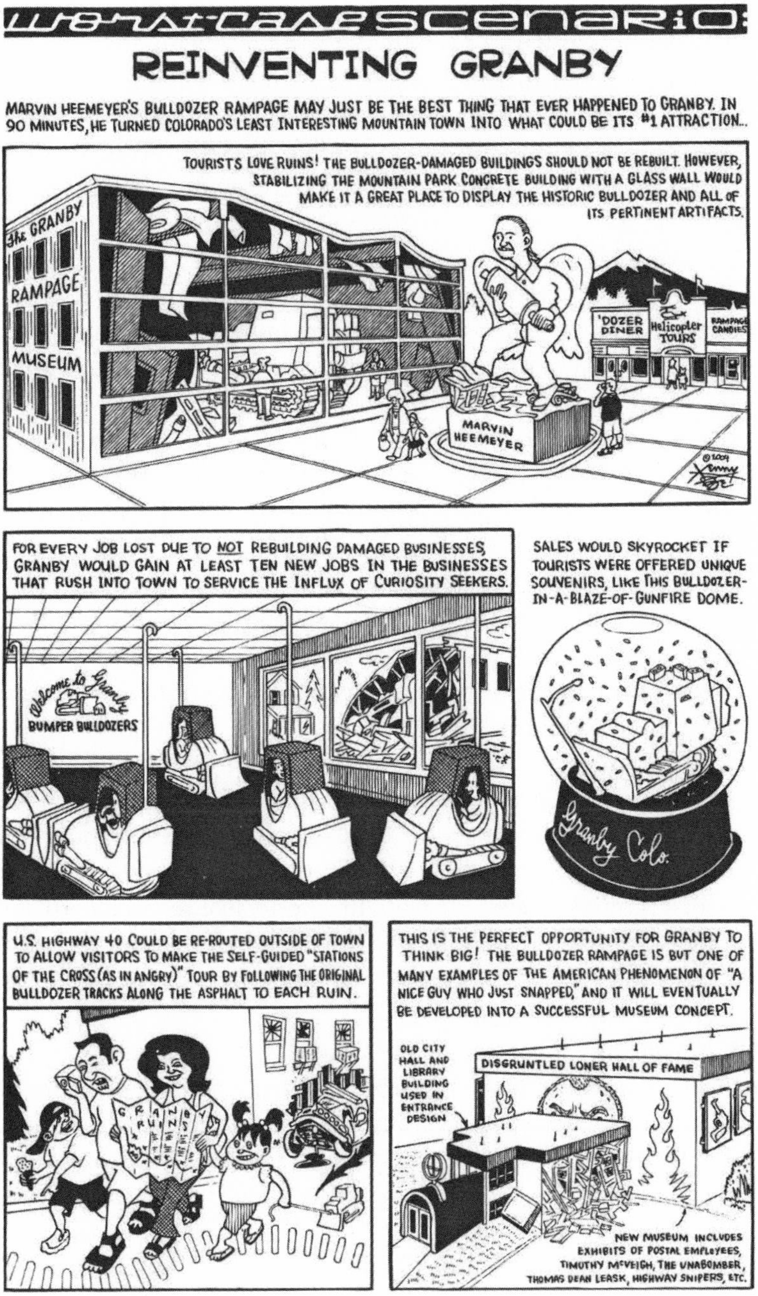
WORST-CASE SCENARIO:
REINVENTING GRANBY
MARVIN HEEMEYER'S BULLDOZER RAMPAGE MAY JUST BE THE BEST THING THAT EVER HAPPENED TO GRANBY. IN 90 MINUTES, HE TURNED COLORADO'S LEAST INTERESTING MOUNTAIN TOWN INTO WHAT COULD BE ITS #1 ATTRACTION...
TOURISTS LOVE RUINS! THE BULLDOZER-DAMAGED BUILDINGS SHOULD NOT BE REBUILT. HOWEVER, STABILIZING THE MOUNTAIN PARK CONCRETE BUILDING WITH A GLASS WALL WOULD MAKE IT A GREAT PLACE TO DISPLAY THE HISTORIC BULLDOZER AND ALL OF ITS PERTINENT ARTIFACTS.
The GRANBY RAMPAGE MUSEUM
'DOZER DINER
Helicopter TOURS
RAMPAGE CANDIES
MARVIN HEEMEYER
FOR EVERY JOB LOST DUE TO NOT REBUILDING DAMAGED BUSINESSES, GRANBY WOULD GAIN AT LEAST TEN NEW JOBS IN THE BUSINESSES THAT RUSH INTO TOWN TO SERVICE THE INFLUX OF CURIOSITY SEEKERS.
Welcome to Granby
BUMPER BULLDOZERS
SALES WOULD SKYROCKET IF TOURISTS WERE OFFERED UNIQUE SOUVENIRS, LIKE THIS BULLDOZER-IN-A-BLAZE-OF-GUNFIRE DOME.
Granby Colo.
U.S. HIGHWAY 40 COULD BE RE-ROUTED OUTSIDE OF TOWN TO ALLOW VISITORS TO MAKE THE SELF-GUIDED "STATIONS OF THE CROSS (AS IN ANGRY)" TOUR BY FOLLOWING THE ORIGINAL BULLDOZER TRACKS ALONG THE ASPHALT TO EACH RUIN.
GRANBY RUINS
THIS IS THE PERFECT OPPORTUNITY FOR GRANBY TO THINK BIG! THE BULLDOZER RAMPAGE IS BUT ONE OF MANY EXAMPLES OF THE AMERICAN PHENOMENON OF "A NICE GUY WHO JUST SNAPPED," AND IT WILL EVENTUALLY BE DEVELOPED INTO A SUCCESSFUL MUSEUM CONCEPT.
OLD CITY HALL AND LIBRARY BUILDING USED IN ENTRANCE DESIGN
DISGRUNTLED LONER HALL OF FAME
NEW MUSEUM INCLUDES EXHIBITS OF POSTAL EMPLOYEES, TIMOTHY McVEIGH, THE UNABOMBER, THOMAS DEAN LEASK, HIGHWAY SNIPERS, ETC.

The first panel of the cartoon depicts a still-ruined but slightly refurbished Mountain Park Concrete batch plant building on the left of a public square in which a large statue of an angel-wing-bedecked Marv Heemeyer stands. Another panel shows "The Granby Rampage Museum." The Killdozer sits inside. In this rendering, tourists wander about, one snapping photos of the Heemeyer statue while a mother-daughter duo strolls by.

The copy block with that panel reads: "Tourists love ruins! The bulldozer-damaged buildings should not be rebuilt. However, stabilizing the Mountain Park Concrete building with a glass wall would make it a great place to display the historic bulldozer and all of its pertinent artifacts."

Additional panels show plans for a "Bumper Bulldozers" attraction, a "Granby Ruins" tourist map and a Granby Town Hall depiction with the heading: "Disgruntled Loner Hall of Fame." And so on.

Kenny Be felt he had to point out in his drawing that he was using the "Old City Hall and Library Building" for his façade design. He adds in the corner: "The New museum includes exhibits of postal employees, Timothy McVeigh, The Unabomber, Thomas Dean Leask, Highway Snipers, etc."

I thought the cartoon was funny but I also smarted at how it summed up just what was wrong with memorializing the Killdozer. While mocking the idea of such a display and commemoration, it also revealed how the rampage helped make Granby an image of a place where "disgruntled loners" just might like to live, especially if it's in "Colorado's least interesting mountain town." If any single letter or comment exposed clearly how any such memorial would open Granby to ridicule, this was it.

Back on the level of those who weren't feeling particularly sarcastically humorous about the entire affair, many people were dead serious in their beliefs that keeping the Killdozer around was a bad idea. The consensus of the Granby Board of Trustees, for example, was that the bulldozer should be destroyed and that it should not be put on display.

This question came to a head after the rampage when a trustee on the Granby Board said he had been approached by organizers of a

Hawgfest motorcycle rally in Winter Park. They wanted to put the Killdozer in a tent and charge admission for people to come in and view it. Proceeds would go to the Granby Community Relief Fund and people's curiosity would be satisfied, he said.

But the Granby board's opinion was that such a display would send the wrong message. Undersheriff Glen Trainor, who had risked his life by climbing on the dozer and trying to stop it, summed it up. He spoke at the meeting and said such a display might be seen as a glorification of Heemeyer's exploits.

"One thing we don't want to do is we don't want to do anything to glorify or honor the man who built this thing," he said. Speaking from law enforcement's perspective, he added, "We definitely don't want that thing out in the public." Trainor added that there were some people in the public who thought of Heemeyer as a hero. "I don't want to do anything that would glorify this guy in any way."

Ultimately, the board decided that putting the dozer on display, even if it could generate revenue, was a bad idea for the victims of the rampage and for many town citizens. Such a move exposed the town to cynical taunts and rebukes. The town board, the chamber of commerce and most of the town's business leaders also dismissed the idea of the Dozer Days celebration. The event itself was just too traumatizing, and the resultant destruction too expensive, to be thought of as something worth celebrating.

Gary Allison, in a letter to the editor of the *Sky-Hi News*, summed up much of the local feeling against any sort of celebration or display. The headline of his letter read *"Long-time local says keeping the Dozer would celebrate anger."* The letter states: *"I knew Marv and considered myself a friend, but in my opinion on June 4, when he got in his Dozer, he had no friends, only his anger."*

"I don't want my grandkids to grow up celebrating anger, so I don't think the Dozer should be put on display or anything done to recognize that day."

Nonetheless, the public sentiment in favor of celebrating the rampage and enshrining the Killdozer persisted. For the next year, the legal process of figuring what to do with the dozer prompted many suggestions. The Grand County Museum wanted to keep it for posterity's sake as a display. Some citizens thought it should be put on display in the town park. Some proposed selling it to the Army for target practice.

The fate of the bulldozer, as it turned out, wasn't exactly as simple a matter as people voting or not. The Granby Board of Trustees officially petitioned the Grand County Board of County Commissioners to avoid letting the bulldozer be used as a spectacle or display. The board even asked that the bulldozer not be chopped up and sold or auctioned off for knickknacks, doo-dads and souvenirs. The county commissioners, which ended up with the Killdozer temporarily, agreed. But as it turned out, it was the district attorney's office and the county judge who ended up determining the fate of the Killdozer.

Heemeyer's creation was ultimately destroyed, 11 months after the rampage, because it had been used in the commission of a crime.

As if that weren't enough, Granby Mayor Ted Wang wrote a letter to the editor that he hoped would be the last word on the idea for a Dozer Days celebration and preserving the Killdozer in general:

"What cannot be forgotten about last June 4 was the motive for the violence and destruction that occurred: revenge for business dealings gone awry, intolerance for differences of opinion, hatred toward responsible and dedicated public servants, contempt for other's rights and an ultimate viciousness in expressing a 'last word' on it all. This is something we want to commemorate and celebrate? I think not."

So for the time being, the idea of a Dozer Days celebration was dead. The Killdozer itself was gone. But Wang was prescient on two points in his letter. First, one of the lasting images of the rampage would indeed be co-opted by extremists, making Heemeyer a hero. Also, Wang's future use of the rampage to further his political career would come back to haunt him.

35. The Heroic Myth of Heemeyer and His Killdozer Takes Off

The legacy of the rampage and the Killdozer, in fact, has become an example of how such an odd and emotional event can be appropriated and twisted to fit a group's or person's preconceived beliefs and grievances. For many people, Heemeyer became a hero, the rampage an event to be celebrated and the Killdozer something to be enshrined.

For some, Heemeyer morphed into a hero who typified the image of the lone American patriot standing up to the intrusions of government and the media. With guns, God, an armed and armored bulldozer and a list of grievances, Heemeyer became an archetype and a martyr. A sort of low-level cult of the Killdozer that was hinted at the day of the rampage took definite shape and form in the week after the event and has continued to this day.

For others, people like me and the other victims, and even some outside observers, he was exactly the opposite of a hero. But the blogging, Internet postings and letters to the editor extolling Heemeyer's actions have taken root in the American consciousness and have put Heemeyer and his Killdozer on a pedestal.

A letter by Bernd Lindow of Winter Park, that appeared in the *Sky-Hi News*, stated that I was wrong in some of my conclusions about Heemeyer.

> *"I have (sic) met him (Heemeyer) four years ago when I came to Colorado," he wrote. "I had business with him. He was just minding his own business, and he was an American."*

"I was reading your story on Marv in the Daily Tribune from June 17 (a reprint of the Sky-Hi News) and I think you are wrong. You got the facts wrong. I don't want to condone Marv's behavior but he had the right to do whatever he had done. Maybe 100 years ago it would have changed America through this act. But what he did showed only that there was something wrong. Did he shoot somebody? No, only equipment. Did he try to kill people? No, people can leave buildings."

Lindow goes on with a general attack on local government and concludes,

"I think he, Marv, deserves a medal."

Lindow started his letter by writing that he didn't think I would print that letter, but I did. I wanted all the viewpoints about the event out there in front of the public.

And it wasn't uncommon to hear Heemeyer defended by people in Grand Lake who knew him and by others who hadn't the faintest idea of what had transpired and why. They merely liked the idea that he lashed out and was taking a stand, of sorts, against "government."

Grand County Sheriff Rod Johnson puts it this way: "The funny thing about these types of things that is a phenomenon . . . it's just hard to understand. You just have to accept it. (This) Is when you find somebody that kind of flips their finger off at government, you will find people that will praise or align with him that just is a bizarre 'feeding,' I will call it, of emotions — not really thinking, well, the guy was just a nut. He was a crazy bastard, you know. He wasn't a genius . . . He didn't fight the system in a way that makes any sense. He didn't have any sense about what he was doing. But I'm telling ya, there's a lot of people that were like, 'yeah, that's the way to go Marv.'"

Other commentators also noticed the swell of opinion that wanted to make Heemeyer a hero.

Perhaps the best illustration of the sort of Internet, blogosphere response to the entire episode (and there were many) was written very shortly after the rampage. On the website called "No B.S. News and Commentary," a series of articles were written under the heading "Marvin Heemeyer — The Truth!" The writer, the so-called publisher Russell R. Bingman, pours forth two screeds that basically say that all of the mainstream media articles and broadcasts about the rampage were full of lies.

Bingman writes:

"Heemeyer's rampage, as press and news media have widely reported, was precipitated by a four year losing battle with the town council of Granby, who, despite widespread opposition from residents, altered town zoning codes and ordinances, to allow Mountain Park Concrete to build and operate a cement batch plant next to Heemeyer's muffler shop, a move which forced Heemeyer out of business due to the dust and pollution of the plant. Mayor Wang presided over most of the council's forceful actions. One thing that Colorado news media has not reported, is that Wang, according to many Granby residents, has a very angry and hostile attitude toward all of the residents of Granby and Grand County who opposed Mountain Park Concrete. Many residents have been and still are contending that Wang and the Granby Town Council accepted bribes and payoffs from Mountain Park Concrete, to alter zoning codes and allow them to build and operate . . .

The statements made in this paragraph, which goes on and on with other outrageous claims, could easily be challenged and rebutted. Zoning codes were not altered. Heemeyer was not forced out of business. Wang did not preside over the town actions. He wasn't mayor until after all the hearings were conducted and he recused himself from most of the voting at that time. Bingman's claims to the contrary, no investigation of the town was conducted relating to the batch plant deliberations.

The rest of the website's first entry contains misstatements, outright distortions and unwarranted attacks on the town and the town board. He contends that the town of Granby had an "enemies list," which it did not have. It claims the CBI (Colorado Bureau of Investigation) had a file on Heemeyer, which it did not have before the rampage. He asserts that people involved in responding to the rampage demonized Heemeyer, but that many others said Marv was "the kind of guy who'd do anything to help anybody — but he was just simply a nice man. He was pushed into this by these people . . . Marvin Heemeyer was a 6 foot-4 inch 230-pound gentle giant, according to most of the people in Granby and Grand County who have bothered to speak up."

He assails his own made-up quotes that asserted people said Heemeyer was shooting at "everybody." Heemeyer wasn't shooting at "everybody" with his .50-caliber, that's true. But he certainly was shooting it, endangering many. The idea that the town of Granby and Mayor Wang were lusting for money is certainly a stretch since Wang's pay has no relation to the batch plant decision and the town's gain from sales taxes from the batch plant was to be minimal, at best. It would be fair to say the board was acting partially in a desire to keep jobs and perhaps add a few jobs in the Granby area. But for Bingman, it was all inspired by "greed."

The notion that the town of Granby and its Mayor compiled an "enemies list," in the tradition of President Richard Nixon, J. Edgar Hoover and the FBI, is laughable at best. The idea that this list was something done in collusion with the Colorado Bureau of Investigation is a stretch of the imagination also. I have not been able to find any credible evidence of such an "enemies list." It seems that when Bingman wants to introduce some outrageous fact to bolster his point of view, he makes up comments from anonymous "concerned citizens."

The website's writings continue in this vein. Anonymous friends of Heemeyer are quoted as saying that government bowled over Heemeyer and pushed him too far. One "fact" stated was that two or three toilet flushes into Heemeyer's leach-field was seen as too much. Interesting, since he didn't have a leach field at all at the muffler shop property. The sewage went directly into a buried concrete truck mixing tank, that's it.

Bingman's opinions weigh heavily on the side of being part populist manifesto and part Patriot Movement attack on government.

In another article on his site, entitled "The real Marvin Heemeyer — Friends Speak," Bingman goes even further. He assails Denver radio broadcasters who stated the facts about the rampage (that there were guns, that Heemeyer fired at the police and gas tanks, etc.) and again raises several conspiracy theories about how government conspired against Heemeyer with an "enemies list." He quotes people who thought Heemeyer was a great guy.

So there you have it: Bingman would have his readers believe that Heemeyer didn't kill himself, that the police shot him once in the head through the mouth while he was inside the tightly sealed bulldozer. That's his version of the truth. And anyone trolling the Internet about the rampage and Marv Heemeyer, and who didn't have any other information, just might believe it, especially if they are predisposed to think that government, the police and American society are corrupt and out to get the little guy.

And that's why it's important to see what's being disseminated on the Internet about Heemeyer. And why it's important to understand that there is a real trend of belief and thinking in America that wants to believe that Heemeyer was a hero trod upon by "big" government. They relish the idea that he got back at government and the "establishment." He was a hero they want to believe in and the facts can't be allowed to get in the way of their adoration. It's a real phenomenon in this country.

Many other website postings echo comments from the Bingman site. It's clear they get most of their "factual" information from it. The "Heemeyer as Hero" mythology is going viral. It builds, expands and multiplies, thanks to some of the uncritical, easily duped readership that can be found on the web, where many people choose to read only what they agree with or want to agree with. If it doesn't reinforce their preconceived beliefs, then it must not be true. It's a lie. It's a government conspiracy.

They can't see that they themselves are perpetrating a hoax of their own imagining. Even worse, these sorts of blog postings don't allow for the complexity of Heemeyer's predicament and personality. They don't question the grey areas of his motivations. They end up being one-sided diatribes that don't allow for the honest examination of the rampage and its causes that really could help "society."

There are other postings on the Internet about the rampage, many of them wrong in little ways but almost all of them buying into the Heemeyer as Hero Mythology; that he was pushed too far by government, robbed of his fortune and somehow justified in the way he lashed back.

There are also *You-Tube* postings about Heemeyer and the Rampage. Almost all of them use the footage shot by Grand County Sheriff's Department Investigator Leo Piechocki as he watched the last third of the rampage. Many appear to relish the sheer mechanical audacity of Heemeyer's action. That he could build such a Killdozer and actually use it to enact his revenge is, in and of itself, for some people, worthy of admiration. For people inclined to adore mechanical power and wherewithal, the Killdozer and its rampage are worth veneration, regardless of the rationale or facts about the case.

This trend of worshipping Heemeyer as a hero and defending his actions was noticed. Mike Rosen, a statewide *KOA* radio commentator and columnist for the *Rocky Mountain News*, then a major Denver daily newspaper that covered the entire state, expressed his critical take on the Heemeyer hero worship.

Under a headline that stated "*Granby madman no hero for Rosen,*" he wrote:

"Gadflies feel for Granby attacker."

"So proclaimed a recent headline in The Denver Post. *To drive home the point, two subheads intoned: 'Rage understood' and 'Local critics say although they may not agree with his action, they can empathize with his frustration.' The story's lead proceeded to paint Marvin Heemeyer as some kind of backwoods folk hero."*

"I wonder how many of his empathizers would feel the same way if it were their property he bulldozed. Or if one of Heemeyer's bullets had succeeded in exploding the propane tanks he fired at, killing their spouse or child in the process."

"Personally, I'm pickier about my heroes. I don't romanticize rampaging, suicidal psychotics. It was only sheer luck that no one was killed. Heemeyer's deranged behavior was only different in degree and no more justified than that of the 9/11 al-Queda terrorists or Unabomber Theodore Kaczynski. When asked, point blank, if they agreed that his actions were unjustified, some Heemeyer apologists resort to the Yeah But Gambit: 'Yeah, he was wrong, but . . .' A yeah but isn't really a 'yeah,' it's usually a convoluted 'no.' One such equivocator described Heemeyer as 'a man done wrong who done wrong in return.' By this twisted reasoning, the Columbine killer struck a commiserative blow for anti-social high school misanthropes everywhere. Heemeyer was flat out wrong — period! Our compact with fellow citizens in this constitutional republic included the understanding that we can't all have our own way all of the time.

The curious yet nearly overwhelming way in which the Killdozer rampage morphed into an act of honor worshiped by Patriots and anti-government types didn't escape the attention of national-level media observers either. An article by Martin J. Smith appeared in the *Los*

Angeles Times Magazine of July 25, 2004. It was featured on the cover with this teaser heading: "The Man, The Myth, The Bulldozer." Its subhead read: "How the Struggling U.S. Patriot Movement Conjured a Western 'Hero' From One Man's Sad Tantrum." Inside, with the body copy of the story, the headline reads: "Martyr Without a Cause." Another subhead: "The Antigovernment Crowd Declared Marvin Heemeyer a Hero After He Died Trying to Level a Colorado Town With an Armored Bulldozer. Never Mind that the Patriots Got It All Wrong."

Smith's article states that outside of Granby — "Out there in the ideological abstract, where mythmaking continues apace and details don't much matter — 52-year-old Marv Heemeyer was being celebrated in terms that suggest he'd pitched his bizarre fit at precisely the right time and in precisely the right place."

Smith continues: "The antigovernmental crowd that historically has flourished in the Western U.S. had been in slow retreat since true terrorism came to America in 1995. But last month, it suddenly resurfaced and exuberantly embraced Heemeyer as a fellow warrior against bureaucratic tyranny. That he'd managed to kill no one other than himself during his rampage was certainly a plus."

He mentions the opinion stated in another pro-Heemeyer website: "When a man has had it 'up to here' with all the bull that the corrupt officials dish out, he can do things others may find unreasonable yet are totally justifiable. This man will go down as a folk hero, not just in Granby but across the nation . . . This is the beginning of a new revolution by those of us who are tired of 'taxation without representation.' Let the battle cry be: 'Remember Marvin Heemeyer!'"

Smith then notes another: "A 17-year-old senior at John F. Kennedy High School in Granada Hills (California) immediately registered the domain name www.killdozer.us and began building a website to honor Heemeyer and his machine, complete with written and video tributes from 'fans.' He anchored its temporary home page with a photograph of Heemeyer's now-legendary armored bulldozer and the somber incantation: 'Never forget.'"

Smith notes a comment on the site, referring to Heemeyer's actions as "the American West outlaw thing. Jesse James. Billy the Kid."

Smith points out that these are clear articulations of a sympathy with the western myth of the justified vigilante. That's how people saw Heemeyer. They also saw him as a hero, but they wouldn't have called him an antihero. But that's clearly what he is. Like Jesse James, who is an antihero because he is a murderer, Heemeyer is an antihero because he was violent, destroyed property and certainly tried to shoot people. And yet Heemeyer is embraced. He becomes the noble martyr for a righteous antigovernmental cause.

And yet, in comments Smith got from Heemeyer's family, they said: "He paid his taxes. He wasn't antigovernment at all. His problem was with just a few people."

Even Heemeyer's family could see beyond the myth. But the cult of the Killdozer had already taken off into the consciousness of many Americans, creating a myth-based story about it all. The facts would have to be ignored, twisted or forgotten.

36. Heemeyer's Tapes Released A Crisis of Confidence — Time to Quit?

I sat down in a former science classroom in the old Middle Park High School building in a pod next to the area where we had been operating our newspapers for two months. Old Bunsen burners sat randomly on the black stone countertops, remnants of labs conducted years ago. A torn poster of the periodic table of elements leaned in a forlorn curl over a podium once used by a teacher. Stacks of mimeographed lessons sat piled under the counters. I occupied an old student's desk that was too small for me. My laptop, with the digital recordings of Marv's tapes, sat open in front of me.

The printing presses had been installed a month earlier and now our entire operation was humming along in an asbestos-plagued and leaking former high school. Aside from working to get our four newspapers out each week, combined with struggling in our new facility, I was also working with the newspaper owner, Bill Johnson, on the plans and preparations for rebuilding the *Sky-Hi News* building.

The national and international interest in the Killdozer rampage had waned to a mere trickle of phone calls and e-mail inquiries, but Heemeyer's fans continued to send letters urging celebrations and memorials for the dozer, not to mention anonymous mailed-in letters attacking me, the newspaper and the town in general for "making Marv do it."

And yet, after three months of waiting, I was ready to listen to the two and a half hours of monologue Marvin Heemeyer had recorded on April 13, 2004 and left behind. I felt as if I were sitting down to have a chat with Marv. I was nervous.

Adding to my apprehension was the phone call I had just received from Bill Johnson, the owner of the newspapers. He wanted to have an important meeting with me when he arrived in two days and he wanted to be sure I would be available. He was vague and all I could think at that moment was that he was about to ease me out. After all, it wouldn't take a genius to think I had run the paper in such a way that his building had been demolished and the business nearly destroyed. Maybe he was thinking it was time to make a change and cut the already significant losses.

And I was beginning to think, sadly, that it might be time to leave this place I had called home for 25 years. Quit the job, dodge all the hard work ahead and forget about rebutting all the Killdozer criticism.

It was a beautiful fall day. I wistfully looked out the large pane windows that faced west, like a daydreaming student who wanted nothing more than to skip school and play in the woods. Music Mountain, the broad expanse of hillside, ridge and table-like promontory overlooking the Colorado and Fraser River Valleys, loomed invitingly. How quaint that the mountain of Heemeyer's secret powder stash, a little side-fact I had learned in interviews with his friends and enemies, was a place that figured so prominently in Granby's western panorama.

In that frame of mind, I sat down to listen to Marv.

As Heemeyer's matter-of-fact voice resonated through the small speakers, his one-sided indictment of me, my community, the town and the world in general depressed and worried me. It was as if I were going through the rampage all over again, but this time it was a rampage of words and invective. Through these tapes, Heemeyer was haunting me and throwing into question much of what I believed to be true and honest in the world.

Here was Marv, echoing, but from the past, the sentiments and comments his defenders had been uttering since the rampage. It was as if he had known how the world would latch onto his rampage and his mission. It was as if he were a man latching on to his own truth about his facts leading up to the event. He was something like a

Truther and conspiracy theory advocate for his own predicament, for his own rampage, but all before the event that made him a hero.

What he said about me grabbed my attention.

"Anyway, we've got this lawsuit going on (the batch plant lawsuit) and this newspaper guy Patrick Brower, this guy's the scum of the earth also. Which is most, most, some of these people here are for different reasons. Because when I first came up here in '91 the gambling issue was getting started up here and I'm just sitting around my condo reading this newspaper and this guy is just blasting, I mean he's just belittling them and slandering them as far as I'm concerned. He just made the pro-gamblers look like fools and I thought that 'What's wrong with these people? They've got no economy up here. Here's something that's happened down there in Blackhawk and over at Cripple Creek. And it was doing good economic things for those communities. Why is he so against this?' I never could understand it."

"So I finally, after he blasted some people I knew here in town, I wrote him a letter and you know told him 'Hey this is America, you know. Leave these people alone, you know. You don't have to be making them look like some kind of fools,' was the whole gist of my letter. Anyway, he just didn't know who Marv Heemeyer was. He definitely hated me because I, you know, said some things in the paper that were right on the money."

And then I learned how Marv believed I had intentionally slighted him.

"This newspaper guy Patrick Brower had told me, after I started the muffler shop, on a couple of different occasions, I called him. And I was advertising with him and so forth. He said that he was going to come down and he'd do an article on my little business. Well he never did do it. You know. He was doing everything he could to keep me from getting any additional publicity. It's a kind of a community that in order for you to get ahead you have to keep the neighbor down."

And then he just had to attack me in other ways.

"Anyway, this Patrick Brower, I mean he's a pot head, of course you can't tell anybody that. A big liberal. Army brat. He's had everything in his life given to him. But he knows how to abuse the power of the pen, and that's a big thing up here, abuse of power. They said that to me one time, that I didn't have any respect for authority. And that's not the truth at all."

"The truth is I have the utmost respect for authority, but they don't. They didn't respect the FDIC or the procedures. They don't respect our good people coming into the community. They only respect what they want . . . Well, I guess, that's their right in America. But, I've got my rights too. Maybe they're wrong. When I exercise these rights, but I really don't care. I am going to exercise these rights because we are given this freedom to do what we want to do. Until you do something wrong, and then you have to pay for it. Well, these people have figured out a pretty good way in a small community how to get away with doing things wrong, and doing it legally."

All those sinking feelings of doubt and fear came back with a rush as I sat there listening. Heemeyer, the hero for many people out there in the world who had adopted him and the Killdozer as a symbol of all that was wrong in America, was saying I was basically a lying jerk, yellow journalist, spoiled brat and a part of the Granby backstabbing community who had set out to ruin him. Oh, and I was a pot head, to boot.

But there was more, just not about me. Larry Thompson was a Catholic, Heemeyer intoned in his tapes, suggesting that was just another reason he had been misused in Granby. And Heemeyer berates Catholics in general in his tape, saying they are the "worst." He says Casey Farrell, a friend of mine and a good person, was just another lying backstabber. And this despite the fact that Farrell had actually leaned to the side of respecting Heemeyer's wishes in the batch plant debate more than others.

His comments on the tapes reveal his mistaken belief the town had schemed against him with the Docheffs, "pre-approving" it all in secret. Judge Doucette is depicted as a hypocrite in the tapes. His lawyer is a liar who set out only to milk Heemeyer of his money. It went on and on. Anyone who had disagreed with him or crossed him comes out sounding like a jerk on Heemeyer's tapes, his version of the world.

And while Heemeyer convinced himself to believe all those "facts" about his alleged adversaries (and allies), he also convinced himself to believe that "God wanted" him to carry out his rampage, avenge his enemies and teach the town of Granby a lesson. He became the victim of his own conspiracy.

But the tapes also revealed a sinister and vindictive side of Heemeyer that his friends and advocates may have found disturbing.

While it could still be debated ad infinitum as to whether Heemeyer intended to kill anyone in his rampage, comments he makes in his taped musings suggest that he was nonchalant about the prospect of killing.

Pondering his plight in getting back payments from people to whom he had sold one of his muffler shops, he says, "I'm not going to chase him down. I'm not going to find his Dad and shoot him. I'm not going to shoot (this guy). I'm not going to shoot his kids. I'd like to. I guess if the opportunity put itself in front of me in the next 60 days, 50 days, whatever it is, I might do it. I have the wherewithal to do that. But I don't think that's going to happen."

Heemeyer frets over the fact that he has lost money on business dealings in his life, saying he doesn't want it to happen again. But he also reveals a sternly moralistic point of view in explaining the failings of people who couldn't pay him.

"I bent over backwards to help this guy down there in Boulder make it. He had it for seven years. How can you fail after seven years? I'll tell you how you can fail. Drugs. Alcohol. Prostitutes. An over-sized ego. I don't know. There's many different ways. That's why this guy failed. He stole some of my equipment. He owes people money down there. He left the place a filthy mess. That evil will be returned to him. If it hasn't already."

Heemeyer rationalizes away the fact that he had finally achieved the very goal he had set for himself when he bought the property in Granby. Most people believed that Heemeyer's real reason for fighting the batch plant was to force his neighbors into paying top dollar for the land he had purchased at the auction in Denver so long ago. Heemeyer himself pleads in his tapes for the Docheffs to buy his property, but always at inflated prices. Ironically, it was only after Heemeyer had convinced himself he had to get back at the town and the community that he sold the property for very close to what he had wanted from the Docheffs three years earlier.

He rationalizes that away by saying he gave the money and property away.

"You know, I sold the property for $400,000. I mean, I had to pay taxes on it, which I did. But I stuck $360,000 in my pocket. You know. I didn't stick it in my pocket. I gave it away. You know it's gone because now money means nothing to me. I've given my house away. I do not need this cabin here in Grand Lake. I've given my snowmobiles away. I've given my snowmobiles away this year. Everything has gone. What I own is just going to be a pittance compared to what I'm going to take."

The tapes reveal that at times he hoped and wished he'd get caught ahead of time, before starting the rampage.

"I've wrestled with it for years," he says. "You know God gave me this last winter off again because he knew that I wasn't strong. And, that was so unique that this didn't get done last year. How, the sale of the business kind of interrupted my progress on my Marv's Komatsu – what did I call it – I've got a name for it. My MK Tank. That I didn't get the ole MK tank done last fall is amazing because it should have happened. But, you know, God has his timing, his plans made out. And, they're to be. And it looks like it's going to be because the one thing that I have wanted to do is to get caught. I had hoped that somebody would catch me and this whole thing would stop and that would be a good sign for me not to do it. I hoped. I haven't played the lottery a lot, but I've hoped that I would win the lottery and I could forget this whole thing. I could move on because then I would have my $300,000 and I would have my life back and I could live the way I want to live."

He comments that he thinks Granby will be a better place "if they ever hear this tape, if they ever hear the truth, if they're ever willing to listen."

He repeats that the town board would never listen to him. He says, almost in a confessional tone, that he was "weak" and "fearful" in his fight against the plant and the town by paying a lawyer and getting "milked." But "I fought the good fight to come to realize that I have to do what I have to do now. It's a sad, sad way to do it. But it's a cross that I'm going to have to carry. And I'm carrying it in God's name, I believe. I truly believe this. I would have been caught, something would have happened. I mean there's still some time left. It still may not happen. It could be that the day it does start the machine quits before I can even get out of the building. Or it may quit right after I get out of the building. It may quit, halfway through what I want to do. You know, and that's where it's supposed to stop. Because God will have stopped it."

The tapes also revealed that Heemeyer knew that if he started on the rampage, it would be a suicide mission.

Listening to the tapes that autumn day sent me into a downward spiral emotionally.

An anonymous letter to the editor praising Marv and shaming us sat open on my desk. With that letter in mind, Marv's taped musings freshly heard, and the prospect of losing my job, I debated in my mind the role I had played in Heemeyer's plight and his downfall. I wondered if my version of the facts surrounding his rampage were the "facts" at all. Heemeyer's assertions in the tapes represented the other reality that I was hearing day in and day out from his defenders and hero worshippers. It was the town's fault. The community and the newspaper set out to get Heemeyer. He wasn't welcomed and the community conspired to get him. Heemeyer, clearly, believed this. His coterie of admirers and followers and just chance observers believed it too.

I felt challenged. My truth, my facts and my version of reality were being turned upside down. Did I really have it that wrong? How wrong had I been? How had we ruined Marv Heemeyer? I was wondering if it were true that we had driven him to it all — that we were, in fact, to blame.

Earlier that week, after the "God Wanted Me to Do It" paper was published, I learned that a Grand Lake gallery owner, angry at our newspaper's coverage of Heemeyer and the rampage, was setting out to write a book about "the truth" on Heemeyer and reveal him as a victimized hero. He would tout Heemeyer as a rugged individual who was merely out to "get back at the Man" and "strike out against small-town prejudice."

He was already conducting interviews.

It all depressed me even more. And despite the chorus of friends, fellow journalists and locals who understood the truth of it all to be what I had seen and reported, I was feeling like giving up. Once again, I felt as if I were on the wrong side of this narrative and the truth was hopeless. Perhaps it really was time to take that job at a big city daily in Denver, like the *Rocky Mountain News* or *The Denver Post*, where my new-found celebrity as a rampage victim might help get my foot in the door for a new job in a new place.

I felt as if Marv were winning the second rampage. That Friday afternoon, I had to do something, anything, to clear my head. I looked back out at Music Mountain. I had only one way of coping with worry and angst, and that was to run.

The mountain is on BLM land. The access is from U.S. Highway 40 west of Granby. I parked and started a slow jog up what was mainly a horse trail into an expanse of already discolored lodgepole pine. The mountain pine beetles were killing trees by the thousands and windrows of rust-colored pine needles that had fallen from the trees softened my footfalls, white pockmarks of sap and diminutive mounds of sawdust marked the fatal wounds to the straight and narrow trees.

The trail began to climb and in two switchbacks, all leading generally to the northwest and not straight up the broad incline that I had observed from Granby so many times, the pines gave way to scattered stands of aspen trees. They had lost most of their leaves by then and the trail, now a single-track, was carpeted with thousands of leaves like dollops of yellow, red and orange paint. The aspen stands thinned as I climbed and stunted and scraped small trees faded into the wide expanse of sage, scrub oak and scrub weeds that now were the only plants on the increasingly steep trail that led straight up the ledge at the promontory of the mountain. The running was difficult now and I dropped my pace to a jog and a walk. All I could think about was my breathing and my pace.

I remembered that Marv had ridden his sled on this very mountain, the place of his secret powder stashes. Perhaps he had ridden through this very spot where I labored to climb. But he would have mounted the steep hillside with ease on his snowmobile in a land of white.

The sky was a dark blue and the air had crispened into a liquid chill around me. I was in the shadow of the setting sun on the other side of the mountain, but I was hot from running and the crest was close. It was an anticlimactic gradual series of switchbacks to the top ridge. Once at the top, looking west, the neighboring small mountains and hills faded toward the giant volcanic caldera that was the basin of Hot Sulphur Springs.

The sun, burning brightly at its low western angle into my eyes, disrupted my view. But when I turned around, breathing hard, I saw the expanse of Middle Park and Granby below me and on the other side of Windy Gap, the reservoir and the Colorado River. The town rose in steps from the meandering Fraser River to the butte where the old high school and my office sat. I looked toward the old high school building, which looked like nothing more than a smudge in the brown and green expanse, and imagined the room where I had sat and listened to Marv's monologue only four hours ago. Marv, perhaps, had enjoyed the same view on one of his snowmobile rides. If he had looked, he most certainly would have looked toward his property in Granby. It was a splendid view.

My only solace as I remembered Heemeyer's rant and my tenuous plight in this place that I loved was the coming easy run down the mountain in cold air with a view in front of me much of the way, back down through the aspens and the pines to the old horse trail and the soggy stream bed of black mud. I had earned the ease of the descent and I cared less about Heemeyer and my job then. If I must leave, well, then I would. I thought of that as a matter of fact. I could accept it now.

I had been to the top of Music Mountain.

Two days after listening to the tapes Bill Johnson arrived. I went to our lunch meeting with a feeling of dread.

"Patrick," he said, "you'll be getting a certified letter in the mail from our attorney."

My heart sank. Maybe I wouldn't have to quit after all. I'd just be fired. For a brief second a glimmer of hope revealed itself to me in this feeling of dread.

"It's an offer to make you a partner in the company. This is the first time I've ever done this. You deserve it. Read it and give it to your lawyer and we'll talk more about it in two weeks."

I was stunned and elated all at the same time. It was a delicious lunch.

But the debates continued about Marv Heemeyer. I thought it was time for me to write another article "setting the record straight." This time the assertion was made that Heemeyer had been mistreated by the town staff and for that reason he didn't feel welcome to plead his case. Once again, it was the town's fault and the mean people who worked at the town.

I thought I knew the answer to this assertion was the town staff had always tried to treat Heemeyer with respect whenever he came by the town hall, which was often during the heated days of the batch plant debate. I remembered hearing Town Clerk Sharon Spurlin explain how at times the staff had felt intimidated by Heemeyer when he came in to demand copies of town meeting tapes and the minutes the very morning after a late evening meeting.

"But don't ask me," Spurlin said. "Talk to Faye. Faye Rumsey. She was the clerk pro-tem and she dealt with him more than anybody."

Faye Rumsey had moved to Nebraska. I called her. Her comments, since she no longer lived in town and since she had no town reputation really to protect, would at least seem more objective and impersonal than the comments of current town staff members who were still reeling from the attack on the town hall.

"Do you think Marv was treated fairly and honestly by the front office staff at the town Hall?"

"Oh, I'm so glad you called," she said. We were longtime acquaintances and had worked together on many news stories and town events over the years.

"Oh, how could they say that? Why, we were the ones who were intimidated and cautious around Marvin Heemeyer, not the other way around. Mind you, we didn't let that affect the way we did our jobs, but Mr. Heemeyer could appear a little bit bossy and overly demanding, but we handled his requests by the book and as efficiently as possible."

One celebrated incident was when Heemeyer demanded the tapes of the previous night's meeting, she said, and the town staff refused to give them to him at that time.

"Why, his face turned red and he accused us of trying to circumvent the First Amendment and that he had a right and all that."

She paused.

"But we said we'd give him the tapes, but we had to transcribe them first and they just weren't ready yet. With his lawsuit and all that, well, we had to be certain we recorded the meeting's proceedings accurately. That's all."

She paused again.

"So we offered to dupe the tapes for him if he needed them right then and there. You know, just make duplicate copies of those cassettes and give him the copies. But we said it would cost, you know, for the cassettes and for the time. Or he could sit down and listen to the original tapes the very moment the minutes were made. You know, the town has to approve its minutes but the tapes, well, they're available to be heard by anyone.

"At that he huffed, sort of, and said something like 'You're abridging my rights!' That was it, 'abridging.' He turned on his heels and walked out in a hurry. A week later he showed up with his own tape recorder and he went off to the little public office we had and he just made a tape of the tapes himself. He just held his tape recorder's microphone over our little cassette player and he made his own recording. That was OK. We treated him like anybody else."

I knew this to be true for I had been through the exact same exercise with the town hall when I had requested tapes or meeting documents.

"He always got what he requested, if we could. And we'd do it right away, or as soon as possible. The truth is, we were intimidated by him a little and we wanted it done right. We knew he was the suing type."

Had he ever screamed or shouted?

"Oh never to us. But he did corner Deb once and gave her a finger-wagging."

I had known about that and said so.

"Now you listen to me, Patrick," she said. "No matter what they say, he was no angel. In fact, like I wrote to you in that letter to the editor, he was out to extort money from the Docheffs. That's all. It's in the record."

"And then he even got his money and his reward, and he still attacked the town. Now that's just crazy spite."

I audibly laughed a little over her summation and she heard me.

"Well, I know. It's just the way it is."

"Can I quote you on this," I asked.

And she laughed.

"You already ran my letter."

"Yes, I did."

"But you can quote me to high heaven on that."

I wrote a story about Faye's point of view, complemented by my column for that week. But they never saw publication. I decided that maybe it was true that we had done "enough already" in challenging Heemeyer's situation.

But after talking to Faye that day I felt much better about how I had seen the world during the days when Heemeyer was attacking and then suing the town and the Docheffs.

And with a new partnership in the works, well, maybe I would just stay on at the newspaper.

After that tumultuous week when we had been assailed again, when I thought I'd lose my job and when the sound of Marv's voice on his tapes sent me into a defensive depression, something changed. A week after the first time I endured listening to the tapes, I listened to the tapes again, but this time at night in the old school when I couldn't be disturbed. His lecturing tone and at times angry voice affected me differently this time.

I hadn't set out to get Marv. In fact, I bent over backward to try to help him. Yes, we had missed an appointment for his free new business story. But that was largely his fault, not mine. And then I made it up to him with free advertising. I hadn't set out to misrepresent or denigrate his positions on gambling, the batch plant or his water lines. In fact, we had gone out of our way to present his point of view clearly and prominently. There were even times on the batch plant debate when we believed Heemeyer had good points. I worked with Marv to get his point of view across, going out of my way to get his side of the story in print and in front of the public. I even criticized the town for some of its handling of the debate and the issues.

I did business with Marv and asked for his help on a special project of mine. What I got in return was snarling threats and a bill for damage that wasn't really my fault. I felt I had been set up.

I had to ponder if the town board had actively worked against Heemeyer. And really, what I saw in all those hearings and countless interviews was that the town honestly wrestled with the batch plant and the process. The town made honest mistakes but they weren't deliberate efforts to hide the truth or conspire. And yet once Heemeyer sued the town and the Docheffs, it became more difficult for the town to deal with Heemeyer in any way other that at arms length but still in deference to him.

Had the Docheffs and the Thompsons and all the other town leaders worked to push Heemeyer down because he was a newcomer? As much as I could see how a person might imagine there was some back-room cabal of local good ol' boys scheming to screw the newcomers (that's a stereotype harbored about small towns the world over), it just didn't exist in this case. In fact, there were many times when the Thompsons and the town officials disagreed with each other. There were many times when the Docheffs and the Thompsons disagreed over business and other issues. They were hardly the coffee-Klatsche buddies scheming away. They were more frequently scheming to find ways go get one up on each other! And yet Heemeyer insisted they schemed to get him when they could barely scheme to protect themselves from each other.

Heemeyer convinced himself that they had worked to deprive him of a business income that would pay for his retirement. In fact, Heemeyer did sell the property for what he wanted, but it was after his meeting God in his hot tub. Never mind the fact that he had succeeded in speculating on his property, he still had to believe he had been victimized.

What about the water and sewer lines? Heemeyer was convinced politics and meddling had prevented him from getting the water and sewer lines he needed. But I know that he had been proud of "getting away with" dodging the sewer issues. Friends of Heemeyer at the time would relate how he boasted of going along for a long time with a non-conforming septic system. I knew he could have paid for sewer lines, connections, and a lift station and had been in legal compliance for many types of uses as early as 1992. But he just didn't want to pay what it would cost. Nobody prevented him from stepping up to pay his way. He was treated just like anybody else would have been treated in the same position.

He just didn't see it that way. He didn't want to pay.

And I saw how for more than two years the town waited for Heemeyer to come into compliance with the water and sewer lines when he could do so for a lot less money, hoping he'd do so on his own, without a fight. But Heemeyer just flat out refused and he basically challenged the town, after considerable leniency, to enforce its codes and laws. Heemeyer, in other words, screwed himself on the water and sewer lines.

And yet the town board was actually reluctant to proceed in a forceful way on those issues. Finally it did so, but only as a last resort, and only when it was forced to do so.

In an odd way that can't be proven, it was as if Heemeyer wanted to lose that fight, too.

In fact, the town had done many of the things Heemeyer's defenders had claimed it hadn't done. It had given him chances to resolve the differences without a court fight. It had compromised on several points regarding the batch plant, insisting on mitigation from the Docheffs that wouldn't have been agreed upon without Marv's intervention. The town even voted closely in Heemeyer's favor on two occasions.

From where I sat, I saw where the town had "tossed Heemeyer a bone."

He didn't want a better batch plant next to his property. He wanted to stop it completely. He didn't care about environmental issues or impacts on the nearby neighborhood, the condition of his own property bearing witness to that. He merely wanted to get back at the Docheffs and force a higher price for the land he owned. He wanted to force them to buy it at a high mark-up. And when that failed, Heemeyer started to lose his moorings.

He wanted to sue. He did sue. He lost but by then it was too late. He had convinced himself that Granby and the town and the Docheffs and the Thompsons were all out to get the newcomer. It was a convenient fiction that justified even the most fantastical thinking, in which Heemeyer indulged.

I had to admit that the world according to Heemeyer and his defenders simply wasn't the real world. It simply wasn't the way it really happened. I knew what I witnessed.

I trusted my facts, once again.

While I knew I couldn't accept Marv's version of the world, I knew I had to accept that many others were going to accept his version no matter what. The facts of the situation didn't matter to them. The truth was meaningless for his supporters, as it was for him.

Many would indulge the visceral appeal of the cult of the Killdozer. That's just the way it was.

But I was never going to be a part of that cult. I know what happened. I had seen it with my own two eyes and heard it with my own ears.

Yet for many, who had only a sketchy and incomplete knowledge of the facts and circumstances, Marv would remain a hero.

And it would only get worse as time went on.

Ladies for Granby

In the hum and buzz of the conflicting opinions about Heemeyer's "heroism" that fall, another event took place that gave me and the victims confidence in our point of view and reassurance as members of the Granby-area community.

A group of well-intentioned and enterprising women who lived in and around Granby launched a new fundraising effort for the victims of the rampage. They named themselves the "Ladies for Granby" and wanted to pose semi-nude or suggestively on a calendar for 2005. The idea was inspired by similar efforts elsewhere and the hit movie "Calendar Girls." But this would be featuring local models and the proceeds from the sale of the calendar were to go to the victims.

Once the idea of the calendar started to circulate, one of the organizers, Karen Bloomfield, said they ended up with more women wanting to participate than there were months in the year.

The project was carried out with taste and restraint and by November of 2004 a calendar had been printed.

But like with many good deeds, this effort didn't get done without some punishment. Pickets were organized to take place outside the theatre where the first calendars were introduced in a well-publicized signing event. The protesters, some from local churches, assailed the use of nudity and "pornography" as immoral and they discouraged people from buying the calendar. Letters to the editor ran voicing similar sentiments. And yet many other letters ran in support of the Ladies for Granby.

Not only that, the effort garnered yet more national publicity for the Killdozer rampage as papers across the country ran stories about the Ladies for Granby. *The Denver Post, Rocky Mountain News* and the *Boston Globe* all interviewed the Ladies for Granby and the story was picked up and TV stations in Denver, which made the story available for national distribution through their affiliated networks.

Calendars were sold in Grand County and at the Tattered Cover bookstore in Denver. It sold out in a month and raised nearly $40,000 for victims of the rampage.

IV: Heemeyer as The New American Antihero

37. Celebrity, Empathy and Respect for Heemeyer

Matt Reed, a friend of Heemeyer's from Grand Lake, helped to organize the special memorial in Marvin Heemeyer's honor. They had his ashes. Word had been sent to riders in Grand Lake and across Colorado.

Forty snowmobiles headed out of the Idleglen parking area near Grand Lake the morning of January 15, 2005, filing up into the mountains west of Grand Lake where Marvin Heemeyer loved to snowmobile. Their destination, appropriately enough, was Gravel Mountain, the high-mountain promontory where Heemeyer and his beloved Thursday ride snowmobile group had ridden and played for years. The whine of the snowmobile cortege rang through the air. The day was cold and blustery.

Three riders who had wanted to attend the service got a late start and they pushed their sleds at top speeds to get to the memorial up on Gravel. At the North Supply intersection they came across Chris Ruske, a one-time champion snowmobile racer from Grand Lake, and invited him to attend Marv's "memorial." But Chris said he didn't care to go, not after what Marv had done to Thelma Thompson, Casey Farrell, and to the town of Granby.

The three riders looked at each other, shrugged almost in unison, gunned their sleds and then headed off fast up the main trail, sending rooster tails of snow high into the air behind their roaring snowmobiles. They caught up with the stream of sleds and the entire group arrived near the broad expanse of terrain at the top of Gravel Mountain. Stunted fir trees no taller than four feet bent to the east. Large boulders stuck out of the snow and the upward arcing mass of tundra and rock that defined the peak seemed to float in the air as its image merged in and out of the fog and blowing snow. The weather had turned blustery, cloudy and cold at the top of the mountain.

The snowmobilers reassessed their plans for the ceremony, shouting back and forth over the din of their idling engines and the hissing wind. The original plan had been for a group of the better snowmobilers to ride up to the prominent ridge on Gravel Mountain where an overhanging cornice formed to the eastward side. This was the place where, many times in the past, Heemeyer and his friends would high-point the massive hillside in their sleds, climbing in screams of power as they rode higher and higher before gravity and momentum stopped the climb and forced a thrilling descent back down the steep incline. They had planned to high point their sleds off the top cornice and each rider would release a handful of Heemeyer's ashes in the cold snowy air to settle in the snow fields, forest and streams far away down the mountain.

But the clouds were thick and the wind was blowing, adding to the difficulty of executing the original plan.

The core group of Marv's friends turned their backs to the wind. The bag holding Heemeyer's remains was opened and the wind whipped a few whisps of grey ashes out of the bag, like smoke. They took turns plunging their hands into the bag. They trotted to the sleds and in a line drove the snowmobiles over to another drop-off on Gravel Mountain called Dead Sled, a less precarious spot. They screamed over the edge and released Heemeyer's ashes into the wind, fog and snow.

The sleds returned to the sheltered spot in the lee side of a ridge and stopped in a ragged circle. Many of the riders then wiped the remaining ashes of Heemeyer off onto their coats and snowmobile bibs, vowing never to wash the ashes off.

After the ceremony the long line of snowmobiles headed back down the trails. Most of the people convened later at Pancho and Lefty's, a Mexican restaurant and bar in Grand Lake where Heemeyer used to gather with the Thursday riders. The group enjoyed a meal and

Matt Reed presented a power point show about Heemeyer. Once again, it was an emotional, bittersweet event.

Heemeyer was praised and remembered with fondness.

Even several years later, television and bloggers continued to follow any bit of news on the rampage. *Shockwave*, a show that appeared on the History Channel, did a segment during the winter approaching the three-year anniversary. The show highlighted the "shock and awe" of the event, presenting quickly the two sides of the story, but emphasizing the sheer novelty and strangeness of the event. That show was quickly followed by a series of interviews by Japanese television networks. They too, in the final product, emphasized the fright factor and the strange nature of Heemeyer's efforts. The Japanese show took a slightly different approach from others. I was surprised to see that more than three-quarters of the show was nothing more than a not-so-great dramatization of the rampage, told from the perspective of the police.

It was odd to see Japanese actors acting out the roles of people like Glen Trainor and me. They were, in general, running in fear from the Killdozer, with some clips of actual rampage footage thrown in for verisimilitude. To me, the real clips served only to emphasize how tacky the rest of the dramatization had become. The rampage, at least, if not Marv, was becoming celebrated in Japan, too.

In light of this renewed interest in the rampage, and to mark the three-year anniversary of it, I wrote a column in the *Sky-Hi News* about the good and bad legacies of the dozer rampage. It got a response. Grand Lake resident Lenny Brooks wrote a letter to the editor, which I published on June 17, 2007:

> *To the Editor:*
>
> *It takes two to tango.*
>
> *"Me Thinks Thou Doest Protest Too Much."*
>
> *Speaking not only for myself, but also for the entire county of Grand — minus the Good Ole Boy connections — stop berating Marv Heemeyer like he was just an evil-doer.*
>
> *Marv had friends, good ones, ones that could always count on him to help them. He was loved and the people he loved are offended by your complete denial of any complicity that drove Marv over the edge.*

Marv had a relatively normal life until he moved to Grand County. Everyone I've talked to about Marv and his situation has felt that if they had been in Marv's shoes, they too would have felt wronged. Everyone has limits and when you're pushed into a corner, you fight. Everyone fights with the weapons at hand.

Fortunately, I have a relatively objective view of the entire situation. I don't even know Marv Heemeyer. He was a motor-head, heavy into snowmobiling, and probably not a fan of the spotted owl. I must say, your one-sided coverage of "Marv, the Madman" has left me bewildered.

Regardless of your contentions, Marv was pushed over the edge by "Powers that Be." Fact, pure and simple. The fact that the town of Granby didn't realize that they were dealing with a perhaps unstable and passionate man, that had nothing left to lose, is certainly not to the town's credit. The law is not always black and white. Abuse of power can be subtle. All the town had to do was "Throw a Dog a Bone."

So please, if you can't report objectively like a newspaper is supposed to do, don't report at all. Let Marv Heemeyer rest in peace. Even Jesus forgives Marv, so why don't you find it in your heart to do the same. Remember the Amish.

Lenny Brooks
And everyone else that is sick of your tirade
Grand Lake

The headline for the letter, which I wrote, stated: "Lenny Brooks comes to rousing defense of Marv Heemeyer."

Shortly after the paper came out I got a phone call from Brooks. He was irate because I had called him a defender of Marv Heemeyer in the headline. At that point I thought it was Brooks who was suddenly protesting too much. The letter certainly sounded like a defense of Heemeyer to me.

It was then I started conducting more interviews. And it was unsettling for me to discover that many people in Grand County, including people he could have killed, began to harbor a peculiar sort of empathy for Marv Heemeyer with the passage of time. Some people feel sorry for him. Maybe it's just a form of pity. Maybe it's the enduring power of the Cult of the Killdozer.

I've noticed in the course of many interviews, and just from casual conversations with local residents, that many people who have legitimate reasons to hate Heemeyer don't. I didn't find anyone who expressed a denunciation of Heemeyer like the one uttered by Granby Mayor Ted Wang the day after the rampage. Instead, I've discovered a sort of head-scratching bewilderment about his actions that include respect for his success in life and sorrow over the spectacular and deranged conclusion to it.

Many ponder the rampage and try to find acts in it that suggest Heemeyer liked them or sympathized with them. Maybe they still feel so mesmerized by his actions that they want to find common ground with the man that essentially held Granby hostage for many hours. To me it resembles a variation of Stockholm Syndrome, a loosely corroborated phenomenon in which kidnapping victims feel sympathy and even respect for their captors, sometimes even to the point of defending them, despite the danger and pain endured in their captivity.

Of course, many feel he must have been mentally ill, but they temper that judgment with empathetic comments that surely he must have suffered in that state.

Keith Klingbail, the owner of the Blue Spruce Motel in Granby at the time, felt that Heemeyer had done him a little favor by plowing down the aspen trees Granby had planted on the sidewalks in front of his business. He had always liked Heemeyer and remembers sharing a few casual complaints with him over the years about the arbitrary and frustrating constraints of local government. He remembers seeing Heemeyer in the Country Ace Hardware in Granby store not too long before the rampage. Heemeyer, usually fairly talkative, wasn't himself that day. He seemed reserved and even a little anxious.

Keith says he didn't give that interaction a second thought until he learned of the rampage.

When I told Klingbail I was writing a book about the rampage, he ended his comments about Heemeyer with a plea: "Take it easy on Marv."

Law enforcement officers who were by circumstance Heemeyer's intended victims also voice this peculiar sort of sympathy for Heemeyer. Heemeyer shot at State Trooper Dave Batura with the .50-caliber rifle, but Batura thinks that later in the rampage Heemeyer nodded in approval to the Colorado State Patrol by going out of his way twice to avoid smashing up state patrol vehicles.

Lt. Walt Eldridge of the Grand County Sheriff's Department, who certainly could have been killed by Heemeyer if he hadn't run from those concrete barriers, also ascribes to Heemeyer seemingly less malign intentions than you'd expect from a potential victim. He contradicts himself in interviews, saying that Heemeyer was intent only on property destruction, then only seconds later acknowledging Heemeyer tried to kill him and others throughout the rampage.

Another law enforcement officer who was fired upon was also inclined to downplay what was apparently an attempt to shoot him. Sgt. Rich Garner knows he was shot at twice by the .308 that was mounted in the front of the Killdozer while the machine was on the north side of the batch plant. He saw the puffs of smoke. He heard the rounds whiz by over his head.

"I couldn't tell you whether he was trying to kill me," Garner says. "He fired the .308 from the front. They went zipping right over my head. Whether he was trying to kill me or just sent some rounds out there . . . " He adds that at the time he felt Heemeyer was trying to hit him, but he doesn't know that he feels exactly the same way now.

Despite these reservations about Heemeyer's intent, Garner is not hesitant to ascribe an indifference on the part of Heemeyer about any deaths or casualties in general.

"I've often thought that if Marv wanted to kill somebody, he really could have," Garner says. "But I also think that Marv was perfectly willing, that if someone was in the wrong place at the wrong time, and something happened to them, that he was willing to accept that as well."

He says this in connection with Heemeyer's attack on the Town Hall and the library, where children had been present just minutes before the Killdozer struck. "That was the one there that really made me stop and think that he didn't care . . . If somebody got hurt. If someone was stranded in the building there, so be it."

Garner also says that in the eyes of some people, shooting at a law enforcement officer isn't the same as shooting at a civilian, suggesting that for some shooting police isn't as reprehensible. "A lot of people see cops in a different light than other people," he says. In that way he also downplays the shots fired at him during the battle at the batch plant.

In these odd sorts of contradictions I find the power of the Killdozer mythology. The mythology gives Heemeyer's violent and life-threatening actions a cloak of benevolence, even among erstwhile victims. It's as if they give Heemeyer a hall pass and want to let him off the hook. This is despite the fact that Heemeyer could have killed or gravely injured them. That's the power of the Cult of the Killdozer.

Rhonda and Casey Farrell, the owners of Gambles, despite their losses and emotional trauma from the event, still feel bewildered. "I can't for the life of me think of anything we might have ever said or done to Marv, other than me being on the town board, that would have justified this," Casey Farrell says. "I'm baffled. Confused." Farrell is quick to add, as well, that he feels sorry for Heemeyer.

"To have that much bitterness and anger built up in him, it just must have been awful," says Rhonda Farrell, echoing her husband's sympathy for Heemeyer's bitter plight.

But Heemeyer was a success!

Investigator Piechocki, though, sums up a common sentiment about Heemeyer that many people voiced in a variety of ways. It is, in essence, a statement of respect for Heemeyer that acknowledges his prowess and success. Rather than outright criticism of Heemeyer, it's more of a back-handed compliment. Heemeyer painted himself in his tapes as the victim, ending up poor and broke. But the fact of the matter was that Heemeyer ended up with a good amount of money, and he could have ended up a fairly wealthy man.

"It just keeps getting rehashed on the Internet or on TV shows and stuff," Piechocki says. "It's almost become folklore, you know, at this point. You know, that's the guy that was screwed over by the town or screwed over by the judge, and this and that. None of these people have any inside information on, you know, whether or not he was actually screwed over or not. And my opinion was, boy I wish people would screw me over like that."

"It just shows how you know what can go wrong when somebody lets something eat at them instead of allowing yourself to move on," Piechocki says. "If I could have sold a muffler shop for $400,000, I would have been real happy with that . . . Alright so you buy something for $42,000, own it until 2004, make money off it during that time, and then sell it for 10 times what you paid for it. Tell me how that screws you over."

Piechocki speculated that with the sale of his house in Grand Lake, the sale of his muffler shop property in Granby, and with the proceeds from his auction, Heemeyer could have walked out of Grand County with a million dollars in his pocket. I think that's true and it points to the contradiction behind Heemeyer's view of his plight. I think he was a successful man who did well in his business dealings in Grand County. He made good money, he expanded his property holdings and he was able to enjoy doing things he loved. Some would say he had it made. He was able to turn on its head the standing joke about Grand County which goes like this: How do you leave Grand County with a million dollars? …Arrive with two million.

Heemeyer invested far less than a million and he certainly could have left with a million. But he instead chose to either see himself, or selectively portray himself, as "losing too much."

People respect Heemeyer because in many ways he actually was a success. They're confounded by his claims that he wasn't.

I too must confess a certain sort of sympathy and respect for Heemeyer. I often wonder how sad and contradictory it was for a man like Heemeyer to be so vulnerable. He was imposing, intelligent and resourceful yet he was also easily and irrevocably hurt by perceived financial and political defeats. He felt publicly humiliated. To be so plagued is a curse, in a way. I don't envy him and his tortured plight.

By June of 2008 the old lot at Gambles had started to sprout a few weeds and stray plants. It still looked like a glaring hole in the fabric of business in downtown Granby. By then, Casey and Rhonda Farrell had been running an appliance store out of two different locations. It wasn't worth it to rebuild.

But then something odd appeared on the lot. A crudely fashioned cross, made of wood, poked out of the soil. On it was written, barely legible: "Marv Heemeyer. Hero and Martyr. Rest in Peace."

I was surprised at the appearance of this poorly done memorial so close to the place where Heemeyer had died. But I wasn't surprised over what it said or the sentiment it expressed. Four years after I was jaded to the public perceptions of the rampage and Heemeyer and had just come to assume that much of the world sympathized with the words scrawled on the cardboard. But it was in awfully bad taste to rub these thoughts right in the faces of Casey and Rhonda, right on their property where they had lost so much because of Heemeyer. I just shook my head over it.

Casey yanked the little shrine out of the ground as soon as he saw it and chucked it into the trash.

Five months later I'm at the baths in Hot Sulphur Springs, soaking in the hot pool that sits highest in the rambling little hot springs resort. The cold air smells of sulphur, like rotten eggs, but the hot water feels good. The small pool has six people sitting in it, all of them relaxing and getting warm. I'm with my friend Bill Anderson.

We start talking to one of the young men sitting across from us. He looks to be about 30 years old, works at a pole yard and lumber mill close to Granby. He shares his tribulation with finding jobs over the last year. He's a local, born in Kremmling and a graduate of the high school in Granby.

"I know you," he says to me. "You're from the paper."

"Not anymore. We sold."

I tell him I'm working in consulting and doing research for this book.

"Oh yeah. Marv. He got screwed."

I say nothing, surprised that he would just say this so openly to me, one of the victims of the rampage. Didn't he think I might feel differently about Heemeyer? Perhaps he was hoping for a confrontation. I let it rest. But I couldn't resist.

"Well, some people think so. But I don't. I was there for all the hearings. I saw it all. Marv wasn't screwed and he made out in the long run. He just lost it."

I looked more closely at this young man. I didn't recognize him. But he seemed happy. My comment didn't seem to bother him at all.

"You know he just got treated wrong. The town. All that water stuff. He just fought back. He did what he had to do."

This time I just let it ride.

"I'm amazed how people come to his defense," I said, after a pause. The two other people in the hot pool weren't listening. They seemed occupied and in their own worlds of hot water and vapor.

"I did," he said.

I said nothing.

"You remember that cross and memorial put up over there at Gambles?"

"Yes, I do."

"That was me. I did it. It was for Marv. Somebody had to remember him. His suffering. I'm glad I did."

"I don't think Casey was at all happy about that — what you did. You just don't know the story."

"Oh, Hell, Casey'll be alright. I know what I need to know. Everything's for the better."

"Well, to each his own."

We sat there. I felt uncomfortable and amazed all over again. With only the vaguest sense of the facts, the story or without even knowing Heemeyer, people rushed to his defense. It was an instinct.

The topic of the conversation switched over to other local topics, like the coming winter and the prospects for a winter of deep snow and great skiing.

The power of the Heemeyer American antihero myth has even recently been used to inspire international cinema. The Russian film *Leviathan*, released in the United States in November of 2014, was inspired by stories the film's producers had heard about Heemeyer's Killdozer rampage.

That inspiration was explained in an article by James Rann that appeared in an on-line journal of New York University's Jordan Center for the Advanced Study of Russia: "Before the screening in a central London cinema, to an audience of cinephiles and *bien pensant* Russian expats, producer Alexander Rodnyansky gave the film an eloquent introduction in which he emphasised the universality of its themes and repeated the story of its genesis: while in America in 2008 filming a section for *New York, I Love You*, Zvyagintsev (the director) was told the story of Marvin Heemeyer, a mechanic who, aggrieved by a dispute with local authorities, went on a bulldozer rampage, leveling buildings in his hometown of Granby, Colorado. This origin story has been told repeatedly, by both Rodnyansky and Zvyagintsev, seemingly as part of a campaign to prove the international relevance of their version of one little guy's struggles against the implacable might of indifferent government."

In an article in *The Calvert Journal*, Director Zvyagintsev states the film's "idea is based on a particular story in America, as soon as it was brought to our territory it acquired certain details that managed to pass on the message about our own circumstances very precisely."

The Heemeyer myth bolsters, in the producers' minds, the international relevance of their version of one little man's struggles against the power and corruption of indifferent government, in this case, the corrupt government of Russia.

Never mind that the little governmental entities of Granby really weren't so indifferent to Heemeyer's plight. Never mind that they weren't corrupt at all. But such is the power of the Killdozer's antihero myth.

Heemeyer continues to live on Facebook

Heemeyer may have died in the flesh on June 4, 2004, but he continues to live in the virtual world of Facebook.

I learned that lesson on the ten-year anniversary of the Killdozer rampage in 2014. After being interviewed by the local newspaper for a rampage anniversary story, I got a worried call from the Granby Chamber of Commerce.

"Marv Heemeyer lives," Cathie Hook, the chamber director, told me.

She waited just long enough for me to respond: "What?"

"That is, on Facebook."

A virtual Marvin Heemeyer had risen from the dead to appear on Facebook several days prior to the 10-year anniversary of the bulldozer rampage in Granby, posting a question to the Granby chamber and "liking" a negative post about Granby.

The post, by a W. Ryan Krauss of Seattle, Wash., states: "Small Business killers. I hope your whole town withers."

But what really got Hook's attention was when that negative post was "liked" by a Marvin Heemeyer. Facebook has a Marvin Heemeyer page, complete with a profile photo of Heemeyer in the foreground, behind which is a photo of the Town of Granby parking lot taken just after the rampage, showing a damaged building and two smashed-up police cars. This is not a Facebook page about Marv Heemeyer. Rather, it's a Facebook page created to look as if Marv Heemeyer was still alive and he was managing the page himself.

That incarnation of the Heemeyer Facebook page appears to have been created May 8, 2014. Two other apparent Marvin Heemeyer pages that have gotten less attention were created earlier that same year.

Shortly after the negative Krauss posting, another negative post appeared on the Granby Chamber of Commerce's Facebook page wall. Edward Kelly's post reads: "Why didn't you horrible people leave Marvin an outlet to address his grievances? You are the worst sort of politicians . . ."

Another posting to the Granby Chamber of Commerce page two days prior to June 4, 2014, reads: "Any fun celebrations happening on the 4th?" That posting came from the Marvin Heemeyer Facebook page and has the name Marvin Heemeyer attached to it. That question was clearly a taunt at the Granby community.

One of the Facebook "friends" of Marvin Heemeyer is a bearded Justin Popp. A post from "Marvin Heemeyer" on his page states: "Shirt looks good on you bigot."

The shirt worn by Popp is a green T-shirt with a line drawing of Heemeyer's bulldozer tank on the front, above which is written "Never forget" with the date "6/4/04" below it. The photo has 23 "likes."

In the world of social media, it appears that many of Marvin Heemeyer's fans never will forget their hero, bolstered by the narrative that he was victimized by a corrupt small-town government and snickered at as a newcomer by narrow-minded locals.

Heemeyer "lives on" for his story to be reinvented day after day in the digital, on-line world.

As if it wasn't enough that the long-dead Marvin Heemeyer had his own Facebook page, hero-worshipping praise for him appeared again in a big way on Facebook in 2017. A posting about Heemeyer appeared on the Facebook page of a Tyler Macfarlane, listed as being from Pittsburgh,

Pennsylvania. His posting was placed on the 13th anniversary of the Killdozer rampage in June of 2017.

It deserves to be repeated here in full as it fairly well summarizes the false narrative and antihero myth that has elevated Heemeyer in the eyes of many people in the general public. In it, Macfarlane shows how he was completely taken in by the myth Heemeyer:

Today is a special day. June 4th 2017 marks the 13th anniversary of the Killdozer's rampage through Granby Colorado.

Sit down kids and let me tell you a tale, about a reasonable man driven to do unreasonable things.

Marvin Heemeyer was a man who owned a muffler shop in Granby Colorado. The city council ordained to approve the construction of a concrete factory in the lot across from Marvin's shop. In the process this blocked the only access road to the muffler shop. Marvin petitioned to stop the construction to no avail. Petitioned to construct a new access road, and even bought the heavy machinery to do so himself. Denied.

The concrete factory went up in disregard to the ramifications on Marvin's business. To add insult to injury, the factory construction disconnected the muffler shop from the city sewage lines. An indifferent city government then chose to fine Marvin for this.

His business and livelihood were in ruin. Rather than lie down and die, Marvin chose to fight back. Over the course of a year and a half Marvin secretly outfitted the bulldozer he bought to save his business with three foot thick steel and concrete armor, camera systems guarded with bulletproof glass.

On June 4th 2004 Marvin Heemeyer lowered the armored shell over top of himself, entombing himself inside the Killdozer to make his last stand.

He burst fourth from the walls of his muffler shop and straight into the concrete factory that ruined his business. Over the course of the next several hours Marvin drove his Killdozer through 13 buildings owned by those officials that had wronged him, including the city council building itself.

Swat teams swarmed the dozer, but it proved immune to small arms fire and even explosives. Another piece of heavy machinery was even brought out to fight the Killdozer, but it too fell to the dozers righteous fury.

In the end, Marvin's Killdozer became trapped in one of the buildings it was built to destroy. Marvin chose to take his life, the only life he took that day.

Today we celebrate Killdozer day and Marvin Heemeyer, the last great American folk hero. A man driven to the brink who chose to fight back against an indifferent system.

From notes left behind after his passing: "I was always willing to be reasonable until I had to be unreasonable. Sometimes reasonable men must do unreasonable things." *HAPPY MOTHERFUCKING KILLDOZER DAY EVERYONE.*

In the three days after the posting went up, Facebook stats on the page show that there were 76,000 positive responses to the post. It was shared 95,083 times and there were 7,758 comments. The majority of the comments are along the lines of statements like "This is what happens when government pushes a man too far." Or "right on, the little man fights back and defeats town hall."

A few comments attempt to present a more balanced point of view, suggesting that the violence wasn't justified and that perhaps Heemeyer was deranged. One poster, Martin Smith of Granby, who had written an article about the rampage for the *Los Angeles Times Magazine* in 2004, attempted to inject some balance into the long string of mostly pro-Marv comments. As he told me, he was "shouted down" by other comments that followed his attempt to present a point of view that painted the truth about the incident.

The string of simply false statements in Macfarlane's post repeat and again exaggerate the mythical narrative that shrouds the Killdozer incident. For starters, the town did not ordain anything that blocked access to Heemeyer's shop. The shop's main access was in place up until the day of the rampage. Heemeyer never petitioned to build a new access road since he never lost his access road. To suggest that the concrete batch plant went up without regard to the ramifications on Heemeyer's business is certainly a stretch, since the concrete batch plant plans were modified many times to conform to concerns that had been raised by Heemeyer in the many public hearings. The plant was improved, thanks to Marv. But Heemeyer's goal wasn't to improve the plant — it was to stop it completely. The goal of stopping the plant was to force the Docheffs to pay the exorbitant price Marv wanted for his two lots.

Macfarlane's post then twists the facts entirely to suggest the town disconnected Heemeyer from sewer lines by allowing the batch plant.

Heemeyer never was on any town or regional sewer system. Instead, he used (and bragged about to Mel Waggoner) an out-of-compliance sewer tank on his property for years, which the local authorities essentially ignored until easily accessible sewer and water lines were put in place because of the construction of the batch plant.

Heemeyer was offered free easements to the new lines for his service connections by the Docheffs if he'd drop his lawsuit. He refused. And he never made a move to connect to the new water and sewer lines despite more than a year of patience by the town of Granby after he was given notice and gently reminded several times by Granby Town Manager Tom Hale. He was fined only after 17 months of forbearance by the town and the court. He just flat-out refused to cooperate.

The notion that his business was in ruin is also a canard foisted upon the world by the Heemeyer fans and by Heemeyer himself. By his own actions Heemeyer decided to ramp down his muffler business and auctioned it all off. And then, to cap off his success at the site, he managed to sell his muffler shop property for $400,000. This was the property he had been trying to sell to the batch plant owners at inflated prices ever since he had bought the property at an FDIC auction in 1992. His gain was nearly ten-fold, as he bought the property for $42,000. As many people have noted, Heemeyer actually made out quite well with his business and his real estate investment. He was hardly in "ruins," other than by his own actions.

Marv is then referred to as the last great American folk hero.

How is it that this heroic myth persists?

38. Explaining Heemeyer as a New American Antihero

"This is the West, sir. When the legend becomes fact, print the legend."

— Newspaper Editor Maxwell Scott in the classic western film *The Man Who Shot Liberty Valance*

Why do many Americans embrace an antihero like Marv Heemeyer? How is it that antiheroes like him are becoming more common and accepted? Why do people increasingly accept these violent, anti-social loners? How is it that fact-challenged and mean-spirited narratives are inching closer and closer to the mainstream?

At the most basic level, this tendency could be explained by what Daniel Kahneman, the Princeton economist and psychologist, presents in his book *Thinking, Fast and Slow*. Kahneman sees that our minds operate under two systems, called System 1 and System 2. System 1 is based on emotional and intuitive feelings, reacting on instinct. System 2, however, is less instinctive and more cognitive. System 2 thinking takes its time to evaluate any problem and weighs the evidence in a deliberative manner. It judges, based on input. System 1 is much more reactionary.

System 1 thinking can lead to an embrace of myth and an antihero like Heemeyer.

Cass Sunstein, a Harvard law professor who has written numerous articles on American behavior for respected journals, has emerged as a leading thinker on the origins and causes of myth-based and fact-challenged opinion in America. One of his books, called *Conspiracy Theories and Other Dangerous Ideas*, explores how people acting under

System 1 tend to formulate far-fetched conspiracy theories and act on impulse rather than thought. Under Kahneman's system these people have been primed by their biases to facilely believe in what they've emotionally been conditioned to feel is true. In this way of thinking, people can believe that the CIA killed Kennedy, the FBI plotted 9/11 and President Obama was born in Africa.

With Kahneman's and Sunstein's thinking in mind, people would end up lionizing Marvin Heemeyer because they feel and believe Heemeyer had to have been victimized by government, the press and xenophobic locals to carry out such an act. Heroes being victimized by government or the establishment is a key trope of this story line. These odd hero worshippers indulge their deepest longings as a way to co-opt the truth. In this way they create corrupt American antiheroes.

And they create a seriously fact-challenged environment.

The Internet plays a critical role in the growing prominence of these fractured facts and the corrupted hero phenomenon. It's important to remember, however, that when Marv Heemeyer plowed through Granby in his tank, social media on the Internet was just barely a reality. But the Internet was still a place where news and myths could go viral through blogs and a wide range of "news" sites. People shared and discussed information that appealed to their biases, but it wasn't as easy to do in 2004 as it is today with sharing, liking and tweeting on social media sites.

Back in 2004 and 2005, when the Killdozer became an on-line myth, songs, videos and stories in general could go "viral" on the Internet when they become extremely popular and were shared millions of times. When it comes to this sort of twisted hero worship bolstered by bogus facts, I like to think of it as going "tribal" — but not tribal in the sense of ethnic similarity. It's tribal in the sense of a unified, paranoid ideological consensus — a sort of like-minded grouping around conspiracy that Sunstein discusses in his book. I feel this is what happened early on with the Heemeyer incident.

As Sunstein states, conspiracy theories blossom and expand when people of similar beliefs listen only to what other people of similar beliefs spout in the echo chambers of web pages and social media sites. In the wide open world of the Internet, people can create a blog or web page post in which they say anything they want, true or not. Most of these web pages and blogs aren't fact-checked or edited. So people can spout their half truths and lies and find, through the miracle of excellent search engine technology, people who have similar interests and who want to nurture similar illusions. In this way people create groups of like-minded thinkers and bloggers.

In writing for the *Bloomberg View*, Sunstein presented evidence about new research that backs up the assertion that confirmation bias spread through the internet enables a new sort of fact-challenged reality.

The study addresses the question of why misinformation spreads so quickly on social media. It hints at an explanation of why there are so many hoaxers, anti-hero worshippers and antigovernmental conspiracy theorists. Why do people accept these falsehoods spouted on-line? The study focuses on Facebook users and provides strong evidence that confirmation bias plays a strong role in this phenomenon. Confirmation bias is a person's tendency to seek out information that confirms their belief and feelings while ignoring contrary information. When there are groups of like-minded people, the numbers grow.

The study was led by Michela Del Vicario of Italy's Laboratory of Computational Social Science. It looked at the postings of Facebook users from 2010 to 2014. The researchers found that there are many communities of like-minded people, which isn't surprising. But these groups tended to accept baseless conspiracy theories as they spread in these echo chambers of like-minded biases. These users chose and shared information they accepted and neglected information they rejected. Sunstein writes that "The consequence is the 'proliferation of biased narratives fomented by unsubstantiated rumors, mistrust and paranoia.'"

The study doesn't make any attempt to compare the numbers of such like-minded groups and echo chambers to an earlier period, when there was no Facebook or Internet blogosphere. But I feel that the existence of social media and the Internet makes it easier for such misinformed groups to spread and breed, if you will, certainly at a rate higher than before the days of blogs and social media. This could explain the rise of corrupt antiheroes like Heemeyer and the spread of hoaxers and far-fetched conspiracy theorists.

Sunstein expands greatly on the idea that social media and Internet connectivity in general result in echo chambers among like-minded believers in his book *#republic*, published in 2017. This echo chamber effect tends to create even more extreme partisan positions and more reliance on ideology over facts. In this book Sunstein expands on this notion and explains how this phenomenon can be bad for democracy and society in general. His book is subtitled *Divided Democracy in the Age of Social Media.* In essence it describes how the way in which people use the Internet today, largely through social media, results in a truth-challenged media landscape that causes new levels of political conflict, polarization and violent extremism.

The broader trend Sunstein notes in his book *#republic* is what I feel happened with the myth of the Killdozer rampage that created Heemeyer as an American antihero.

Sunstein proposes legal changes and structural changes in the Internet that will allow people to get out of their echo chambers and see and experience other points of view, allowing for honest democratic deliberation that won't be so polarizing or blind to the truth.

The Decline of Facts

Micheal P. Lynch has written a book called *The Internet of Us: Knowing More and Understanding Less in the Age of Big Data.* Lynch was called a "philosopher of truth" in a *New Yorker* review of his book penned by Jill Lepore. Lynch's book explores the way in which most people today use Google or the Internet to establish the truth of a fact. Lynch writes that most people's knowledge today is "Google-knowing — knowledge acquired online." Facts aren't observed, they are downloaded. This, I believe, allows for an easy way for people to find "factual" validation for their biases and beliefs without really knowing they are merely confirming their misconceptions. Lynch makes it clear that the Internet didn't create or cause this problem, but he notes that the Internet exaggerates it.

In a world where extreme websites spout their ideologies to tribes of like-minded believers, facts and the truth have become compromised. Just consider the many fact-checking websites out there on-line. Some do a good job, but many have cropped up to cater to the site's own partisan or cultural biases. These partisan sites create fractured, fact-checked facts that make truth elusive.

The Cultural Antihero

Then there are the new American heroes of television and film. Long gone are the days when we could venerate a pure sort of hero like Superman or Roy Rogers of 50 years ago. It's been as if television and cinematic scriptwriters have taken too far the dictum that a plausible hero should have flaws and imperfections. Think of Clint Eastwood's character in *Forgiven*, a renegade killer who nonetheless redeems a town. Or Patrick Bateman in the novel and film adaptation of *American Psycho* by Bret Easton Ellis. Here's a successful New York investment banker living the good life who is also a sadistic serial killer who even engages in cannibalism. The film ends with Bateman as a banal American success despite his murderous and sadistic acts. He's a survivor, somehow, with fatal and grievous flaws. He is corrupt, but he's the hero — a new American antihero.

On television these flawed heroes thrive. Consider Dexter Morgan in the popular TV show *Dexter*. He's a blood spatter analyst by day who's also a serial killer, but with a twist. He only kills people, usually in profoundly awful ways, who he can prove are guilty of murder and heinous crimes themselves. So he's a lawless, craven redeemer — an ambiguous and corrupt hero. Or consider the hit show *Breaking Bad*. The show's hero is Walter White, a high school chemistry teacher who is diagnosed with cancer. To secure extra funds and guarantee his family's future, White starts manufacturing and selling crystal meth. In the process, he becomes deeply corrupted by the ins and outs of the illicit drug trade. He's lawless, a murderer, yet he's also a noble redeemer for his family. He's ambiguous and corrupt, and yet he's the hero of the show.

America has been given permission to love corrupt and even craven heroes.

Roots in America's Founding Document

It's not as if every American alive rushes out and praises the most recent mass killer. But there is something disturbing to me about some reactions to the latest Heemeyer-like rampage, the latest mass killing, the most recent horrific event or the latest renegade patriot, anarchist or political zealot challenging government. First, the events are seemingly celebrated on all media simply through exposure. Secondly, the facts of the exposure are then twisted or denied to meet the ideological bent of a group or a person. And then victims and witnesses are maligned and the perpetrators lionized or ignored, giving an odd sort of tacit approval.

Then consider the ingrained influence of the founding element of the constitution of the United States: The First Amendment to the Constitution.

This amendment is unique as a foundational, fundamental right. It was based on a deep suspicion of government. The right to a free press and free practice of religion came about as a reaction against the governments of Europe, where government controlled or prosecuted the news outlets of the day and where government and religion were commingled, much to the distress of the common man. Thomas Jefferson, in framing the First Amendment, felt that the monarchical and dictatorial tendencies of government could be reined in by the practice of a free and independent "press" that could question, attack and even ridicule government without fear of confiscation or arrest.

This skepticism expressed through speech is deeply rooted in the American consciousness. With the advent of the Internet, wide-open blogging, un-edited "web newspapers," social media and electronic information dissemination of all kinds, this skepticism about government and the "official" line of "mainstream media" has resulted in an emotional free-for-all on-line when it comes to facts and opinion. Many people, inspired by a vague understanding of the First Amendment, feel it's their God-given right and duty to spout their beliefs, many times buttressed by questionable facts, on-line. These are citizen "journalists" of the sort not envisioned by Thomas Jefferson more than two centuries ago. These are also people simply spouting their thoughts of the day on Facebook, Google Plus or any other of the many blogging platforms.

This skepticism is a part of our consciousness. So as people search for explanations to the vexing issue of the notoriety that surrounds mass violence perpetrated by gun-toting rampagers it's not far-fetched for them to grasp at the nearest emotional solution. It's vaguely appealing for some to see "government" conspiring in the background. It's vaguely appealing to share as citizen journalists, bloggers and Facebook posters these baseless but reassuring suspicions. And suddenly there are like groups of hoaxers, antihero worshippers and conspiracy theorists, spouting as gospel one-sided and bogus information that seems more real because there's a group or community of like-minded opinion.

That's how the outlandish slowly but surely gets closer to the mainstream.

Our Superheroes Are Antiheroes

And yet, there is something heroic, almost superheroic, about an antihero like Marv Heemeyer. The appeal of this new national heroic ideal is explored in a book called the *Myth of the American Superhero*, by John Shelton Lawrence and Robert Jewett.

Lawrence and Jewett address the growing popularity of vigilante-style narratives in American culture and how they blend with a sort of instinctive adoration of people standing up against government. The Heemeyer narrative, and the narrative of other recent new American antiheroes, mesh well with the myth of the superhero, which can be traced back to the cowboy stories of the Old West.

There is something irresistibly attractive to the American psyche about the persona of Heemeyer and his Killdozer and these other corrupt heroes.

As described by Lawrence and Jewett, Heemeyer and many of our new antiheroes reflect the new American heroic paradigm distinguished by disguised origins, pure motivations, a redemptive task and extraordinary powers. This superhero "originates outside the community he is called to save, and in those exceptional instances when he resides therein, the superhero plays the role of the idealistic loner. His identity is secret, either by virtue of his unknown origins or his alter ego; his motivation is a selfless zeal for justice."

"By elaborate conventions of restraint, his desire for revenge is purified. Patient in the face of provocations, he seeks nothing for himself and withstands all temptations. He renounces sexual fulfillment for the duration of the mission and the purity of his motivations ensures his moral infallibility in judging persons and situations. When he is threatened by violent adversaries, he finds an answer in vigilantism, restoring justice and thus lifting the siege of paradise. In order to accomplish this mission without incurring blame or causing undue injury to others, he requires superhuman powers. The superhero's aim is unerring, his fists irresistible, and his body incapable of suffering fatal injury. In the most dangerous trials he remains utterly cool and thus divinely competent."

Heemeyer, like our other antiheroes, has come from outside the community. He hails from South Dakota and the Front Range of Colorado near Denver.

Heemeyer played the role of the idealistic, non-sexual loner well. In his tapes he states that if he had been married or had children, maybe this wouldn't have had to happen. Our other antiheroes were unmarried and childless.

Heemeyer showed elaborate conventions of restraint in not lashing out at town government during the public meetings over the batch plant. Several of our antiheroes seem restrained in the way they waited to carry out their extreme violence.

Heemeyer, for example, held back and seemed almost passive in his dealings with the town over the sewer and water lines. He waited. He appeared patient in the face of the perceived provocations. In this way, Heemeyer also imbued his judgments against the town and the community with a sort of moral infallibility, at least from his perspective. He patiently endured loss and wrongdoing for years so suddenly it was OK to lash back with vindictive fury. Since no one was killed, he shows even more elaborate and admirable "restraint."

Our heroes give themselves superhuman powers. Heemeyer wrapped himself in an impenetrable cocoon of armor.

Heemeyer is disguised and his identity is a "secret," like that of most superheroes. Heemeyer concealed the construction of his machine. The window-less steel shell of the Killdozer is Heemeyer's disguise. It's Spiderman's costume, Superman's Clark Kent, Batman's mask and the Lone Ranger's covered eyes.

Heemeyer found a reason for his mission in "vigilantism," going outside the law to restore "justice" and "lift the siege of paradise." As he says throughout his tapes, he's going to "teach" the people and government of Granby a lesson and perhaps keep it all from happening again. Heemeyer is the self-fashioned redeemer, hoping to bring about a twisted sort of justice.

Heemeyer believed his act was a mission of vigilante like justice and redemption. Others perceived them in the same way and were able to interpret his violent act as a form of corrective justice that aspired to a purer, better world. Some can see the acts as noble.

Heemeyer, at least, even did a good job of carrying out his mission without incurring blame or causing undue injury to others by using the Killdozer to attack only his perceived targets. He *seems* selective and not random in his task. He *appears* to be intent only on property damage to those who have done (him) wrong. He opens the door for dodging blame.

It's no accident, I believe, that the Vin Diesel film, *A Man Alone*, was found in the videos Heemeyer had in the shed where he built the Killdozer. The movie reflects in many ways the mythic structure of the American Superhero as spelled out by Jewett and Lawrence.

The reality behind Heemeyer's story reveals that the Heemeyer heroic myth is distorted. There was no conspiracy of government, lawyers and locals united against Heemeyer. The town may have been clumsy and inept at times in its dealings with Heemeyer, but it wasn't out to get him. The town, actually, was afraid of and deferential toward Heemeyer.

Heemeyer's efforts aren't the noble quest to teach Granby a lesson and redeem the town of its crimes against him, because no actual crimes were committed. Heemeyer invented town crimes and acts against him to justify his spree. In this light his righteous vengeance becomes nothing more than sour grapes and he looks less like a hero and more like an extremely inspired and obsessed sore loser. He invokes God as a buttress to his righteous rage, but the fact is that divine inspiration was an indulgence of his imagination as well. He created it to give his petty gripes Divine significance, a key ingredient of the superheroic paradigm.

In essence, this American monomyth of the superhero revealed in Heemeyer's followers is anti-democratic, anti-government and destructive. Heemeyer literally and figuratively attacked and destroyed small town democracy, defying it first and then attempting to destroy it. He attacked the town hall of Granby. He attacked and attempted to destroy the instruments that make democracy work, such as a free press. He attacked independent businesses simply because he disagreed with them. But the myth of the wronged superhero redeeming himself and a community wronged by government corruption makes him appealing.

Many people are biased in favor of the Killdozer-as-hero explanation because it helps to explain the problem (man goes berserk in armed bulldozer, destroys town and shoots at people) with an attractive and readily remembered narrative of the noble victim.

The tragedy of this new antihero mythology goes beyond the tragic violence perpetrated by the antiheroes. It's the revelation of how vulnerable the American psyche is to a narrative of selfish, corrupt and divinely inspired lone vigilantism against community, a free press and democratic government.

This is the social and cultural tragedy of Marv Heemeyer as a new American antihero.

Epilogue

"I think he (Heemeyer) will always be admired," Matt Reed of Grand Lake said in an interview. "I think anybody, you know, short of a couple of people in Granby, should be all proud and happy of Marv too. Look at how much better their town is now because of what he did. Granted, it was kind of a wreck at first, and it was a big deal. . . . They went from being kind of the armpit of the county to being on the map, in a big way. They got all new buildings. Everybody that got affected they got a building out of it."

Reed's comments conform with a version of events adhered to by the Killdozer Cult that purports Granby got urban renewal and "free" buildings (because of insurance and donations) as a result of the rampage. This line of reasoning contends that the rampage was a huge blessing in disguise. This false narrative claims that in one fit of violence, Heemeyer gave Granby a town that was so much better; that he really did somehow redeem, purify and improve the corrupt town.

In other words, Marv was a hero.

The facts paint a different picture.

Each target of the rampage went through its own unique process in rebuilding. Some received fair insurance payouts while others didn't. For some, the insurance dealings were acceptable, for others they were a nightmare. After rebuilding, Granby ended up with new and remodeled buildings it hadn't had before the rampage. But that came with a cost both financial and emotional.

A tally of the real costs and long-term impacts of the rampage, offset by insurance payouts and charitable gifts, shows that Heemeyer succeeded in costing the businesses and people of Granby a lot of money, even with the facelift. The added costs, in some cases, are likely to continue until 2025.

By my accounting, the total financial cost is $10 million. A new library, a new Town Hall and repairs to streets and other infrastructure represent the taxpayers' contribution to that number. The cost to private businesses and individuals is also significant.

Emotional scars persist as a result of the rampage. For people like Casey and Rhonda Farrell, owners of Gambles, there's a lingering feeling of sorrow and loss. They did, after all, lose their longstanding business. Unpleasant memories spawned by the event remain.

It was, for many, a traumatizing event. For some victims, who buried themselves in the hard work of recovering, the initial impacts might not have been as obvious. For me, I know I was so immersed in simply getting my job done and rebuilding, it was as if I had no time to dwell upon it all. But I'd be a liar if I didn't say that feelings of anger and fear were common reactions I felt for two or three years after, whenever topics relating to the Killdozer rampage arose.

Many times, when discussions of the rampage come up, they are informed by false narratives that assert the town was corrupt, that it mistreated Heemeyer and that people in town were out to get him as a newcomer. From what I saw, that narrative simply was not true. That narrative foreshadowed the post-truth America of today.

Which is not to say there weren't a few jokes to arise from the rampage.

My favorite goes like this.

A month after the rampage, a man walks into the local heavy equipment store. He's interested in buying a new bulldozer for his excavation company. He checks out the models on the lot and he picks out a sturdy, mid-sized model. It's used. He works out the price with the dealership's manager and then says he'll pull around back to drive it onto his trailer.

'You can't do that,' the dealer says.

'Why not?'

'I thought you knew.'

'Knew what?'

'The town just passed a new law. There's a 45-day cooling off period on dozer purchases.'

Or there's the story told by Lana Mills, a hairdresser who was working at a salon in Grand Lake the day of the rampage. She says she was busy doing someone's hair, when news started to come in about a person going crazy in a bulldozer tank in Granby.

She says she, her co-workers and patrons, after feeling alarmed about the event, started to speculate on who it could have been inside the bulldozer tank. This was before people really knew details about what was happening.

'The funny thing is,' she says, 'we came up with about six names before we even got to Marv Heemeyer.'

Or there was the proposal for a new town slogan voiced at a town meeting two weeks after Heemeyer had demolished the town hall. A wag at the meeting said the town slogan should be: 'Granby's not just a great town. It's Marvinless!'

I also liked the short poem dreamed up by Dan Schneller and Don Dailey, two longtime Grand County locals. They composed it while sitting in the Lariat Saloon in Grand Lake:

By the sewer he lived,
By the sewer he died,
Some say it was murder,
Others say it was sewercide.

I remain puzzled after the rampage. I still wonder about the sheer power of will and determination that drove Heemeyer to his task. I wonder if he was driven only by a motive of revenge justified by God's will to teach us a lesson. I think pride played a role in his actions. I have deliberately avoided speculating on his sanity or wondering about what psychological malady may have prevailed in his life that could have allowed him to go so far with his rage. Was he overly narcissistic? Was he a sociopath? It's impossible to know. Suicide, in my mind, is the ultimate statement about his overall psychological state of mind. I still have pangs of doubt about the role I played in it all, but those pass when I look at the facts.

The true lasting impact of the rampage to me is the curious nature of the way people react to it. Yes, there are many who see it as the act of violence and terrorism that it was, roundly condemning it, although not without a feeling of awe over Heemeyer's accomplishment.

What puzzles me is the continued celebration and even defense of Heemeyer from people all around the world and locally. Many know the facts and choose not to heed their import. Most don't know the facts of the event and don't care to know them. They just want to celebrate and even venerate anyone who would "get back at the man" in such a glorious and bizarre manner, immediately creating a fictional narrative to justify the event.

I've now seen similar reactions to any number of national crises and watershed moments. People deliberately or unwittingly fracture the facts of a trauma, create a conspiracy to explain those events and then venerate unworthy heroes. It's not only violent rampagers who gain positive acclaim. Politicians and cultural leaders also benefit from this tendency to believe false narratives. In these contexts, the facts take a back seat to personal bias.

I'm still puzzled, and alarmed, by that.

In this sense, all of us who live and function in today's society are the ongoing victims of the distortions, conspiracies and depraved role models foisted upon us. A critical eye, an appreciation of the facts and honest skepticism about our own biases are the ways we as a nation can triumph in this age of fractured facts and flawed American antiheroes.

I now know that I had an early taste of this post-truth America as I lived through the saga of Marv Heemeyer and his Killdozer.

A man and his revenge machine

It took a considerable amount of time and planning for Marvin Heemeyer to convert a used bulldozer into a tank and then use it to destroy specific buildings in Granby on June 4.

The armament

Entry
There was a hole through the top of the armor, much like a manhole, that Heemeyer bolted shut after he was inside.

Steering
Heemeyer could tell where he was going by watching three video monitors in the cab of the bulldozer. Five video cameras mounted around the vehicle sent images to the monitors.

Portholes
Multiple pieces of 1/2- to 3/4-inch-thick plexiglass were used in the viewing ports and in front of some cameras for protection. In addition, the viewing ports had sliding metal plates inside the vehicle.

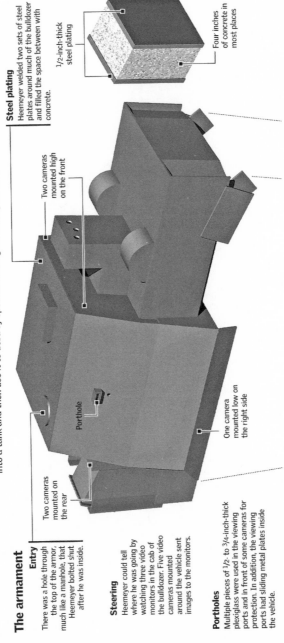

Steel plating
Heemeyer welded two sets of steel plates around much of the bulldozer and filled the space between with concrete.

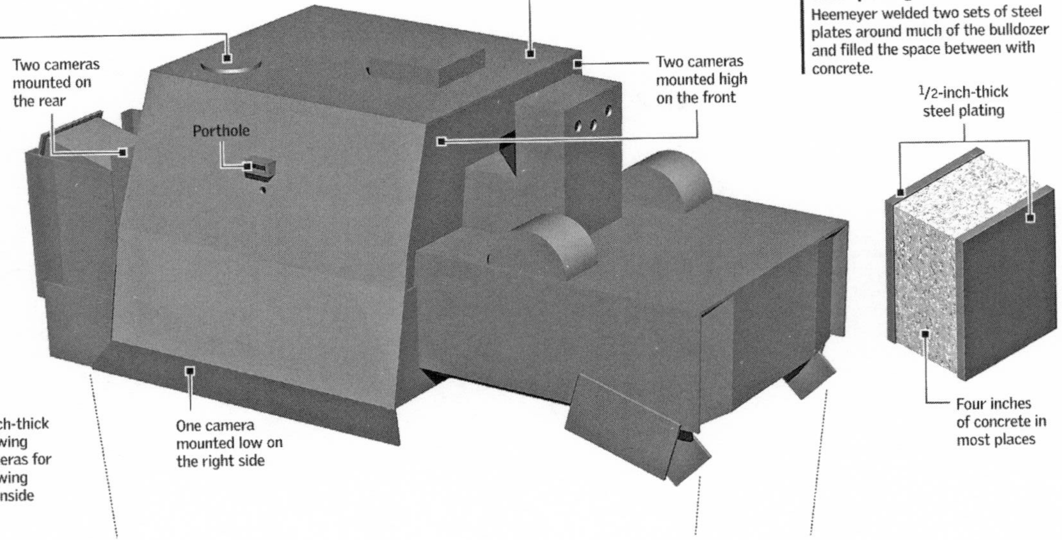

KILLDOZER Schematic

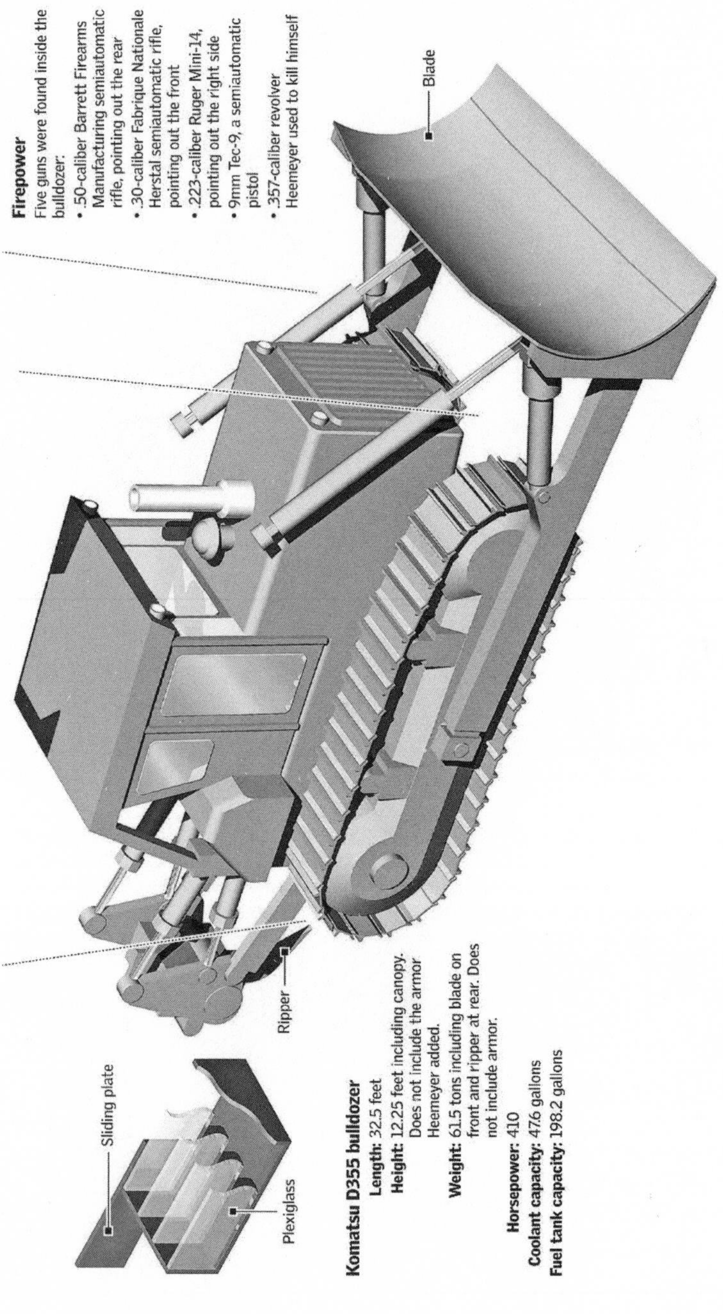
Firepower
Five guns were found inside the bulldozer:
• .50-caliber Barrett Firearms Manufacturing semiautomatic rifle, pointing out the rear
• .30-caliber Fabrique Nationale Herstal semiautomatic rifle, pointing out the front
• .223-caliber Ruger Mini-14, pointing out the right side
• 9mm Tec-9, a semiautomatic pistol
• .357-caliber revolver Heemeyer used to kill himself
Blade
Ripper
Sliding plate
Plexiglass
Komatsu D355 bulldozer
Length: 32.5 feet
Height: 12.25 feet including canopy. Does not include the armor Heemeyer added.
Weight: 61.5 tons including blade on front and ripper at rear. Does not include armor.
Horsepower: 410
Coolant capacity: 47.6 gallons
Fuel tank capacity: 198.2 gallons

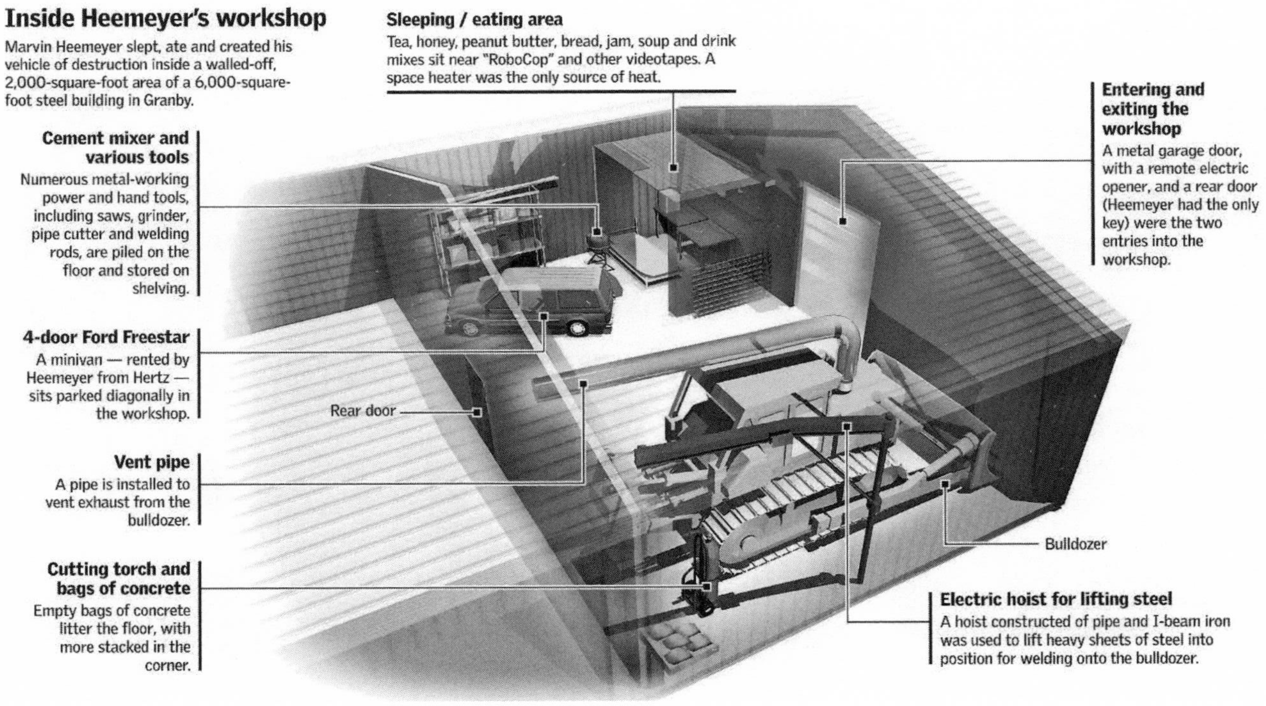
Inside Heemeyer's workshop
Marvin Heemeyer slept, ate and created his vehicle of destruction inside a walled-off, 2,000-square-foot area of a 6,000-square-foot steel building in Granby.
Sleeping / eating area
Tea, honey, peanut butter, bread, jam, soup and drink mixes sit near "RoboCop" and other videotapes. A space heater was the only source of heat.
Entering and exiting the workshop
A metal garage door, with a remote electric opener, and a rear door (Heemeyer had the only key) were the two entries into the workshop.
Cement mixer and various tools
Numerous metal-working power and hand tools, including saws, grinder, pipe cutter and welding rods, are piled on the floor and stored on shelving.
4-door Ford Freestar
A minivan — rented by Heemeyer from Hertz — sits parked diagonally in the workshop.
Rear door
Vent pipe
A pipe is installed to vent exhaust from the bulldozer.
Bulldozer
Cutting torch and bags of concrete
Empty bags of concrete litter the floor, with more stacked in the corner.
Electric hoist for lifting steel
A hoist constructed of pipe and I-beam iron was used to lift heavy sheets of steel into position for welding onto the bulldozer.

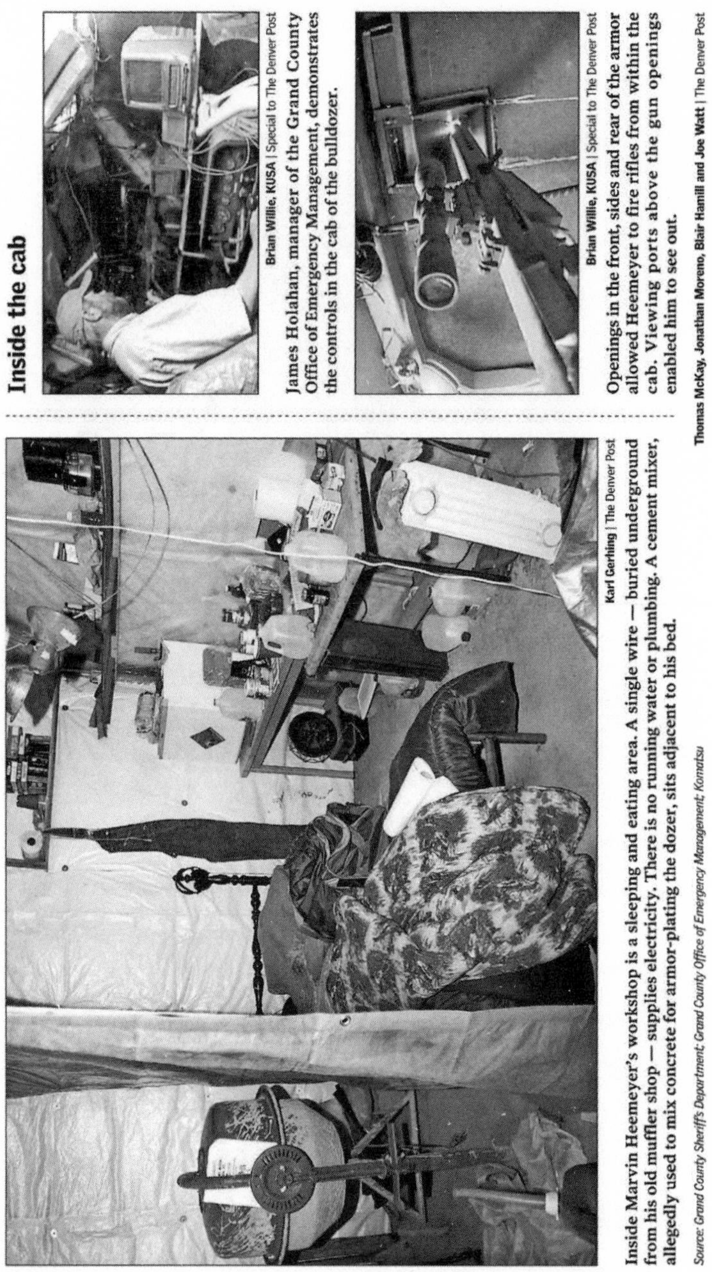

Inside the cab

Brian Willie, KUSA | Special to The Denver Post

James Holahan, manager of the Grand County Office of Emergency Management, demonstrates the controls in the cab of the bulldozer.

Brian Willie, KUSA | Special to The Denver Post

Openings in the front, sides and rear of the armor allowed Heemeyer to fire rifles from within the cab. Viewing ports above the gun openings enabled him to see out.

Thomas McKay, Jonathan Moreno, Blair Hamill and Joe Watt | The Denver Post

Karl Gerhing | The Denver Post

Inside Marvin Heemeyer's workshop is a sleeping and eating area. A single wire — buried underground from his old muffler shop — supplies electricity. There is no running water or plumbing. A cement mixer, allegedly used to mix concrete for armor-plating the dozer, sits adjacent to his bed.

Source: Grand County Sheriff's Department; Grand County Office of Emergency Management; Komatsu

Schematic illustrations and photos used with permission from *The Denver Post.*

Orientation Map of Granby

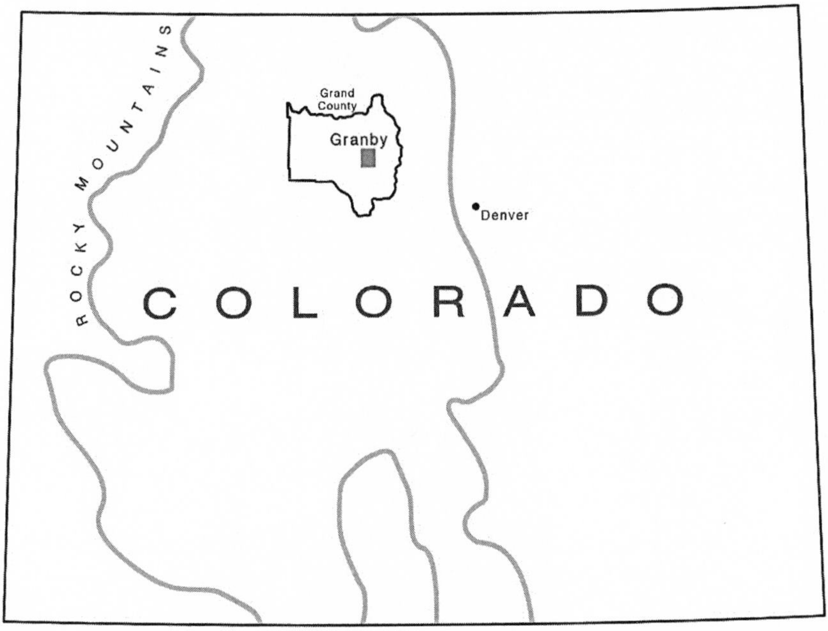

Granby, Colorado

Elevation: 7,935 ft.

U.S. Census Population

1930	90
1940	251
1950	463
1960	503
1970	554
1980	963
1990	966
2000	1,525
2010	1,864
2016 est.	1,916

Orientation Map of Granby

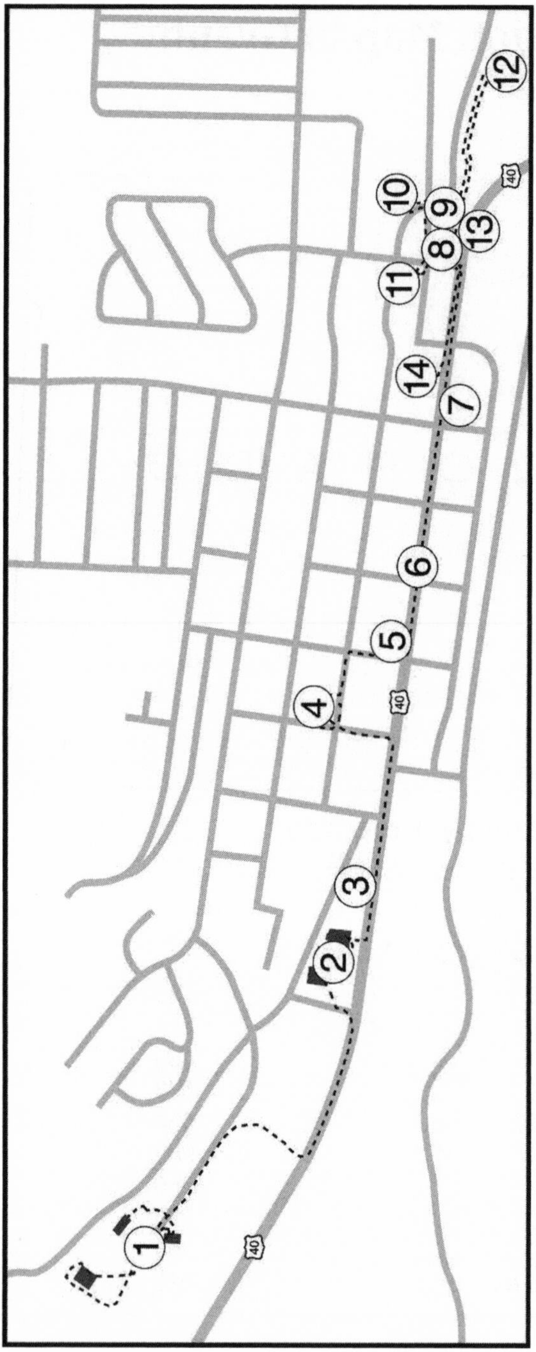

Path of the Killdozer rampage June 4, 2004.

Map Key

1 — Mountain Park Concrete, where two buildings were damaged by Heemeyer. The concrete forming building was the first structure hit and it was completely destroyed. Next was the concrete batch plant itself. The plant was severely damaged. Gun battles between the Killdozer and law enforcement took place at Mountain Park Concrete. It's also the place where the Killdozer was futilely attacked by Cody Docheff in a front-end loader.

2 — After the battles at the batch plant the Killdozer worked its way over to the offices of Mountain Parks Electric on U.S. Highway 40. There, the dozer caused massive damage to garage entrances and to the main office building and reception area. This was the area where Grand County Undersheriff Glen Trainor was atop the Killdozer trying to figure out a way to disable it.

3 — After damaging Mountain Parks Electric the Killdozer headed toward downtown Granby and on the way it took a detour and slammed into the front of the offices of Maple Street Builders on U.S. Highway 40. A truck was destroyed in the attack and the building was severely damaged.

4 — The Town Hall of Granby was completely destroyed by Heemeyer in a fit of motorized rage that lasted 20 minutes. Police fired sporadically at the machine while it was destroying the Town Hall. Police cars were flattened in the parking lot of the Town Hall and a toddlers playground was crushed.

5 — While heading back toward Granby's main street, which is U.S. Highway 40, Heemeyer takes a grand swipe at the offices of Liberty Savings Bank, smashing in walls and ripping out a corner of the building. He also slams into a traffic light pole, failing to knock it over, and he destroys a water hydrant, leading to a flow of water onto the main drag of Granby.

6 — Heemeyer mows down aspen trees that had been planted along the sidewalk in front of what was then Alpine West Office Supply and the Blue Spruce motel.

7 — Heemeyer levels the *Sky-Hi News* office building and central production plant for all the Grand County newspapers.

8 — The Killdozer heads over to Xcel Energy and destroys its office building and garages. While there, Heemeyer and his machine battle it out with Grand County Road and Bridge Superintendent Clark Branstetter, who took on the dozer in a massive scraper. The scraper did not prevail against the Killdozer.

9 — The dozer then destroys the home of Thelma Thompson, the widowed wife of a former Granby Mayor.

10 — The main storage facililty of Thompson and Sons Excavation is then smashed up by Heemeyer.

11 — An outside storage yard owned by Thompson and Sons is then attacked by the Killdozer. The machine destroys equipment and knocks over trailers.

12 — The Killdozer then drove back in front of the Xcel Energy building and headed down a service road to the Inpendent Gas Company bulk propane storage facility. There, Heemeyer parked the Killdozer and fired numerous rounds from his .50-caliber rifle at propane tanks and electrical transformers. He managed to hit the electrical transformers but he did not hit any of the large propane tanks that appeared to be his targets.

13 — At the top of the service road Heemeyer has another battle with a county scraper, once again driven by Branstetter. The Killdozer prevailed again.

14 — After retracing some of its path on U.S. Highway 40, the Killdozer experienced a massive loss of coolant before slamming into the Gambles store. The store was completely destroyed before the machine stopped moving near the rear of the structure. It was here that Heemeyer turned off the engine of the dozer and then killed himself.

Acknowledgements

Many people and agencies helped me greatly in the process of researching and writing this book.

I never would have experienced this strange event if I hadn't been given the opportunity to write for, edit and manage the newspapers in Grand County. Bill Johnson, the owner of the papers, gave me that chance and stuck with me as a publisher and editor even after Heemeyer had destroyed the newspaper building (which Bill owned) and severely crippled — if only for a year — the business of his newspapers.

The staff members of the newspapers were hit particularly hard by the rampage and they worked selflessly to make sure we didn't miss an edition. They slaved away under extremely difficult circumstances, particularly during that month after the rampage. As well, the original and on-deadline reporting of many of my staff members was the basis for lots of my research. They include Cyndi McCoy, Will Bublitz (reporter), Tonya Bina (reporter), Harry Williamson (*Winter Park Manifest* editor), Cece Krewson (reporter and columnist and now deceased) and Larry Banman (Kremmling *Middle Park Times* editor). Other people with whom I worked at the newspapers were also of great help: Jean Landess (photographer), Jennifer Anderson (office manager), Mike Garcia (head pressman), Eric Vandernail (pressman), John Marte (production manager) and Jennifer Larsen (pressroom). I will never forget how Dick Little came to our rescue to help salvage our presses after the rampage. Ken Langley came through to help with both of the press installations after the event.

Lauren Gompertz, who also worked at the paper as an artist, has also been a great help as a sounding board and general advisor during this project.

Acknowledgements

Tom Hale, former Granby town manager, was generous with his time and insights relating to the event and its aftermath.

Martin Smith, who recently moved to Granby from California, was an insightful friend and mentor as I moved forward with this project. An article written by him for the *Los Angeles Times Magazine* shortly after the rampage was one of the key inspirations for this book as it solidified my suspicion that something bigger happened in Granby that day when Heemeyer destroyed much of the town.

Many of Heemeyer's victims were generous enough to let me interview them about their experiences. Rhonda and Casey Farrell, then Granby town manager Tom Hale, George Davis, Cody Docheff, Joe Docheff, Tom Sifers, Dick Broady, Sharon Spurlin, Deb Hess, Ted Wang, Tess Riley, Terry Lange, Keith Klingbail, Larry and Gary Thompson, Clark Branstetter, Lurline Underbrink-Curran and Duane Dailey all shared their thoughts and memories of the event.

Law enforcement personnel put their lives on the line during the rampage and they were generous in talking to me about the rampage. These include Rich Garner, then of the Grand County Sheriff's Department, Dave Batura of the Colorado State Patrol, then Grand County Undersheriff Glen Trainor (now chief of police for Winter Park and Fraser), Sheriff Rod Johnson, Granby deputy Jim Kraker (who is now Chief of Police for Granby) and Mike McGinley of the Colorado State Patrol. Investigator Leo Piechocki of the Grand County Sheriff's Department was generous with his time and insights, openly sharing his thoughts and information he gathered as the lead rampage investigator for the Grand County Sheriff's Department.

Friends and acquaintances of Marv, some who unwittingly became his enemies, were kind enough to indulge my questions and interviews. Some of these people are Chris Ruske, Ian Daugherty, Ted Kellner, Mel Waggoner, Lana Mills, Trisha MacDonald and Mike Garrett. Matt Reed, a friend of Heemeyer's, offered great insight into Heemeyer. John Linton also helped greatly in gaining a broad perspective on Heemeyer as an expert snowmobiler.

Blair Corder, who helped to disassesemble the Killdozer, was also generous with his time and insights about Heemeyer's machine.

In the editing department I must give credit to Ellen Haight, who helped with copy editing and text review in the final stages. Editor

Coralie Hunter of Coralie Hunter Editorial helped greatly to winnow and focus what was at first an ungainly manuscript. Martha Williams, a former reporter at the Grand County newspapers, was also instrumental in early manuscript review. Doug Freed also helped greatly with editorial review and conceptualization early in this project. Jonathan Black also helped me crystallize the overall editorial vision for the book. Mark Swanson of Deer Track Publishing was also a great resource in helping to craft this book.

My wife Lydia Castiello was patient and honest in her observations about the book. My sister Anne Brower also offered priceless insight as I worked through the manuscript.

The Colorado Press Association was an important resource in helping us find assistance after the rampage. Robb Rankin and the East Grand School District also helped us greatly. The Lighthouse Writer's Workshop in Denver also offered me valuable insight and assistance throughout this project.

Sharon Brenner, former executive director of the Granby Chamber of Commerce, was a great source of information relating to her tireless efforts to raise money for and assist the victims of the rampage.

I also want to thank the Ladies for Granby, who stuck their necks out, and other parts, to raise money for the victims of the rampage. They took some grief for their efforts, but they should know that their project was greatly appreciated by me and other victims of the rampage.

About the Author

Patrick F. Brower is uniquely qualified to write this book. He is the former editor and publisher of the *Sky-Hi News*, and a group of weekly and daily newspapers, in Granby, Colorado. He was published extensively for 28 years, as a reporter, editor and columnist and has received numerous statewide and regional awards for his writing. He's also had short fiction published in the *Redneck Review of Literature.* His news articles have also been published in the *Denver Post* and the *Rocky Mountain News.*

Brower personally covered almost all of the hearings and interactions relating to the Killdozer rampage before it took place. Brower was also a victim of the rampage and extensively covered the event itself as well as its aftermath. After the newspapers were sold in 2007, Brower owned and operated his own public affairs consulting firm before working in grassroots economic development with the Grand Enterprise Initiative in Grand County. He continues to write.

Brower graduated from the University of Virginia with a B.A. in American Studies.

He is an accomplished jazz drummer, an avid cross-country skier, runner and a masters level national champion biathlete. He has three children and continues to live in Granby, Colorado.